Derivatives and Development

Derivatives and Development

A Political Economy of Global Finance, Farming, and Poverty

Sasha Breger Bush

palgrave
macmillan

DERIVATIVES AND DEVELOPMENT

First published in 2012 by
PALGRAVE MACMILLAN®
in the United States—a division of St. Martin's Press LLC,
175 Fifth Avenue, New York, NY 10010.

Where this book is distributed in the UK, Europe and the rest of the World, this is by Palgrave Macmillan, a division of Macmillan Publishers Limited, registered in England, company number 785998, of Houndmills, Basingstoke, Hampshire RG21 6XS.

Palgrave Macmillan is the global academic imprint of the above companies and has companies and representatives throughout the world.

ISBN: 978–0–230–33892–0

Library of Congress Cataloging-in-Publication Data

Breger Bush, Sasha.
Derivatives and development : a political economy of global finance, farming, and poverty / by Sasha Breger Bush.
p. cm.
ISBN 978–0–230–33892–0 (alk. paper)
1. Derivative securities—Developing countries. 2. Finance—Developing countries. 3. International finance. 4. Agriculture—Economic aspects—Developing countries. 5. Economic development—Developing countries. 6. Developing countries—Commerce. I. Title.
HG6024.D44B87 2012
332.64'57091724—dc23 2011051409

A catalogue record of the book is available from the British Library.

Design by Integra Software Services

First edition: July 2012

10 9 8 7 6 5 4 3 2 1

Printed in the United States of America.

Contents

List of Figures

List of Tables

Acknowledgments

Huge thanks to Bill Bush, Paul and Debra Breger, Ilene Grabel, George DeMartino, Martin Rhodes, Randall Dodd, and Dr. Cakes for their help and support. Thanks also to Julie Dana at the World Bank, Marcelo Gualda and Marizette Browne at the BM&F, Colleen Herbert at LIFFE, and Mary Ann Ogasawara at the TGE for assistance with the data.

CHAPTER 1

Introduction

The position of the rural population is that of a man standing permanently up to the neck in water, so that even a ripple is sufficient to drown him.[1]

One in five people on Earth is a small farmer.[2] And for small farmers, these are difficult times. While farming has always been a risky proposition—what with the weather, pests, and disease—it has grown more so over the past several decades. In addition to dealing with the usual challenges, small farmers today must also battle volatile and falling prices, deteriorating ecological conditions, fierce and lopsided global competition, and suffocating pressures from the big companies that provide farm inputs and buy farm products. Making matters more difficult still, governments of developed and developing countries alike no longer provide the assistance and support to smallholders that they used to offer in the past. Indeed, "Problems of poverty, marginalization and disempowerment connected to processes of globalization have resulted in small-scale farmers in both the North and South becoming the weakest players in the global market."[3]

In Mexico, small corn farmers have been struggling to compete with mega corn producers from the United States since the North American Free Trade Agreement (NAFTA) deregulated and opened agricultural trade between the two countries in 1994. Mexican corn farmers working small plots of land face high input costs (e.g., credit, fertilizer) and low prices, owing partly to the substantial public subsidies paid by the US government to its biggest corn farms. However, the Mexican government pays no such subsidies to its farmers, a key provision of the 1994 agreement. Many operators of small corn farms in Mexico have been forced to forgo basic necessities, sell off land, move to the cities, and/or migrate to the United States in order to survive.

José Guadalupe Rodríguez, a corn farmer from Chiapas, states, "While the price of corn has fallen, the cost of producing it has hit the roof. We no longer have enough for our family."[4] Alfonso Garcia of Puebla works two jobs in addition to growing corn in order to support his family, and he believes that he will have to migrate elsewhere soon to look for work: "When my children are ill, I have to work like crazy. If I don't even have enough money to look after them, how can I buy chemicals to improve my land? I can barely grow anything on it anymore . . . I know that soon I will have to go, and it saddens me to leave my family behind."[5]

In India, peasant farmers are increasingly stuck in a lethal trap of low crop prices and high input prices (especially for seeds), resulting in large debts that are impossible to repay. Whereas prior to the early 1990s agricultural prices were managed by the government and credit was subsidized and lent on more lenient terms, today government has come to play a smaller role. Thus, prices now are relatively low and volatile, and farmers must often procure loans from informal moneylenders at usurious rates. Since the late 1990s, indebtedness has led to tens of thousands of suicides by male heads of household.

Kusumbai Waghmare of the state of Maharashtra, the widow of a deceased cotton farmer, explains the difficulties her family has experienced since her husband took his own life. When the monsoon wiped out the year's cotton crop, the Waghmare family was suddenly unable to repay its debts. "I have no money for sowing. My husband had already incurred a loan of Rs.40,000 which he could not pay back, and the bank had refused him any more credit. Now I do not know where to get more money. Maybe next year someone will be willing to lend me some money."[6]

Likewise, in the United States small farmers often face low and volatile prices, and confront the rise of big, commercial agribusiness along with government favoritism toward these larger enterprises. In the 1970s, US secretary of agriculture Earl Butz undertook to revolutionize food and farming in the United States. Telling farmers to "get big or get out," Butz intended to streamline US food production, and thereby reduce the costs of food for the average American. Corn, soybeans, and other industrial food crops were planted "fencerow to fencerow" on ever-larger plots to maximize production levels. Aided by government subsidies and huge quantities of industrial pesticides and fertilizers, the largest farmers in the United States began turning out unprecedented amounts of food for domestic consumption and export.[7] For smaller farmers, however, these changes resulted in enormous insecurities as competition grew fierce, prices fell, and subsidies continued to be channeled to the largest, most influential farms.

George Naylor, an Iowa corn farmer, notes how lower corn prices since the 1970s perversely result in even higher levels of corn production and still lower prices: "Farmers facing lower prices have only one option if they want to be able to maintain their standard of living, pay their bills, and service their debt, and that is to produce more."[8] Fred Stokes, retired Army officer-turned-Mississippi cattle rancher, explains the difficulties small ranching operations have today competing with large, industrial ranching and meat processing operations, which have become more concentrated and powerful over the past several decades:

> We're in a death struggle out here, and we're getting our butts kicked . . . . The thing that bothers me most is the Big Brother aspect of this deal. It is clear the government is more concerned with the mining big profits for these corporations than it is with food security or family farmers. It's all about the money for a handful of guys who will be the elites. The rest of us wind up swinging machetes. You talk about feudalism. This thing makes farmers indentured on their own land; they're going to be the new serfs.[9]

In Uganda, coffee farmers struggle with volatile and low prices for their crop, pressure from big multinational coffee traders and roasters, as well as the loss of government assistance that was provided previously. Since 1989, when the world coffee market was freed from the grasp of an intergovernmental cartel, coffee farmers have suffered through two severe price crises, a testament to the increasingly volatile market environment they contend with today.

Lawrence Seguya, who lives in the Mpigi District, implored during the 1998–2002 crisis: "I'd like you to tell people in your place that the drink they are enjoying is now the cause of all our problems. We [grow] the crop with our sweat and sell it for nothing."[10] Bruno and Michael Selugo, aged 17 and 15 respectively and also from the Mpigi District, discuss the impact of the crisis on their education:

> I can't be successful if I don't go to school. I will just be left here, growing a little food. I have been sent home again and again from secondary school . . . . They just send you away if you don't have the fees . . . . This is the main coffee season. Everyone used to go back to school with the money from coffee, but now the money is not there. The price is so low people are not even picking coffee . . . I wish the people who use our coffee could give us a better market. All I want is to go to school.[11]

There is a growing recognition—one that has grown sharper with the global food price crisis that began in 2007 and continues today—that the changes wrought over the past several decades in how we, as a global community, produce, transport, distribute, and consume food and drink have introduced serious insecurities into the lives of billions of people around the world.

At least four interconnected dynamics have characterized these changes. Since World War II, if not earlier, our food systems have gradually become more globally integrated—that is, *globalized*—as governments reduce barriers to global agricultural trade. They have also been *liberalized* as governments increasingly refrain from interfering with agricultural commodity prices; dictating production levels and processes; and providing various supports to farmers, ranchers, and poor consumers.

Over this period, food production has also *commercialized* to a great degree—it is more oriented toward production for the market rather than for consumption at home—and today it is dominated by sophisticated multinational producers, traders, processors, and distributors who are uniquely positioned to navigate the intricacies and complexities of the new global system. Finally, food production, trade, distribution, and consumption have, especially over the past decade, been increasingly subject to the logic and power of the financial sector—food and drink have been *financialized*. While finance has always kept one foot in agriculture—for farming and food trading requires credit—the industry is today expanding its influence on agriculture as multinational financial firms hoard commodities, speculate on commodity futures markets, and purchase broad swaths of farmland across the developing world.[12]

The insecurity of small farm life is but one of many indications that the global food and farming system is in crisis. As small farmers are marginalized, so too are poor consumers across the global South, as market volatility pushes food prices out of reach. As of late 2011, global food prices have risen almost 140 percent over their 2002–04 average, driving many millions of people worldwide into hunger and misery.[13] Many developing countries have, over the past several decades, become reliant on imported food, exacerbating the negative impact of rising world food prices. While the urban poor have been widely cited as the primary victims of the food price crisis, small farmers and agricultural laborers suffer as well. In one of global capitalism's cruelest ironies, those who produce our food are among those most likely to go hungry. Dependent on the sale of only one or two commercial export crops, many small farmers and agricultural laborers have been unable to afford rising food costs as the price of food outpaces that of coffee, cocoa, or cotton sold for export.

In places where food is generally more affordable, as in many countries of the rich North, it often contributes to a wide variety of health problems. Contamination of meat, fruits, vegetables, and even peanut butter by mad cow disease or nasty bugs like *salmonella*, and *E. coli* has become commonplace. Health problems associated with food quality—like obesity, diabetes, and heart disease—are now regular features of the food landscape in the

North, and increasingly in some parts of the South as well.[14] Yet, even in the richest nation in the world, food insecurity has been growing. In 2010, an unprecedented 40 million residents of the United States received assistance through the food stamp program, almost half of them children.[15] Nor has the Earth been spared, as industrial agriculture claims more land and pumps out more pollutants, contaminating the very soil, water, and air upon which the food system relies. It would appear that small farmers are in good company.

Even as the momentous economic changes of the past several decades jeopardize small farm lives and livelihoods, these changes generate new, profitable opportunities in other parts of the global economy. Especially significant has been the explosive growth of the global financial sector. Of the many new avenues globalization has opened for financial interests, derivative markets are among the most fascinating.

Difficult to conceptualize, even harder to regulate, and often troublesome for even the most savvy traders, derivative instruments have nonetheless become a powerful and growing force in global economic relations. As recently as 1986, global derivatives markets were valued at close to US$1 trillion. By 2010, this figure had risen to US$670 trillion, almost nine times global GDP.[16] Feeding this growth, the derivatives industry has turned out a spectacular array of new products to complement the more mundane and traditional futures and options. Commodity-index, credit default, and interest rate swaps are joined by even more exotic contracts with cryptic names like PERLS, KIKOs, and TARNs.[17] These complex financial derivatives are complemented by an equally impressive array of unique commodity contracts, many of which have only recently been offered by emerging derivatives exchanges across the global South—for example, contracts on steel rebar in China and on cardamom and chickpeas in India. In fact, of the top 50 derivatives exchanges in the world in 2010, ranked according to trading volumes, 23 are located in emerging markets across the developing world.[18]

When derivatives are discussed in the business presses and academic circles, the conversation often revolves around the spectacular failures of big firms—such as Barings Bank, Long Term Capital Management, Enron, and AIG—and the correlate threats posed to international financial stability. As with recent commentaries about the role of exotic derivatives in the ongoing global financial crisis, these markets are generally pictured as the stomping grounds of an elite group of financiers whose intricate and complicated gambles threaten systemic ruin.

Speaking on the role of derivatives in precipitating the meltdown of the US mortgage market, Schwartz and Creswell note:

> On Wall Street, of course, what you don't see can hurt you. In the past decade, there has been an explosion in complex derivative instruments, such as collateralized debt obligations and credit default swaps, which were intended primarily to transfer risk.... Used judiciously, derivatives can limit the damage from financial miscues and uncertainty, greasing the wheels of commerce. Used unwisely—when greed and the urge to gamble with borrowed money overtake sensible risk-taking—derivatives can become Wall Street's version of nitroglycerin.[19]

Similarly, with a Greek sovereign default imminent in late 2011, media commentators turned their gaze to the backroom derivatives deals that Greece had made with Goldman Sachs, allowing the Greek government to incur more debt than was permitted by European Union regulators:

> Greece's debt managers agreed a huge deal with the savvy bankers of US investment bank Goldman Sachs at the start of 2002. The deal involved so-called cross-currency swaps in which government debt issued in dollars and yen was swapped for euro debt for a certain period—to be exchanged back into the original currencies at a later date... this credit disguised as a swap didn't show up in the Greek debt statistics.[20]

By these lights, derivatives are catalysts of crisis.

Yet, derivatives are also starting to spring up in other sorts of conversations. Rather than being relegated to the elite corridors of finance, it is argued that derivatives can help ordinary people manage some of the risks associated with economic globalization. Yale economist Robert Shiller stands out in this growing cohort: "We need to democratize finance and bring the advantages enjoyed by the clients of Wall Street to the customers of Wal-Mart."[21] Among his suggestions are proposals for individual use of home equity derivatives to secure against declining home values,[22] the use of derivatives on occupational indexes to secure against declining individual incomes, and the use of gross domestic product (GDP) derivatives to offset the impact of cyclical downturns in aggregate economic activity.

This movement to democratize derivatives has made larger strides in developing country agriculture than in any other area. A growing group of advocates suggests that derivatives might be harnessed as development tools, instruments for reducing poverty among struggling small farmers across the global South. Specifically, derivatives markets may be able to provide much-needed insurance for producers confronting price and weather volatility, and help to mitigate the resulting financial insecurity. This insurance is all the more critical, it is asserted, given that governments no longer provide the social insurance that they did in past times.

For example, the United Nations Conference on Trade and Development (UNCTAD) argues: "When evaluated through the prism of poverty reduction, the notorious price volatility that has long plagued world commodity markets is among the most pressing of challenges facing developing countries. Price volatility breeds risk, and vulnerability to risk is recognized as one of the four dimensions that constitute poverty. Commodity exchanges can help . . . ."[23] The World Bank's International Task Force on Commodity Price Risk Management (ITF) agrees, "Unlike government supports that artificially prop up prices, these instruments [derivatives] can provide some protection for producers using sustainable market-based tools."[24] UNCTAD and the World Bank are joined by the United Nations Food and Agriculture Organization (FAO) and the United Nations Development Program (UNDP), among other segments of the development establishment, as well as a host of governments, aid agencies, and financial firms, in their advocacy of derivatives for small farmers.

Paradoxically, as derivative instruments stand trial for their role in the global financial crisis, they are simultaneously hailed as solutions to small farm poverty and insecurity across the developing world. Whether the markets are well-suited to this critically important social task remains to be seen.

The story of coffee contains within it these broader narratives about the changing, complex, and increasingly interconnected worlds of food and finance. Since the late 1980s, the coffee market has become more globally integrated and subject to lower levels of government regulation. Responding to these changes, coffee prices have generally become more volatile and fallen lower, punctuated by two severe price crises. Coffee producers, the vast majority of them small farmers, have been encouraged to specialize in coffee production for export, thus reducing and sometimes eliminating the production of subsistence food crops. Large multinational exporters, traders, and roasters have secured their dominance over the global coffee commodity chain. And finance, particularly the derivatives industry, has drawn closer to the global coffee economy as coffee firms trade the instruments to reduce risk, speculative financial interest in coffee grows, and development organizations urge the integration derivative instruments into development policy agendas in coffee-producing countries.

Small farmers who are dependent on coffee sales for their survival are exceptionally vulnerable to volatile and falling prices, dynamics that impoverish farmers and introduce enormous insecurities as procuring food, water, fuel, education, medical treatment, and farm supplies becomes difficult. It is in this context that suggestions to "democratize derivatives" have recently gained traction. Derivative instruments can, in theory, help traders to manage price risk. They are frequently used by large, commercially oriented coffee firms to hedge the risk of rising, falling, or volatile prices. The World Bank and UNCTAD, among others, have suggested that small coffee farmers might also utilize these instruments to their advantage. Protection from falling and volatile prices can stabilize farm incomes, help smooth consumption, and promote investment in the farm, contributing to greater family security and well-being, and thus reduced levels of rural poverty.

Paralleling broader global trends, derivatives for development recommendations represent a new kind of thinking about the most appropriate ways to manage agricultural commodity price risk. Indeed, the past several decades have seen significant shifts in policies and programs for risk management across the global North and South. Be they private unemployment accounts, private retirement accounts, or private health insurance programs, the developed countries are increasingly privatizing social risk management (the welfare state) in a process that political scientist Jacob Hacker calls "risk privatization."[25] In the South, risk privatization is ongoing, especially in agriculture, as governments disengage from price and supply management, subsidy programs, and other supports to farmers. Derivatives are increasingly a mechanism for agricultural risk privatization, as development institutions recommend substituting these financial instruments for the public institutions that previously dominated agricultural commodity policy.

In the coffee context, derivatives recommendations represent a shift away from the previous regime that focused on government control and international cooperation as mechanisms for risk management. As with the two recent coffee price crises, the 1930s Great Depression was a terrible time to be a coffee producer. World coffee supplies had grown in the years prior such that when the Depression hit and demand plummeted coffee prices fell quickly and far. Producers across the coffee-growing world clamored for relief. Pervading the ideological climate of the 1930s was the idea that market problems required social, public solutions. "The economic system [ceased] to lay down the law to society and the primacy of society over that system [was] secured."[26] Such was the case with coffee. After several failed attempts, an international, governmental, cooperative solution to coffee price volatility took shape with the 1962 ratification of the International Coffee Agreement (ICA). The ICA constituted a commitment by importing and exporting nations to manage coffee supplies through quotas and stabilize and raise coffee prices. Ensuring farmer well-being was among the stated goals of the system, although it was not the only reason to socialize coffee price risk.

The year 1989 marked the end of the ICA's quota clauses and publicly managed coffee prices. The two crises since have led to renewed interest in the very same issues that policymakers were contemplating in the Great Depression era. Distinguishing contemporary debates from these older ones, however, are assertions that in derivatives markets a solution might be found. Rather than socializing coffee price risk, increasing numbers of researchers and development institutions argue that price risk management should be marketized. As one recent commentator notes about this application of derivatives to social policy, "Personal life circumstances have become commodified; your well-being is being traded."[27] Coffee price risk does not have to be prevented as the ICA sought to do; instead, it can simply be sold.

This book sits at the intersection of the global food and financial systems, at the crossroads of global finance, farming, and poverty. In the chapters that follow, I undertake a critical examination of the integration of derivatives markets into development policy and the capacity of these financial instruments to address poverty among small Southern coffee farmers. Of the 1.5 billion small farmers that live and work in the global South, roughly 25 million of these are coffee smallholders trying to sell their crop in a turbulent global marketplace. With the collapse of other forms of social insurance, and the volatile and crisis-prone nature of the global coffee market, small coffee farmers are, according to derivatives advocates, among the intended beneficiaries of integrating derivatives into development.

The complex story of global farming, finance, and poverty that I present below is fertile ground for exploring what Gray calls the global "politics of insecurity."[28] This story unearths fierce debates about the causes of insecurity and poverty in Southern farming communities, and equally ferocious disagreement about the proper way to contain, manage, and prevent the pervasive risks small farmers confront. These discussions bear strong resemblance to other ongoing debates about insecurity and risk management—for example, the continuing disagreements surrounding the causes and management of the global food and financial crises. Indeed, the story I tell here exposes dynamics—political, social, economic, and ideological—that illuminate the widespread phenomena of insecurity and vulnerability to risk in the global economy and may assist policymakers, academics, and other interested parties in navigating critical, contemporary policy debates.

The deployment of derivatives to help poor farmers manage the uncertainties associated with globalization also provides an interesting and timely case through which to explore several other significant dynamics, features, and contradictions apparent in the contemporary global economy. The case of derivatives for development provides an opportunity to examine the phenomenon of "financialization" in the development context, and the growing influence of financial interests in the development enterprise. Financialization, or "the increasing role of financial motives, financial markets, financial actors and financial institutions," is increasingly recognized by scholars as a defining feature of the global economy over the past several decades.[29] While the financialization process has been explored extensively in the US and European contexts, only recently are scholars turning to the impact of this process in the developing world. The case of derivatives for development further speaks of the financialization of development policy and the development process, a trend exemplified by the increasing reliance of international development institutions and national policymakers on commodity derivative instruments and exchanges. In Chapter 2, I describe a dimension of financialization in the global South, focusing on the expansion and growing popularity of derivatives markets across Latin America, Africa, and Asia. The chapter also highlights the contemporary applications of derivatives to development and their integration into development policy in a variety of contexts.

Further, the global food and financial crises are connected in complex ways to the recent globalization of derivatives markets. For some, echoing the concerns raised in the popular presses cited above, derivatives markets and instruments are figured as contributors to these twin crises, facilitating product innovations and speculative trading that heighten market volatility and uncertainty. For others, derivatives markets provide an innovative and efficient new means of managing the insecurities associated with globalized agriculture and finance, particularly for smallholder farmers. Yet, as I detail in Chapter 3, the theoretical benefits of derivatives for smallholders are not often borne out by reality, while concerns about their dangers are quite real.

The analysis of derivatives for development in subsequent chapters also provides a case study in the processes of globalization and the impact of these processes on rural communities. As will be seen for coffee, globalization of coffee markets has facilitated rising levels of price volatility, fierce competition among producers, and the consolidation of wealth and power in the hands of an elite group of multinational coffee agribusinesses. The development mainstream agrees that agricultural globalization has not been easy for small farmers, and argues that derivatives market globalization provides effective means for countering some of the problems they confront in the coffee market. Yet, the commodity chain analysis I perform in Chapter 4 suggests, in contrast to these assertions, that derivatives market globalization and integration into development policy actually reinforces and magnifies global inequalities in wealth and power and exacerbates poverty and insecurity among small coffee farmers. These unintended consequences transform derivatives from tools for poverty alleviation into mechanisms for impoverishment, insecurity, and ultimately, "de-pesantization."[30]

Finally, the case of derivatives for development opens a window onto the contemporary development orthodoxy. The development mainstream has since the 1990s been subject to growing criticism and efforts to reform the misguided market-based policy recommendations that were espoused previously. Among many other important criticisms, international development organizations were accused of misunderstanding and ignoring the special position of small farmers as agricultural markets opened and globalized in the early 1980s. Today, debate rages about the extent to which the mainstream has learned from its past mistakes. Paradoxically, derivatives for development represent a concerted effort to specifically address the insecurities and uncertainties that plague small farm life today, all the while allowing continued adherence to traditional neoliberal policy prescriptions. As I discuss in Chapter 5, derivatives for development permits the mainstream to address critics and generate new sources of political legitimacy, all the while maintaining the promarket and high-tech core of past agricultural policy agendas. This is troubling, not least because it forecloses consideration of innovative and imaginative alternatives for coffee price risk management that do not conform as neatly to the ideological biases and political needs of prominent international development organizations.

As such, the analyses and discussions that follow contribute to a large and growing academic and policy literature on policies and programs for reducing poverty and vulnerability, the nature and consequences of financialization and economic globalization, crisis and insecurity in agriculture and finance, and the evolution of the development enterprise. Throughout, I contribute a variety of original data and evidence that shed new light upon the deployment of derivatives for development. I also draw extensively on existing research authored by academics, policymakers, and practitioners. The book is specifically designed to be accessible to those without a finance background and of use to policymakers considering employing derivatives as poverty alleviation tools.

CHAPTER 2

Derivatives and Development: Contemporary Applications

The farmer that is smart on finance as well as on fields and food is the farmer that survives.[1]

In this latest phase of globalization, derivatives markets are springing up like toadstools across the global South, in Latin America, Africa, and Asia. A testament to the global process of financialization, the fastest growing derivatives exchanges in the world today are located in China and India, with many of the Southern exchanges nonexistent only 20 years ago. While complex financial derivatives on interest rates, equities, and foreign exchange are most popular in the Northern markets, in the Southern markets agricultural contracts like those on sugar and soy are among the most heavily traded. It is here, in the context of futures and options markets on agricultural commodities, that one finds an important intersection between development and global derivatives markets.

The globalization of derivatives markets is opening new avenues for development thinking and practice. No longer exclusive to the needs of financial elites and the global business community, derivatives markets are currently being harnessed as tools for agricultural development and instruments for poverty alleviation in rural communities. Just as big business has successfully managed its risks and generated profits by derivatives trading, so too might small farmers, processors, and traders in Southern agriculture, along with their governments, apply similar techniques to protect their increasingly fragile livelihoods. For big businesses, derivatives have provided a means to compete more successfully in the global economy and have helped to shore up revenues in the face of volatile economic conditions. A growing cohort from the international development community hopes that derivatives may do the same for poor farmers and others in the global South who rely on volatile global agricultural markets for their well-being.

This chapter address three related trends in derivatives markets, providing background and context for subsequent discussions of derivatives and development. First, derivatives markets are rapidly expanding in geographic scope, size, and product offerings. Second, derivatives market expansion is being fuelled by economic policy liberalization; technological change; and promotion by international organizations, businesses, and governments. Third, derivatives are increasingly being harnessed as tools for development and poverty alleviation in the rural global South in a variety of contexts. The chapter is broken into two main parts. In the section directly below I provide general background information on derivative instruments and markets: what derivatives do, the growth and expansion of derivatives markets over the past several decades, and the several reasons for this trend. In the second part of the chapter, I present an overview of contemporary applications of derivatives to agricultural development.

Background to Derivatives

What Are Derivatives? What Do They Do?

Derivatives are financial contracts. They take this name because the value of a derivative (theoretically) is *derived* from the value of some kind of "underlier."[2] Derivative contracts have underliers ranging from commodities (like coffee, corn, gold, and oil) and assets (such as stocks and bonds), to rates (such as interest and exchange rates) and indices (like the Dow Jones Industrial Average and the Case-Shiller Home Price Indices), to economic aggregates (e.g. GDP and nonfarm payrolls), to the probability of certain events occurring (like a snowstorm, more-than-average rainfall, or a terrorist attack). As derivatives markets grow and expand, the list of underliers traded on them has grown more diverse, as discussed in more detail below. The "underlying market" is often referred to as the "cash" or "spot" market.

Derivatives markets are sometimes referred to as "futures markets." This is because "futures" are historically the main type of contract traded on derivatives exchanges, and, more importantly, because derivatives markets represent activity on the basis of economic events *that have yet to happen*. The underlying markets (cash markets or spot markets) trade items available today, while futures markets trade the same items that will be available sometime in the future. While there are some exceptions, derivatives markets usually project at most 18–24 months into the future.

Risk Shifting: Hedging versus Speculation

Generally speaking, derivative instruments represent exposure to economic risks, and derivatives trading represents the shifting around of economic risks among traders. I do not think it is misleading to present derivatives markets as forums for gambling on what will happen next in the global economy. Fischer Black, a towering figure in the derivatives field, writes, "I believe that futures markets exist because in some situations they provide an inexpensive way to transfer risk, and because many people both in the business and out like to gamble on commodity prices."

To buy or sell a derivative contract is to *place a bet*. Instead of betting on NCAA basketball or the Kentucky Derby, the holder of a derivative contract is betting on economic changes or changes that have economic consequences—such as changes in prices, rates, performance of indices, creditworthiness of corporations, GDP, and even changes in the weather. Just as vacationers to Las Vegas gamble on the next card turned or the rotations of the roulette wheel, so too do derivatives traders gamble on the future price of coffee, the future value of a share of General Electric stock, or the likelihood that an unusually cool summer will diminish the revenues of utility companies.

Such gambling serves two major purposes for the traders involved: speculation and hedging.[3] Speculation is most akin to traditional gambling in places like Las Vegas: Speculators in derivatives markets take on risks with the intent of making a profit. To speculate is to attempt to increase one's income by gambling on the future. Speculators generally do not own and do not intend to own the commodity or asset or rate or index that underpin derivative contracts. Indeed, derivatives markets are increasingly a place where "men who don't own something are selling that something to men who really don't want it."[4]

That derivative instruments allow traders to *leverage* their positions frequently recommends them to speculators. Leverage refers to the fact that traders can participate in derivatives markets by posting only a small proportion of the value of their transactions at the outset—a small initial outlay can potentially yield much larger gains in the end. Bryan and Rafferty explain:

> Leverage also facilitates people with no direct interest [in the underlier] *per se* to become involved in the market . . . it is the capacity to obtain exposure to a much greater amount of a commodity, or financial asset, for little investment, and with no necessary interest in the underlying commodity or asset that concerns many worried about their explosive potential.[5]

Indeed, observers of derivatives-based corporate failures note that the small size of the initial outlay masks sizable liabilities should the bet be lost, resulting in a very fragile financial structure with potentially catastrophic consequences should it collapse.[6]

By contrast, hedging is gambling with the intent of neutralizing another bet made previously in another market. It refers to the process whereby a participant in the cash market takes an *offsetting* position in the futures market to insure against changes in the value of the underlying commodity or asset. Rather than take on risk and increase their exposure like speculators, hedgers lay off risk and reduce their exposure by trading in derivatives. The same leveraging that permits cheap gambling for speculators allows hedgers to purchase insurance for a relatively small up-front cost (however, this "cheapness" can ultimately be undermined in several ways, not least by losing the bet later on).

To hedge is to purchase a kind of financial insurance against losses in incomes, asset values, and revenues. By counterbalancing risks in the underlying market with offsetting risks in the derivatives market, traders, in theory, protect themselves from fluctuations in those prices and values that impact incomes and revenues. However, even as hedging protects traders from losses, it also precludes trader gain. It is a technique for *stabilizing* incomes, revenues, and/or asset values, *not* enlarging them. That said, and as discussed subsequently, many proponents of derivatives hedging for farmers argue that short-term income stabilization can lead to long-term income growth.

Several recent examples help to illustrate the difference between speculation and hedging. Consider the market for crude oil. As most of us are aware, oil prices are volatile and are often subject to rapid price increases. Without derivatives, speculating on the price of oil requires one to actually purchase oil. A speculator would have to "short" the market to bet on oil prices falling (sell oil high; buy oil low) or go "long" to bet on prices rising (buy oil low; sell oil high). Derivative instruments, however, allow one to place this same bet *without owning any oil at all.* In this way, traders gain exposure to the price of oil (i.e. they can bet on it) without having to buy, store, or transport any oil (which can be time consuming and expensive). By posting as collateral a small proportion of the value of an oil derivative contract, a trader can speculate on the price of oil without spending the much larger sum required to speculate on oil prices in the cash market (more below on posting collateral, which is called a "margin" in this context).

Other kinds of oil derivatives traders are already heavily invested in the cash market before they begin to trade derivatives. For example, airlines regularly confront the risk of oil price volatility in their operations because oil is a critical input in the production of jet fuel. When oil prices rise, jet fuel prices also usually rise, and airline profit margins grow smaller. In this context, any airline is a potential hedger in the oil derivatives market. The airlines' business—flying people around in airplanes that require jet fuel—involves an implicit bet on the price of oil and jet fuel: It will stay the same or fall or fluctuate within a reasonably narrow band. Southwest Airlines, for example, can protect itself against the risk of rising oil and jet fuel prices and falling profit margins by betting in derivatives markets. When oil and jet fuel prices rise in the cash market, Southwest would then receive an insurance payment of sorts from the derivatives market, a payment that should cover its losses in the cash market almost exactly. Keep in mind, however, that in this case Southwest would not make any gains in the derivatives market should oil prices fall instead. Hedging not only precludes big losses when oil prices rise but also precludes savings when oil prices fall.[7]

To put some real numbers on this, US Airways had estimated that in 2000 their profits would be US$38 million if fuel prices had not risen—instead the airline lost US$88 million, illustrating the vulnerability of airlines to fluctuating oil prices.[8] By contrast, Southwest Airlines recorded a gain of US$87 million in the third quarter of 2005 alone from hedging its jet fuel costs, and expected to pay about US$26 per barrel in the fourth quarter of 2005, less than half the market price at that time.[9] This shows how hedging can protect firms against losses and give them an advantage over the competition.

Another example of speculation versus hedging involves coffee, the case study that focuses my discussion of derivatives and development in chapters 3–5. Coffee farmers are said to be "long in the field." This means that they have bet that coffee prices will rise by virtue of having planted some coffee (who would plant coffee in the hopes that prices fall?). Because many coffee farmers rely on the crop as their only source of income, price volatility adversely affects them. When coffee prices fall, farmer incomes fall, and farmers and their families are deprived of necessary goods, services, and investments. As will be noted at more length subsequently, development researchers are presently recommending that coffee farmers hedge with derivatives to reduce their vulnerability. By betting in the derivatives markets that prices will fall, farmers could be assured a cash payment in the event that future coffee prices do indeed fall.

More specifically, to illustrate how these bets work for hedgers, suppose that it is September and that I am an Arabica coffee farmer. I am planning to begin harvesting my crop in November, but am fearful that prices will fall between the time that I begin harvesting and the time that I finish marketing my crop in February. This is a justified fear as many of my fellow coffee farmers are also harvesting at this time, meaning that by February the market could be awash in coffee beans, driving down the price and undermining my income and livelihood. In theory, derivatives markets can allow me to protect myself from the risk that prices will fall over the harvest and marketing period. In September I could sell one Arabica futures contract for delivery in March at the prevailing (hypothetical) future price of US$1.25 per pound. Selling this contract means that I am selling the crop I have yet to harvest *forward* at a prearranged price. Should prices fall between September and March, the trader who bought my future will pay me the difference between the contract price (US$1.25/pound) and the future price prevailing when I make delivery March (or even late February).

Alternatively, given these same circumstances, as a farmer I could instead have purchased a put option, dated to March, in September as I prepared to harvest. Paying a premium up front, the put option would give me the right to sell my crop at US$1.25 per pound at any time between September and the time that the contract expires in March. (American options can be exercised at any time prior to the expiration date; this type constitutes the majority of exchange traded options.) This arrangement is more flexible because I am given the freedom to choose whether or not to sell at the contract price, and can always choose not to exercise the option should coffee prices rise over the course of the harvest. This freedom is not obtainable with a coffee future (the scenario directly above), as I am bound and obligated in a futures transaction to sell my crop at the preestablished price. However, futures trading does not require a premium to be paid up front. In both of these cases, that is, selling futures and buying put options, hedgers like coffee farmers are engaging in an insurance transaction of sorts. The derivatives market works to compensate hedgers for money lost in the cash market.

That said, recent evidence suggests that most of the trading that goes on in coffee derivatives markets is speculative in nature. For example, Newman estimates that for every kilogram of coffee traded on the world market since 2002, a *minimum* of 8,000 kilos of virtual "future coffee" were traded by people who do not have any coffee and do not want any coffee, for the purposes of price speculation.[10] Hedgers do not generally bet on more coffee in derivatives markets than they have actually grown, meaning that the excess of coffee traded in futures markets over the volume that is physically traded represents a rough measure of coffee traded for speculative purposes. That speculators increasingly dominate global derivatives markets is a point that I ask the reader to keep in mind. Speculative activity has concrete implications for the behavior of future prices and contributes to making derivatives markets unsuitable as poverty alleviation tools (see Chapter 4).

Price Discovery

Gambling on derivatives markets also serves an overarching function, outside of risk shifting among traders. Derivatives markets are forums for gambling on what will happen next in the economy. The markets not only facilitate the gambling but also sum up the wagers of all individual traders such that future economic risks can be *priced.* Future prices represent the market's collective wisdom on the probabilities and likely impact of future economic changes. (This is akin to the "lines" in Las Vegas changing in response to customer bets in the lead up to a sporting event.) These prices are in turn the basis upon which subsequent bets are made. Illustrating the relationship between such "price discovery," hedging, and speculation, Bryan and Rafferty note, "If you could precisely estimate the price of risk . . . [it] would, to all intents and purposes, be reduced to a conscious choice. Risk would cease to be so risky."[11]

Price discovery refers to this process whereby a futures market "discovers," or predicts, future prices, via aggregating the future (price) expectations of traders—for this reason futures markets are sometimes called "prediction markets." In theory, these future price discoveries permit cash market participants to transact and make investment decisions efficiently on the basis of "rational" forward prices—they have a glimpse of what the future holds and can thus make decisions with more certainty. Looking to the prices established in futures markets, farmers, for example, can make better decisions about what crop to plant, how much to plant, the proper quantities of inputs to procure, and about general consumption because the futures market gives a glimpse of future revenues via its future price predictions.

Crucially, the benefits of price discovery are thought to accrue to derivatives market participants and nonparticipants alike. Even if a farmer cannot access the futures market per se to manage risk by hedging, she may still reap gains from futures trading in that her business and investment decisions will be better directed when future prices are used as a guide. Please note, however, that the benefits of price discovery rely upon derivatives traders getting the future "right," that is, upon correct predictions of what will happen next. To the extent that futures markets are inefficient—future prices today do not accurately predict cash prices some time from now (traders' crystal balls are cloudy)—future prices may misguide those who follow them. Indeed, the reader should be aware that while the language of "discovery" implies some sort of scientific unearthing of "true" prices, in reality the situation is not nearly so neat. We shall revisit this issue in chapters 3 and 4, where I discuss the impact of market inefficiencies and speculative derivatives trading on the price discovery mechanism.

Types of Contracts

Notwithstanding the different underliers, derivative contracts come in some basic and standard forms.

The first pertinent distinction among derivative contracts are contracts that are *exchange traded* versus those that are traded *over-the-counter* (OTC). Exchange traded contracts are standardized ones, the trade in which is regulated by exchanges and clearing houses, among other institutions. Exchanges determine product offerings, set down trading rules, match buyers with sellers, and ensure regulatory compliance. Increasingly, exchanges are managed electronically (on electronic trading platforms), such that buyers and sellers are matched via a computer program, rather than via pit trading, which was the norm until very recently.[12] In addition, the electronic platforms of some exchanges are networked with the platforms of other exchanges, allowing clients of one exchange to more easily and cheaply trade in the products of another (e.g. the Chicago Mercantile Exchange has recently entered into such an arrangement with BM&F Bovespa in Brazil). Electronic trading has, in this context, allowed for greater global market integration. Clearinghouses secure market participants against counterparty risk (i.e. the risk that the other party to the contract will default on her obligation). They act as guarantors, ensuring the creditworthiness of traders, and holding and verifying traders' collateral. Exchange traded agricultural commodity derivatives are the primary focus of the discussion in chapters 3–5.

OTC derivatives, in contrast to exchange traded derivatives, are "custom" contracts and are generally negotiated between dealer and client on an individual basis. Crucially, there are no clearinghouses in OTC markets to ensure that all parties meet their obligations nor are there exchanges to promulgate and standardize contracts and trading rules. Many of the corporate derivatives disasters, like those experienced by Enron and AIG, have arisen from OTC derivatives defaults.

A variety of derivative contracts may be traded on exchanges, or OTC, or both. Keep in mind that derivatives markets are growing very quickly and rapid financial innovation is the norm. This means that thousands of different contracts exist, making it impossible to provide an in-depth discussion of all of them here. However, an overview of the most common and basic derivative contracts is given below.

Forward contracts are the most basic and oldest form of derivative and they are OTC contracts. A forward contract represents a deal between the buyer and seller in which the seller of the forward agrees to make delivery of a specific quantity of a given commodity at a specific price at a specific time and place in the future. The buyer of the forward agrees to take delivery of that quantity, at that price, on that date, at that location. Crucially, a forward contract entails an *obligation* on the part of both the seller and the buyer, to make and take delivery respectively, on the terms specified in the contract.

For example, a coffee farmer may sell forward (go short) 1,000 pounds of mild Arabica coffee at $1.08 per pound, to be delivered to the port at Mombasa on November 4, 2012. A coffee exporter, looking to buy some coffee in the future, might take up the other end of this contract, going long (buying forward) the precise amount and quality of the coffee specified in the contract. In terms of the betting analogy made earlier, a transaction like this one implies that two bets are being made. The coffee farmer is betting that coffee prices will fall between now and November 4, 2012. The coffee exporter is betting that coffee prices will rise between now and November 4, 2012. As with futures contracts, discussed below, no money changes hands at the time the parties enter into the contract. The contract is worth nothing (zero) at the outset and gains/losses accrue only as prices diverge from the "strike" price specified in the contract.

Futures contracts are almost identical to forwards, with one big difference. Like a forward contract, a futures contract entails an obligation to sell/buy a certain quantity of a good, of specific quality, at a specific price at a specific time and place in the future. Unlike forwards, however, futures contracts are *standardized* contracts, that is, they all have the same specifications, and they are bought and sold en masse on organized exchanges. For example, coffee "C" futures are sold on the Intercontinental Exchange (ICE; previously the New York Board of Trade), and each contract specifies 37,500 pounds of mild Arabica coffee, deliverable to a variety of ports internationally. Coffee futures are standardized such that five to six trading months are available, depending on the exchange—on ICE, coffee trades for delivery in March, May, July, September, and December. The "trading months" are those months in which delivery of the good can be made and contracts usually expire about two to three weeks into the delivery month, though futures trading occurs during all months of the year. In gambling terms, the buyer/seller of a March 2013 coffee future is betting today on what the price of coffee will be in March 2013. Crucially, futures contracts for agricultural commodities extend, at most, 18–24 months into the future. This suggests that futures can provide only short-term price insurance, a point that will be raised again subsequently (see Chapter 3).

Like a forward, futures contracts are worth nothing (zero) at the outset and gains/losses accrue only as prices diverge from the "strike" price in the contract. Neither of the two parties to the transaction exchange money when the contract is entered into. However, because futures are exchange traded, brokerage, exchange, and clearing fees are levied at the outset. Clearinghouses and exchanges play a similar role to the "house" in any casino, while brokerage firms play the role of the bookie, among other functions. Further, traders on exchanges must post an initial "margin" with the clearinghouse that serves as collateral against any losses incurred.

Options contracts are the last of the most common and basic derivative contracts. Options give the buyer the *right*, but not the obligation, to buy/sell a specific amount of some good at a specific price at a specific time and place in the future. Options may be exchange traded or OTC. *Put* options are options to sell. Someone who buys a coffee put option (is *long* a put option) has the right, but not the obligation, to sell a specific amount of coffee in the future at a specific price. *Call* options are options to buy, and they give the person who buys it (goes *long* a call option) the right, but not the obligation, to buy a specific amount of some good at a specific price in the future. The individual who sells (goes short) the put or call option can be said to have "written the option." The seller (writer) of the option receives a premium from the buyer in exchange for taking on the risk that the buyer will exercise her right. Unlike forwards and futures contracts, then, the amount of the premium is exchanged as soon as the parties enter into the contract. The option buyer is getting a privilege that parties to futures and forwards do not—the right to sell/buy without any obligation to do so—and this flexibility comes at a cost. To "exercise" an option is to assert one's contractual right to buy or sell according to contract terms. American options may be exercised at any time up until the date of expiry specified in the contract. European options may only be exercised on the expiration date.

While forwards, futures, and options are the most basic and most widely utilized derivative contracts, there are a few more complex instruments that are worthy of note. For example, *swaps* are agreements to exchange the attributes of one commodity for those of another at a specific time in the future. Foreign exchange swaps are among the most common, as are interest rate and credit default swaps (as the recent housing market crisis in the United States has miserably highlighted). To give an example, an interest rate swap might involve swapping a fixed principal amount subject to a floating interest rate for the same principal amount subject to a fixed rate. The transaction allows traders to take positions on relative price of credit. *Swaptions* are hybrid instruments that give traders a right, but not an obligation, to swap sometime in the future—they are options on swaps. Derivatives or "derivative-like features" can also be blended either with other derivatives or with commodities or assets."[13] Convertible bonds, for example, give the holder the option of converting the note (debt) into an equity share (stock). In another instance, back in the 1990s JP Morgan issued PERLS, or principal exchange rate linked securities, the payouts on which were linked to the movement of the Thai baht.[14] These instruments looked like bonds in that they promised regular payments to holders, but acted like derivatives insofar as the size of payments to holders were dependent on the relative value of the baht.

Clearing and Contract Settlement

Exchange traded derivative contracts are "cleared" via the exchange's clearinghouse. The clearinghouse, which is usually a large bank or bank-like entity, facilitates and administers credits and debits among market participants according to changing market prices (more on clearinghouses in Chapter 4). This practice is called "marking-to-market." While it has not always been the case, today almost all futures accounts are marked-to-market *daily*. At the end of every trading day each account is marked to market, with gains credited or losses debited. In order to prevent default, clearinghouses require that each trader maintain a "margin account." The "initial margin" is a good faith deposit made prior to commencing futures trading. The amount is specified by the exchange and is usually about 3–10 percent of the value of the contract. Each time the margin account balance falls below the "maintenance" level (which may be the same as or less than the initial margin), the trader must deposit funds to bring the account balance back up to the maintenance level. This is referred to as a "margin call." For example, coffee futures traded on ICE require a US$5,400 initial margin. In addition to all futures traders, traders who sell (write) options on exchanges must also post collateral to cover their obligations in the event that the option is exercised.

For example, a farmer who sells short (bets that prices will fall) in an environment of rising future prices may have to make margin calls daily. His losses are a function of the size of his open position and the daily rise in the future price. Margin calls, in addition to the initial margin deposit, can be costly for market participants and are sometimes a financial impossibility. Recently, the World Bank, among other development organizations, has begun to investigate the potential for developing country banks to incorporate the cost of margins and margin calls into the loans they sell to coffee farmers.[15] The World Bank has also begun partnering with multinational banks to extend lines of credit directly to potential hedgers, partly to cover margin calls (more below).

Exchange traded agricultural commodity futures contracts can be settled in four different ways: physical delivery, exchange of physicals (or actuals), offsetting trade, and cash. Not all exchanges will allow for all of these methods of settlement; the contract specifications available for each product offered by a given exchange delineate the allowed settlement methods. Please note that more settlement options are available in practice for commodity contracts than for financial contracts (like interest rates, forex, etc.) because there is a possibility of delivery. Note also that settlement mechanisms that do not require possession and delivery of an actual commodity permit more speculative activity.

Physical delivery, perhaps the most intuitive settlement method, refers to the settlement of a futures contracts via delivery of the good specified in the contract. Each exchange specifies those ports where deliveries are accepted, and short sellers must give notice of delivery to the exchange before shipment.

Exchange of physicals (or exchange of actuals) refers to the process whereby "two traders agree to a simultaneous exchange of a cash commodity and futures contracts based on that cash commodity."[16] This procedure is almost identical to physical delivery, with the exception that the exchange does not intermediate delivery of the commodity. The two parties who agree to the trade, both of whom have open and opposite positions on the futures exchange, notify the exchange of what has transpired, and the exchange closes the accounts of both the traders.

Cash settlement means that the two parties to the futures contract settle any losses or gains, as well as delivery/acceptance of the underlier, in cash. Both physical delivery and cash settlement are used only rarely.[17]

An offsetting trade, by far the most common method of contract settlement, requires that a trader make a transaction opposite to the position that is open. For example, a farmer who has sold one coffee future can settle her account by buying one future, making her net futures position zero. The farmer captures the gains or losses that accrue due to future price changes from the time the future was sold until the time it is bought back. The farmer would then go and sell her crop in the local cash market at the price prevailing in that market.

Types of Derivatives Exchanges

Derivatives exchanges come in many varieties, differing in size, location, client base, product offering, and contract specifics, among other distinctions. There are global mega-exchanges like the Chicago Mercantile Exchange and NYSE-Euronext that offer a wide variety of products, post massive trading volumes and cater to global investors. There are smaller national and regional exchanges that offer a narrower and more specialized suite of products and often cater more to local or regional traders. For example, the Tokyo Financial Exchange offers only financial derivative products like interest and exchange rate contracts, while the BATS Options Exchange in the United States offers only financial options.

Turning to local/regional commodity derivatives exchanges, the Dalian Commodity Exchange in China offers a small selection of agricultural and energy products, while the Shanghai Futures Exchange is the only exchange globally to offer futures on steel rebar (a construction material in hot demand in rapidly growing Chinese cities). The Indian Multi Commodity Exchange is another great example of a national exchange that tailors its products to local needs, offering contracts on cardamom, turmeric, and *chana* (chickpeas), among other locally important products. Among the commodity exchanges, of which there are a growing number across the developing world, some offer only opportunities for forward contracting (really they just offer a meeting place for buyers and sellers of agricultural goods), while others offer futures and options in standardized fashion. For example, Bourse Africa in Botswana does not currently offer futures and options (though it plans to), with only forward contracting available presently.

Not only might localized commodity exchanges offer contracts on products not available elsewhere, but they may also have contract terms that are more appealing to locals. Often, on local exchanges, lot sizes are smaller and trades are settled in local currencies (lot size refers to the quantity of a given commodity specified in the contract). This allows for greater levels of local participation, as smaller players can trade and local traders can eliminate exchange rate risks on their transactions. In some cases, local futures and options exchanges allow lower-quality products to fill the contract, while the global exchanges often enforce higher-quality standards. This was the case until very recently with Brazilian Arabica coffee. Previously, Brazilian Arabicas were deliverable only locally on the BM&F Futures Exchange in Sao Paulo, with the mega exchange in New York (ICE) refusing to accept Brazilian beans on account of their lower quality. Just recently, ICE added Brazil to its list of "origins tenderable" (these are the places from which coffee is accepted to fulfill a contract), citing quality improvements among Brazilian producers as the main reason for the change.[18]

Like most financial markets, derivatives markets are characterized by constant innovation, new product offerings, expansion into new markets, and new operating rules and procedures and technologies. The reader should be aware of the diversity of exchanges, as well as their tendency to change and innovate very rapidly. As will be seen, differences across exchanges are important in considering the accessibility of derivatives markets to small, local players. That said, it will also become clear that derivatives markets are homogeneous in significant ways, not least in that they are dominated by very large, sophisticated, and wealthy multinational corporations and are generally exclusive of smaller, poorer Southern actors.

Size and Scope of Derivatives Markets

While derivatives have a long history, it is only recently that their growing popularity has captured significant international attention, and for good reason—the pace of growth and the sheer size of derivatives markets today are simply breathtaking. In 1986, the total outstanding notional value of all derivatives markets was US$1 trillion.[19] By year-end 2010, the combined size of global OTC and exchange traded derivatives markets was almost US$670 trillion.[20] By comparison, total global income (GDP) in 2010 was just over US$75 trillion.[21] Recent data further suggest that the spectacular growth of derivatives markets worldwide has not been unduly hampered by the Great Recession. Between 2009 and 2010 alone the number of contracts traded worldwide rose by more than 25 percent.[22]

The measure used above to determine derivatives market size is "notional amount outstanding," referring to face value of the contract (the value of the underliers, e.g. commodity, currency, rate, index, etc.) aggregated across the total number of contracts traded. Put differently, the International Swaps and Derivatives Association (ISDA) defines "notional amount" or "notional principal" as "a hypothetical underlying quantity upon which interest rate or other payment obligations are computed."[23] In the case of interest rate and other purely financial derivatives, the underlying quantity is indeed hypothetical as these contracts are only settled in cash, with no prospect of actual delivery (imagine the difficulty in delivering, for example, the basket of stocks required to settle a contract on the Dow Jones Industrial Average). In the case of commodity derivatives, particularly on storable commodities (like coffee, precious metals, oil, etc.), delivery may be (and sometimes is) made and the underlying quantity is thus part real and part hypothetical. The ability to cash settle and to settle via offsetting trade in commodity markets is the mechanism that allows the quantity of a good traded in futures markets to so greatly exceed the amount of the good that is actually produced globally. Put differently, cash settlement and offsetting trades allow for speculative participation and exponential market growth beyond the limits of the "real" set by global production levels. This is why derivatives markets can trade volumes many times actual production levels. Some commodity derivatives exchanges make delivery compulsory, as a means of limiting speculator participation in the market (e.g. delivery is compulsory for coffee contracts traded on the Tokyo Grain Exchange).

Notional amount outstanding is *not* a measure of how much money actually changes hands between traders in derivatives markets. Recall that it is a characteristic of derivative instruments to enable traders to acquire leverage, which means that the value of one's transaction is more than the amount one pays to enter into the transaction. Further, because so many positions are closed out via offsetting trade, the cash value of the underlier changes hands infrequently. "Gross market value" measures the actual amount of money that changes hands in derivatives transactions. At year-end 2010 the gross market value for global OTC markets was just over US$21 trillion, a mere 3.5 percent of the total value of the underlying principal of the contracts.[24] Gross market value data are unavailable for exchange traded derivatives markets.

While the most notable growth over the past two decades has been in financial derivatives markets, agricultural commodity derivatives markets—which are the focus of this book—have been expanding quite rapidly with growth rates in agricultural contracts overtaking those in financial contracts since 2005.[25] According to the Futures Industry Association (FIA), agricultural commodity contracts accounted for just over 5 percent of contracts traded globally at year-end 2010, with equity, equity index, and interest rate derivatives accounting for over 80 percent of global derivatives trading by volume. However, exchange traded agricultural commodity derivatives volumes more than doubled from 2007 to 2010, rising from roughly 641 million contracts traded worldwide in 2007 to about 1.3 billion contracts in 2010.[26]

As these figures suggest, the growth of agricultural derivatives markets has been particularly pronounced since the onset of the global food crisis in 2007 and the Great Recession in 2008. Between 2009 and 2010 alone, the number of agricultural contracts traded rose by 40 percent. This growth rate dwarfs the growth rates of all other categories of contract noted by the FIA with the exception of foreign exchange contracts.[27] Data from the Bank of International Settlements (BIS) support this trend, with turnover in exchange traded commodity futures rising by 40 percent globally between 2009 and 2010 and turnover in exchange traded commodity options rising by about 17 percent over the same period.[28]

While some of this growing demand can be traced to new and larger "commercial" positions looking to hedge in an increasingly volatile price environment (i.e. participation by firms actually involved in the cash market; speculators hold "non-commercial" positions), much of this upward trend has been traced to the rapid entrance of hedge funds, managed funds, and other financial institutions into the markets (more on this in Chapter 4). Bello notes that global investors moved out of traditional financial and real estate investments en masse in 2007 as the US economy began to collapse, investing instead in commodities that were seen as safer investments with more growth potential.[29] The *Wall Street Journal* explains:

> The commodity futures markets play a key role in establishing worldwide prices for wheat, corn, soybeans and other foodstuffs, as well as energy products like crude oil and natural gas. But in recent years, these markets have also become an attractive haven for investors seeking profits from rising commodity prices and protection against inflation and a withering dollar. As a result, billions of dollars have poured into the commodity futures market—from pension

> funds, endowments and a host of other institutional investors—through the new conduit of commodity index funds. Billions more have come in from investment banks that are hedging the risk of complex bets, called swaps, that these same investors have made in the unregulated international swaps market.[30]

While derivatives exchanges in the global North continue to see the highest trading volumes and largest market sizes, derivatives are now becoming increasingly popular in the global South. The FIA notes, "As the global brokers well know, this business is no longer concentrated in the major European and North American centers. . . ."[31] The most rapidly growing derivatives markets in the world today are located in Asia and Latin America, with these regions posting growth rates (by volume) of 43 percent and 50 percent respectively in 2010. These growth rates are more than triple that of the developed Northern markets, with the North American and European markets growing only between 12 and 15 percent in 2010.[32]

Further, of the top 50 derivatives exchanges worldwide (ranked by number of futures and options contracts traded and/or cleared), 23 are located in the global South in 2010. Looking more closely, seven of the top fifteen exchanges, including the top exchange, are Southern, located in South Korea (ranked #1), India (#5 and #9), Brazil (#6), and China (#11–13). Turning to individual contracts, the so-called "emerging" markets are clear leaders in several product categories. Across six categories of contract—equities, metals, interest rates, foreign exchange, agriculture, and energy—emerging markets offered the leading contract (the one that is most heavily traded) in four of these categories in 2010: equities (Korea Exchange), metals (Shanghai Futures Exchange), foreign exchange (MCX Stock Exchange of India), and agricultural commodities (Zhengzhou Commodity Exchange).[33]

Turning again to agricultural contracts, developing country exchanges are also experiencing more rapid growth in this context than exchanges in the rich countries. According to Gross, between 2003 and 2006 the compound annual growth rate for exchange traded, agricultural commodity futures and options was 26 percent for non-OECD countries compared to only 16 percent in OECD countries.[34] (The OECD is an abbreviation of Organization for Economic Cooperation and Development and it represents 34 countries generally considered to be the world's wealthiest economies.) In 2005–06, non-OECD countries witnessed 38 percent growth in exchange traded agricultural contracts compared to 26 percent in the OECD. More recently, China's Securities Regulatory Commission announced that China had become the largest commodity derivatives market in the world, contributing 43 percent of global volume in 2009.[35]

Derivatives exchanges now exist in the following countries considered to be part of the global South. In Latin America: Brazil, Argentina, and Mexico. In Africa: South Africa, Mauritius, and Botswana (Bourse Africa in Botswana plans to offer derivatives in the future; and Egypt is toying with opening a commodity and financial derivatives exchange). In Asia: Turkey, China, Hong Kong, Taiwan, South Korea, Thailand, Malaysia, Indonesia, India, Pakistan, Nepal, the Philippines, and Singapore. In the Middle East: Israel, United Arab Emirates, and Iran. In Eastern Europe: Czech Republic, Hungary, Poland, Romania, Slovakia, and Ukraine. Most of these "emerging" exchanges have been established since the early 1990s; many have been in operation for less than a decade.

Why so Big? Explaining the Popularity of Derivatives Markets

The growth and expansion of derivatives markets over the past 30 years can be attributed to at least three major factors: widespread trade and financial liberalization since the 1970s in the global North and South; technological developments in pricing and structuring derivative products and in trading platforms; and promotion of derivatives exchanges and risk hedging by government, business, and international organizations.

Liberalization

Economic policy liberalization figures as a cause of derivatives market expansion in at least two ways. First, liberalization has engendered market volatility and entailed a government retreat from risk management, both of which have generated growing demand for the risk management products and speculative instruments offered on derivatives exchanges. Second, liberalization has created a regulatory and policy environment permissive of increasing levels of cross-border financial activity and financial innovation. I ask the reader to keep in mind these connections between derivatives market growth and policy liberalization as they reappear frequently in the discussions that follow.

"Liberalization" refers to the process whereby governments around the world undertook to "free" their economies from government regulation, beginning in the 1970s-early 1980s. Policymakers were motivated to eliminate government as an economic manager by factors including the growing acceptance of neoliberal ideology in policy circles; the opening of the Chinese economy; the faltering of the Soviet economy; the failure of governments to avoid the oil price crises of the 1970s, the recession of the early 1980s, and the debt crisis in the global South; and the rise of Ronald Reagan and Margaret Thatcher in the United States and United Kingdom, respectively. Markets for goods and services of all types were liberalized as tariffs, quotas, and subsidies were reduced or eliminated. Markets for labor were liberalized as guaranteed employment schemes, minimum wages, and labor unions came under more frequent attack. Markets for finance capital were also liberalized as capital controls and other limitations to global financial flows were steadily dismantled. While occurring at different paces and to differing degrees, most countries in the global North and South have liberalized to some extent, generating a significantly more integrated and interdependent world economy. Indeed, economic policy liberalization has been a key driver of economic globalization more generally.[36]

In the derivatives context, liberalization has been pivotal to market growth and expansion by facilitating demand for and the capacity to supply derivative instruments. Turning first to demand, liberalization has entailed the breaking down of public (governmental) forms of economic insurance *and* has simultaneously made economic insurance more necessary by augmenting market volatility. The outcome of this dynamic has been to stimulate demand for alternative forms of insurance, that is, private, market-based insurance like derivatives. Increasing market volatility has also stimulated increases in speculative derivatives trading—the more volatile the underlying markets, the more potential profits to be made anticipating their movements (more on this in Chapter 4).

For example, in the immediate post–World War II period, as for centuries before, governments around the world undertook to stabilize national currency values by pegging exchange rates either to a precious metal like gold or to strong currencies like the US dollar. In this way, a country's economy was largely protected from the risks associated with exchange rate volatility (macroeconomic risks like balance of payments crises and capital flight, as well as microeconomic risks such as fluctuating input costs and revenues). Beginning with US abandonment of the gold standard in 1971, countries around the world undertook to liberalize their exchange rate regimes, moving from a relatively stable, pegged exchange rate system to a more volatile, floating (market-determined) system. Liberalization here resulted in the dismantlement of public insurance (pegged exchange rates) *and* increases in foreign exchange market volatility (as pegged rates changed to more volatile floating rates). Both of these dynamics stimulated increases in demand for foreign exchange derivatives that help firms around manage and speculate upon exchange rate risk. As Melamed notes, "On August 15, 1971, when President Richard Nixon dropped the U.S. dollar convertibility to gold, it led to an irreversible breakdown of the system of fixed exchange rates, initiated the modern era of globalization, and provided the rationale for the launch of financial futures."[37] Today, foreign exchange derivatives are among the most widely traded contracts in the world.[38]

Coffee provides another example of how liberalization stimulates demand for derivative instruments. Between 1962 and 1989, the global coffee market was regulated by the International Coffee Agreement (ICA). The ICA constituted a commitment by coffee importing and exporting nations to manage global coffee supplies through quotas, and stabilize and raise coffee prices. When the Agreement fell apart in 1989, coffee stocks flooded the market and prices fell quickly. Thus, since 1989, the global coffee market has witnessed significantly more volatility than during the ICA era. Jorge Cardenas, former chairman of the World Coffee Conference, states in his 2001 speech: "International coffee prices have shown a fluctuation of more than 50 percent annually in recent years whereas during periods when the market was regulated prices fluctuated between 10–15 percent around their medium-term trend."[39]

Reductions in government-provided price insurance implied by the dissolution of the ICA, combined with higher levels of price volatility, has translated into growing demand for coffee derivatives. For example, UNCTAD argues:

> Commodity exchanges [that offer futures and options] make it possible for farmers to achieve price predictability and security, despite the volatility, over a crop cycle (and, for storable commodities, for a further six months to one year). This is particularly relevant because, with the withdrawal of government support for developing-country agricultural producers, short-term shocks in the prices of key export products are increasingly felt at the level of the farmer.[40]

Not only has liberalization generated demand for derivative instruments, it has also provided the regulatory and policy context within which derivative instruments can be more readily supplied on exchanges and OTC. Prior to the 1970s in many Northern countries and prior to the early 1990s in many Southern countries, governments had in place regulations that prevented or limited cross-border derivatives transactions, as well as outright bans on speculation and specific types of instruments.

In the United States, Markham's history of commodity futures regulation reveals that US regulators frequently intervened in the markets, beginning in the 1920s, to curtail fraudulent practices and curb speculative trading. The Futures Trading Act of 1921, for example, aimed to limit the scope of "bucket shops," brokerage firms who took client orders and held them without placing the orders on the exchange itself. (This practice leaves clients of bucket shops exposed to the risk that the brokerage house will not be able to pay.)[41] Falling commodity prices during the Great Depression of the 1930s led US regulator to implement rules to limit speculative trading. President Roosevelt noted to the US Congress in 1934: "It is my belief that exchanges for dealing in securities and commodities are necessary and of definite value to our commercial and agricultural life. Nevertheless, it should be our national priority to restrict, as far as possible, the use of these exchanges for purely speculative purposes."[42] Consistent with such sentiments, the Commodity Exchange Act of 1934 was passed and the Commodity Exchange Administration (CEA) was set up, with the latter designated as the new agency to oversee prohibitions on speculative activity and other trading regulations prescribed by the former. One key rule established in the CEA era was a ban on options trading in those markets regulated by the exchange, as options were viewed as purely speculative tools. Over the next 40 years, regulators would respond to increasing concern about speculation, and regulatory inadequacies, via a broad array of new policies and rules (e.g. margin requirements, broker and exchange registration, speculative position limits, and product bans like on options contracts).

By the late 1970s and early 1980s, signs of liberalization (deregulation) began to appear. In the 1970s the CEA was replaced by the Commodity Futures Trading Commission (CFTC), which brought more commodity markets under government regulation (many markets were more or less unregulated until this time) and extended the monitoring and oversight role of regulators (previously, regulators had relied on the exchanges to monitor and enforce rules). However, when it came time to reauthorize the CFTC in 1982, the US Congress showed some openness to measures to liberalize the markets. One of the critical measures adopted at this time was "to allow the CFTC to begin a pilot program for exchange trading of agricultural options, which had been banned since at least 1936."[43] Markham also suggests that liberalization of the markets around this time sometimes occurred in a less purposeful way, as the private sector innovated more quickly than the CFTC could regulate. Referring to the rise of "deferred delivery" contracts in the late 1970s, the author notes, "If the CFTC believed that the options suspension had rid it of fly-by-night operators, it was sadly mistaken. They simply shifted their operations to a 'new' product."[44] More recently, the US Congress further deregulated and liberalized derivatives markets by simply affirming their commitment not to regulate complex OTC derivatives. The Commodity Futures Modernization Act was passed in 2001, in the wake of the 9/11 attacks on the World Trade Center, and "It effectively banned regulators from sticking their noses into over-the-counter derivatives like credit default swaps."[45]

The growing permissiveness of US legislators and regulators toward derivative instruments and trading is mirrored in the regulatory moves of other countries. In India, the government removed the ban on the cash settlement of futures trading in 2000 and bans on certain options have also been removed since that time, regulations that had been in place since the 1950s.[46]

Today, Indian regulators are considering whether to allow foreign entities to trade in Indian futures markets. In China, pilot trading programs in the late 1980s resulted in the establishment of multiple commodity exchanges in the 1990s, with Chinese exchanges now among the largest in the world. Further liberalizing the markets would be new rules, now actively being considered, to allow foreigners to trade Chinese futures.[47] Dodd and Griffith-Jones note how liberalization of rules governing options trading in Chile in 2005 is providing an impetus for market growth and expansion.[48]

It is important to note that the financial and food crises have prompted some policy reversals in the derivatives context. In the United States, the Dodd-Frank Wall Street Reform and Consumer Protection Act of 2010 seeks to move OTC derivatives trading onto organized exchanges, in the hopes of preventing the kinds of OTC credit default swap trades in which AIG, for example, was involved in the run-up to the 2008 crisis. Clapp and Helleiner note that the role of financial speculation in the food crisis has led European regulators to consider new rules to govern commodity derivatives trading.[49] The relationship between derivatives trading and food price volatility is discussed at length in Chapter 4.

Technological Change

While explaining the rise of derivatives markets over the past decades, it is also important to discuss the variety of technological developments that have underpinned this growth, particularly developments in information and communications technology (ICT) and several specific innovations in the derivatives field.

Globalization has generally been associated with, and many argue caused by, rapid developments in ICT technology like the Internet. As in most areas of the economy, the rapidity and ease of global communication and information access made possible by the Internet have lubricated derivatives trading and market growth. Economides notes that the Internet plays at least three critical roles in financial markets: allowing information access and exchange; facilitating exchanges among market participants; and providing for the "democratization" of trading, whereby traders can more easily access markets directly. The author further notes that financial markets networked via the Internet, like exchange traded derivatives markets, frequently grow more rapidly and tend toward greater levels of *both* competition and concentration among top firms than do non-networked markets.[50] Please keep this tendency toward market concentration in mind, as it will be discussed frequently in subsequent sections and chapters (e.g. Chapter 4).

An array of more specific technological developments, particular to the derivatives and financial fields, are also worthy of note. These include technological developments in options pricing, electronic trading, and technical market analysis.

In the 1970s, three economists—Fischer Black, Robert Merton, and Myron Scholes—developed the Black-Scholes Options Pricing Formula. Merton and Scholes won the 1997 Nobel Prize in Economics for their method of reliably pricing options contracts. (Black, who died in 1995, did not receive Nobel Prize because it is never awarded posthumously.) Perry Mehrling, Black's biographer, notes, "In finance, he had one spectacular success, when the Black-Scholes formula moved almost immediately from the pages of an academic journal to concrete practice at the Chicago Board Options Exchange."[51] Steinherr comments:

> The development of options, which had existed for a long time, into a widespread, regularly used and traded financial instrument with applications in most financial domains, benefited tremendously from a scientific breakthrough achieved by Fischer Black and Myron Scholes . . . . The Black-Scholes formula is a benchmark for arbitrage operations and a basis for valuing a non-traded option. Without it, option products would not have achieved such an amazing success.[52]

Electronic trading has been similarly influential. As noted previously, electronic trading platforms have replaced open outcry (pit trading) on almost all exchanges globally. Electronic trading platforms provide at least two major benefits in terms of derivatives market growth. First, setting up an electronic exchange is cheaper and easier than establishing the physical presence required for open outcry operations. This has allowed smaller and newer exchanges to proliferate outside of the major world financial centers. Second, electronic platforms allow exchanges to reach a larger client base, thereby facilitating greater market liquidity and growth. In his 2009 book, Melamed recounts the development of the Chicago Mercantile Exchange (CME, aka "the Merc"), one of the world's premier derivatives exchanges. Speaking on the impact of Globex, the exchange's electronic platform, he writes, "It extended the Merc's pits to every nook and cranny of the financial world with live access from more than 80 countries. Its technological evolution is nearly incomprehensible, the stuff of science fiction."[53]

Technical analysis, one of two major ways that traders evaluate financial markets and determine trading strategies, has also benefited enormously from technological change. The other technique, fundamental analysis, involves looking at market "fundamentals," the determinants of supply and demand and thus prices. By contrast, technical analysis "refers to a study of the market itself rather than of the external factors that affect the supply of and demand for the various commodities, currencies, financial instruments, and other items which are traded in the futures markets."[54] Using market data, technical analysts try to "identify turning points in the market's assessment" to maximize profits from changing market conditions.[55] Revolutions in computing power and capability partly explain how technical analysis has become popular among financial market analysts. Melamed comments:

> Computers, no longer acting within the structure of their classical capability, have gained artificial intelligence and assumed a significant role in directing the actions of the traders themselves. Hugely successful proprietary trading enterprises have sprung up in all parts of the globe with jealously guarded algorithms (trading programs) that have achieved a new generation of analytics. These programs, operating at unimaginable speeds, apply advanced mathematical models in order to capture countless sophisticated trading strategies based on price correlations and associations between markets that were never before possible. It has forever changed the definition of a "trader."[56]

While the Internet, derivatives pricing formulae, electronic trading, and computing for technical analysis have all, no doubt, contributed to the growth and expansion of derivatives market, the reader has to keep in mind that many other technologies have also been instrumental, for example, clearing and settlement technologies employed by exchanges and hybridization techniques that combine several financial/derivative contracts into one in order to create new products.

Promotion

A contingent of government agencies, international organizations, and private businesses have been steadily promoting derivative market expansion for the past several decades. International organizations are recommending and financing the establishment of derivatives exchanges in developing countries, and incorporating derivatives into policy recommendations for national officials. Governments are sponsoring new exchanges, providing assistance to prospective traders, and integrating derivatives-based schemes into national policy. Private firms, that is, the exchanges, brokers, and clearinghouses, have been investing heavily in "emerging market derivatives" in the hopes of tapping into a new and potentially very large client base. Combined with the enabling forces of liberalization and technological change, promotion activities appear to have been widely effective in extending the global reach of derivatives markets.

A variety of international organizations (IOs) have been actively promoting the establishment of new derivatives exchanges and the expansion of existing ones. Among others, the International Monetary Fund (IMF), the World Bank, and UNCTAD are active in this context, though to varying degrees. Please keep in mind that derivatives promotion by IOs is one of the major topics of this book; it explores whether such promotion is justified in the agricultural development context, especially with reference to the supposed benefits derivatives can deliver to local agricultural players like small farmers.

Researchers at the IMF have authored several recent papers highlighting the benefits of derivatives exchanges to host economies. Focusing largely on financial derivatives, the IMF has argued that derivatives can provide price discovery and risk management services, increase the pool of investment capital available locally (because risks can be more easily and cheaply laid off by foreign investors), and generate new income and depth for less mature financial sectors (i.e. relative to the mega financial centers of the North). Writing for the IMF, Adelegan concludes that more derivatives exchanges in sub-Saharan Africa (SSA) are desirable: "Despite these current weaknesses [global financial crisis and lax regulation], the advantages of derivatives markets should not be discounted. The main benefit of derivatives markets in SSA countries would be to enable them to self-insure against the volatility of capital flows. Their overdependence on bank credit as a source of funding could be reduced and through the introduction of commodity futures they could improve their management of seasonal risk, albeit with appropriate regulation and supervision."[57] Please note that the IMF here is supporting various types of derivatives markets, financial and commodity derivatives, with the commodities markets justified on the basis that they can help local players manage seasonal price risks. As will be seen throughout the book, it is *very* common for researchers and IOs to legitimize establishing derivatives exchanges with reference to benefits for local participants. As will also be seen, these benefits are not always certain and derivatives can actually do harm to local participants through a variety of channels.

As will be discussed below, the World Bank has also been actively promoting the use of derivative instruments for use by Southern actors for development purposes. While the IMF's research has been rather recent and focused mainly on financial derivatives markets, the World Bank's work on derivatives dates back to the early 1990s (if not earlier) and has focused largely (though not exclusively) on the potential for agricultural and raw materials derivatives markets to foster "development" in Southern economies dependent upon primary product production and export. The World Bank's work in this area is extensive, ranging from research and policy advice to training public officials and running pilot programs in client countries. And, while the IMF directs its recommendations mostly to governments, the Bank is working to integrate commodity derivatives not only into public policy and regulatory endeavors but also into the daily routines of farmers, small processors, traders, cooperatives, and banks, among other actors.[58]

The World Bank itself has also begun to offer hedging instruments to its clients. For example, the International Bank for Reconstruction and Development (IBRD), the central lending division of the World Bank Group, offers several hedging products to its sovereign clients.[59] On a stand-alone or "built-in" basis (i.e. built into loans), IBRD borrowers can purchase commodity, interest, and exchange rate derivatives to mitigate risks associated with loans in foreign currencies, variable interest rates, and governmental commodity dependence. Presumably, the IBRD trades in global derivatives markets to lay off the risks associated with entering into such contracts with clients. One advantage for clients to hedging via the World Bank's facility is that clients do not need to post collateral (margin) to trade.

Similarly, UNCTAD has been a recent contributor to derivatives promotion in the global South, with its advocacy picking up pace beginning in the late 1990s. Like the World Bank, UNCTAD focuses primarily on agricultural and raw materials derivatives and their development potential in commodity-dependent Southern states. However, UNCTAD differs slightly from the World Bank in its focus on establishing "commodity exchanges" in developing countries. A commodity exchange is a central marketplace for agricultural products, designed to make marketing more efficient, that also in some cases offers agricultural futures and options. UNCTAD has been involved in research, government consultations and meetings, and promotion of derivatives/commodity exchanges through pilot programs, cooperation with the World Bank and other agencies, and hosting of expert meetings like the "The Emerging Markets Forum at the 28th International SFOA Bürgenstock Derivatives Conference" held in Switzerland in 2006.[60] The United Nations Development Program (UNDP) and the UN Food and Agriculture Organization (FAO) have further recently produced a few reports that echo the sentiments of UNCTAD on the matter of commodity exchanges.[61]

Like the IOs, governments around the world have supported and in some cases actively encouraged derivative market development. For example, in China and India the major derivatives exchanges are promoted and sponsored by government agencies. The Dalian Commodity Exchange—one of China's largest, established in 1993 and offering agricultural and energy contracts—has recently been incorporated by the Government of China into the "Plan to Revitalize Northeast China" and is being explicitly promoted by the state.[62] In India, the State Bank of India and the National Bank for Agriculture and Rural Development are among the primary shareholders in the Multi Commodity Exchange (MCX).[63]

Other governments are actively assisting potential traders in accessing the markets. The United States Department of Agriculture (USDA), for example, actively supports forward contracting and futures and options hedging by farmers and agribusiness by providing education and technical support.[64] The United States Agency for International Development (USAID) has been promoting new commodity exchanges in the developing world, complementing the efforts of the World Bank and UNCTAD, among other multilateral agencies.[65] In Mexico, the government-operated ASERCA (*Apoyos y Servicios a la Comercialización Agropecuaria*/Agricultural Commercialization Support and Services) program facilitates and subsidizes the purchase of agricultural commodity options for farmers and agribusinesses in the country.[66]

Private firms are the third major group of derivatives promoters. Financial firms are pursuing "emerging market" derivatives opportunities as a means of tapping into new profitable client bases, establishing new trading centers, and unrolling new products.

Developments in India provide a recent example of cross-border derivatives promotion in the global South. The Financial Technologies Group is a private financial technologies firm located in India and is the lead promoter of India's MCX, which opened its doors in 2003. The Financial Technologies Group has, since then, partnered with various foreign firms to open the Dubai Gold and Commodity Exchange (DGCX), the Bahrain Financial Exchange (BFX), the Global Board of Trade in Mauritius (GBOT), the Singapore Mercantile Exchange (SMX), and Bourse Africa. GBOT's website notes:

> GBOT is promoted by the Financial Technologies Group, a global leader in setting up and operating tech centric next generation exchanges in the emerging but fast growing economies from Africa to Asia and Middle East to South East Asia. The Group operates one of the largest exchange networks comprising 10 exchanges and 5 ecosystem ventures which address upstream and downstream opportunities around exchanges, including clearing, depository, information vending, and payment gateway among others.[67]

Further highlighting the substantial cross-border cooperation among firms to promote derivatives exchanges, the MCX in India is itself partly capitalized by large financial companies from the global North, like Fidelity Investments, Merrill Lynch, and Euronext.[68] Please keep these partnerships and joint ventures in mind, as they come up again in subsequent discussions of derivatives market concentration and dominance of the markets by Northern multinationals (see Chapter 4).

International organizations have also begun to partner with select private firms to sell derivative instruments in Southern markets. For example, in June

2011 the World Bank unveiled a new "Agricultural Price Risk Management Product" that will "improve access to hedging instruments to shield consumers and producers of agricultural commodities from price volatility."[69] The World Bank is partnering with US financial giant JPMorgan to provide US$200 million in credit to generate some US$4 billion in price protection for World Bank clients (who may include governments, producers, traders, manufacturers, consumers, etc.). The International Finance Corporation (IFC, one of the five organizations that make up the World Bank Group) is further partnering with global reinsurance giant Swiss Re to extend weather derivatives markets in the global South (more below).

Contemporary Applications of Derivatives to Agricultural Development

Derivatives can help traders manage economic risks. It is this risk management function that makes the markets attractive to development researchers, practitioners, and public officials. Just as businesses protect revenues and profits via derivative hedging, developing country actors might also employ the same strategies to good, poverty-reducing effect. In so hedging, Southern governments and individual players in agriculture might make their tax revenues, incomes, investments, and expenditures more stable and secure. Or so the argument goes.

Tracing poverty and insecurity in Southern states to problems of commodity dependence combined with vulnerability to risk, the development establishment has suggested a growing array of derivative-based policies and programs that might be applied in the agricultural development context. "Commodity dependence" refers to a situation in which an actor relies on the production and sale of only a few goods (or just one good) for the bulk (or all) of its income. Commodity-dependent economies, governments, and individuals are vulnerable to fluctuations in the prices of the goods they produce and sell. "Vulnerability" expresses a combination of exposure to and inability to effectively manage risk.[70] Volatile prices, along with other risks like the weather, can reduce incomes and revenues and render them more uncertain, making it difficult to finance the purchase of necessary goods and services, productive investments, and debt repayment. Many, and this cohort continues to grow, have argued that derivatives markets are well-suited to help commodity-dependent actors, many of whom are poor residents of the rural South, survive and prosper amidst volatile conditions by insulating them from the negative financial consequences of fluctuating prices and changing weather patterns.

What is more, derivatives markets can help the South address its vulnerabilities *without* government intervention in commodity markets and unnecessary public expenditure. This point is key. Consistent with neoliberal ideas about free markets and the proper role of government in the economy, derivatives are posited as *substitutes* for wrongheaded, government-centered agricultural policies of the past (such as public crop insurance, marketing boards, buffer stocks, and international commodity agreements like the ICA mentioned above). Derivatives are *private, market-based* institutions, characteristics that are highly valued in today's political and ideological climate. Indeed, many researchers deliberately juxtapose derivatives markets to the (in their reckoning) less efficient, and more expensive, coercive, and corrupt public systems of commodity management that existed previously.

Since the early 1990s, derivatives advocacy in the development and poverty contexts has gained serious momentum. As the current period of economic globalization has unfolded, the calls of derivatives advocates have grown louder, responding it seems to increasingly volatile commodity markets, more precarious rural livelihoods, the rising prominence and sophistication of global financial markets and actors, and growing discontent with the global economic system among the world's poor, insecure, and dispossessed. However, and as I will flush out in greater length in Chapter 5, derivatives advocacy is also a highly *political* project despite its techno-economic façade. As important as derivatives' risk management functions, or perhaps even more so, is the insurance that derivatives expansion affords the neoliberal project in the global South.

The remainder of this section of the chapter outlines the major contemporary applications of derivative instruments to agricultural development: weather derivatives and crop insurance; commodity derivatives and price insurance; and, price discovery and investment decisions. For each application, I briefly present technical background regarding how derivatives are applied to various problems of rural development and poverty, the benefits of derivatives claimed by advocates relative to publicly centered programs, and information regarding the extent of promotional activity and adoption of derivatives in Southern agriculture.

Weather Derivatives and Crop Insurance

While most of the derivatives-based development initiatives discussed throughout this book are geared toward addressing the problem of *price* volatility, there are a growing number of crop insurance programs across the South based on *weather* derivatives. Weather derivatives, based on indices of relevant weather variables (such as temperature or rainfall), are increasingly being utilized to structure and finance crop insurance schemes in developing countries.

A weather derivative is a "weather contingent contract whose payoff will be in an amount of cash determined by future weather events. The settlement value of these weather events is determined from a weather index, expressed as values of a weather variable measured at a stated location."[71] Like other derivative instruments, weather derivatives are traded on exchanges and OTC. Weather futures and options, and index-based weather insurance policies are the most commonly traded weather derivatives. The reader should be aware that much of the literature on weather risk and rural development discusses weather derivatives in terms of "index-based weather insurance." While there may be important legal and regulatory differences between the derivative and the insurance product, the two types of instruments are virtually identical for our purposes.

The value of the weather derivative or weather insurance contract is based on the deviation of actual conditions from "strike" index level specified in the contract, as well as the specified liability level. In essence, traders pay a premium to an insurance company or derivatives dealer, which agrees to pay a given sum for every "tick" above or below the strike level specified in the contract. Insurance companies and dealers can, in turn, lay off the risks they incur in writing these contracts via contracts with global reinsurance companies and derivatives dealers.

Weather derivatives are rapidly gaining popularity, particularly as the weather becomes more volatile and more unpredictable with climate change. From energy and construction companies to ski resorts, grain elevators, and clothing retailers, weather derivatives are increasingly used as a vehicle for hedging weather-related business risks. According to the Weather Risk Management Association (WRMA), OTC weather derivative trading increased 30 percent in 2010–11, while total market growth topped 20 percent the same year.[72] The CME, the largest exchange to offer weather derivatives, offers futures and options on temperature, snowfall, rainfall, frost, and hurricanes across three continents (North America, Europe, and Asia). Morrison, writing for the FIA, believes that the Great Recession may stimulate more use of weather derivatives: "The trend for using weather derivatives may grow as companies find that the recession gives them less flexibility to absorb a hit from abnormal weather patterns."[73]

As with other derivatives, weather derivatives are no longer the exclusive purview of business and are increasingly advocated as tools for yield, "catastrophe," and disaster risk management in the rural development context. Like price risk, weather risk is dangerous for agricultural producers. For this reason, crop insurance programs that ensure payments to producers when weather conditions damage crops have historically been important components of agricultural support systems in the North and South. Because risk always hits the poor hardest, crop insurance programs also have important antipoverty dimensions, especially in Southern states where agriculture is dominated by smallholders. For poor, commodity-dependent farmers, crop insurance payments can mean a stable supply of food and other necessities during times of crop failure, as well as the ability to reinvest in future crop production. As several researchers recently argued, "Reducing economic vulnerability to weather events in developing countries may very well be the most critical economic development challenge of the new millennium."[74]

Although researchers generally agree on the importance of crop insurance that protects farmers from financial losses associated with weather, they tend to differ on how the insurance should be structured and financed. Traditional, private crop insurance markets have a long history of failure. Among other problems, private crop insurance confronts problems of correlated (i.e. systemic or covariate) risks, moral hazard, adverse selection, and high administrative costs.[75] Private market failure has historically resulted in government guarantees, subsidies, and other supports for traditional crop insurance. Derivatives advocates usually criticize these public (or publicly sponsored) programs as inefficient, wasteful of scarce public resources, and inappropriate for developing countries. Weather derivatives are envisioned by advocates as superior, private, market-based substitutes for traditional schemes.

For example, the World Bank argues that large, government-funded crop insurance programs in countries like the United States and Canada are not replicable in most developing countries because resources are not as readily available, a much larger proportion of the population is involved in farming, and the opportunity costs of expenditures on crop insurance are higher in developing countries (i.e. there are a lot of other important things to spend scarce government resources on).[76] Researchers Hess, Richter, and Stoppa (from the IFC, the World Bank, and Procom Agr in Italy, respectively) argue that weather derivatives markets can insulate Southern farmers from weather risk without the problems associated with traditional schemes: "New WRM [weather risk management] insurance instruments, like area-based weather indices, provide a viable alternative to traditional insurance instruments, and offer real advantages to households, companies and governments in developing countries."[77]

Promotion and use of weather derivatives in the Southern agricultural context is being undertaken by several international organizations working in conjunction with national governments. A host of financial and agricultural multinationals are also involved both separately and in conjunction with the IOs. In 2006, the UN World Food Program (WFP) bought index-based weather insurance (actually, a call option) from reinsurance multinational Axa Re to ensure necessary financing for food aid in the event of drought in Ethiopia. Even though the option was never exercised, "The World Food Program established a mechanism for accessing global risk markets to supplement traditional donor-based humanitarian relief."[78] The World Bank has undertaken weather insurance experiments and pilot programs in Nicaragua, Morocco, Tunisia, Ethiopia, India, Ukraine, Malawi, Peru, and Mongolia, among other countries.[79] In most cases, the World Bank works with other international organizations (like the United Nations); government agencies; and/or local partners, including insurance companies, farmer cooperatives, and microfinance organizations, to implement the programs.

The World Bank (specifically the IFC and IBRD) is also working to create the Global Index Insurance Fund (GIIF) that would "close the gap between the developing country's demand for insurance against severe shocks at public and private levels and the index insurance markets . . . ."[80] The IFC's website on the project notes extensive cooperation among international organizations, and government and private companies to promote weather derivatives: "The IFC and its partners in GIIF would like to work with local insurers and financial institutions, as well as regulatory bodies and organizations from the private sector to build capacity and a suitable regulatory and commercial environment for index-based insurance products."[81] The GIIF is funded primarily by the European Commission, and receives technical and market support from the global reinsurance multinational Swiss Re.

Private companies are also independently pursuing emerging weather derivatives markets, purportedly to further rural development and support poverty alleviation efforts. For example, the Syngenta Foundation, the nominally philanthropic arm of the Swiss agribusiness giant, is actively working to sell weather derivatives in Kenya. "The Foundation is committed to further developing weather index insurance products so that they may protect farmers against agricultural risk more comprehensively and be accessible to many farmers."[82] Micro Ensure, an insurance company dedicated to "serving the poor throughout the developing world," provides another recent example. Micro Ensure provides weather insurance products (along with credit life, funeral, health, political violence, and property insurance products) to the Southern poor. The company's website notes that weather policies are being actively marketed in Malawi, Tanzania, Rwanda, India, and the Philippines.[83]

Commodity Derivatives and Price Insurance

In addition to weather derivatives, commodity derivative instruments like forwards, futures, and commodity-linked bonds are also being integrated into agricultural development agendas across the South. Like weather derivatives, commodity derivatives are thought capable of providing the much needed risk management services to poor agricultural players and commodity-dependent governments facing increasingly volatile market environments. Further paralleling the weather derivatives discussion above, derivative-based price insurance is also seen by advocates as a superior substitute to the government-centered programs popular previously.

Global commodity prices have become more volatile since the 1970s as a consequence of market liberalization and globalization. Severe price volatility is common for a whole range of commodities, including food commodities, beverages, and raw materials. Interestingly, price trends are increasingly correlated across different commodities, an unexpected development given that there is no fundamental reason to think that the price of cotton, for example, should move in tandem with the price of coffee. The growing volatility and correlation of commodity prices over time speaks to the growing influence of speculative investors in commodity futures markets, investors who treat commodities as a single asset class, an issue that will be discussed in depth in Chapter 4.

Speaking on rising volatility in commodity markets over the past several decades, several researchers note, "In the past 30 years, there have been as many price shocks across the range of commodities as there were in the preceding 75 years."[84] A 1999 study of commodity prices by researchers at the IMF concluded:

> First, for the majority of commodities, price slumps last longer than price booms. Second, the magnitude of price falls in a slump is slightly larger than those of price rises in subsequent booms. Third, there is little evidence of a consistent "shape" to the cycles in commodity prices. Fourth, for all commodities, the probability of an end to a slump in prices is independent of the time already spent in the slump, and for most commodities, the probability of an end to a boom in prices is independent of the time already spent in the boom.[85]

Please note that the authors specifically conclude that coffee conforms to all of these general conclusions, along with a number of other commodities.[86] Please also be aware that these findings suggest several important price dynamics, a few of which I highlight here as they will come up again later in Chapter 3: (a) long-term declines in real commodity prices over time; (b) significant price volatility over time; and (c) difficulties predicting future price movements.

Indeed, the past decade has witnessed continued, if not elevated, levels of price volatility across a range of commodities. There have been both severe price rises, as with the food crises of 2007–08 and 2010–11, as well as severe price falls, as with the coffee crisis of 1998–2002. The FAO recently observed, "There is emerging consensus that the global food system is becoming more vulnerable and susceptible to episodes of extreme price volatility. As markets are increasingly integrated in the world economy shocks in the international arena can now transpire and propagate to domestic markets much quicker than before."[87]

Price volatility results in a host of problems in the global South. Rising agricultural commodity prices can lead to hunger for the urban and rural poor, stimulate rapidly rising national import bills, and can put pressure on government budgets as officials scramble to feed their populations and pay their debts. People and governments of import-dependent countries, such as Haiti and Libya that do not grow enough food at home to feed everyone, are particularly vulnerable to rising commodity prices. Falling agricultural commodity prices can lead to dramatic drops in the living standards of farmers, laborers, and small processors; reduced revenues for exporters; and falling foreign exchange and tax earnings for governments. Falling commodity prices are especially dangerous for commodity-dependent countries and peoples, which frequently depend on exports of a single crop for their well-being. In general, price volatility can also create uncertainty about the future, with rapidly changing prices preventing or misdirecting investments in future production.

It is in this context that derivatives advocates offer their wares. It is argued that commodity derivatives like forwards, futures, options, and commodity-linked bonds can provide market-based price insurance, protecting farmers, governments, and other actors from price volatility. Because commodity derivatives allow traders to hedge against price risk, advocates agree that they represent critical tools in the fight against rural poverty. Forward contracting can guarantee a market and a set price for one's crop. Income earned from the futures markets can compensate for monies lost by farmers in the cash market. More stable income streams can also facilitate access to credit markets, allow farmers to pay back loans more reliably, and facilitate investments in future income growth. Governments can hedge against revenue and foreign exchange losses, protecting their budgets and credit ratings when prices fall.

In general, advocates view derivative-based price insurance arrangements as superior substitutes for the public price risk management arrangements that were popular previously. From the 1930s Great Depression to the 1980s, it was common for governments across the North and South to manipulate commodity markets to raise and stabilize prices. International commodity agreements like the ICA were attempted for many commodities aside from coffee, including rubber, tin, cocoa, and sugar. These attempts, some of them successful, involved governments collectively restricting global commodity supplies via trade and production barriers. Governments also erected a host of domestic institutions, such as marketing boards, that were designed to support and restrict domestic commodity production and exchange. Frequently, these domestic crop marketing institutions fixed the prices paid to farmers and small processors thereby generating some price stability and certainty.

By and large, derivative advocates view these prior attempts to stabilize commodity markets via government intervention as wrongheaded, expensive, coercive, inefficient, and frequently subject to corruption and mismanagement. Derivatives, by contrast, allow for some stability and certainty, but do not involve government manipulation of agricultural markets. Rather than managing commodity supplies and creating "artificially" stable and high prices, derivatives compensate traders for financial losses from volatility, all the while allowing commodity markets to do as they "naturally" will.

The World Bank and UNCTAD have been joined by other international organizations in advocating derivatives as price insurance in Southern agriculture. For example, the FAO's Committee on Commodity Problems writes:

> As a proactive approach for minimizing uncertainty, risk management tools are increasingly replacing government support programs as an alternative for raising price predictability and enhancing producer income stability. . . . On a national front, institutional development and legislative measures permitting derivatives trading have paved the way for striking success in managing risks and reducing volatility in many developing countries.[88]

More detailed information on promotion of derivative-based price risk management strategies in Southern agriculture is provided in chapters 3–5.

There are a large variety of specific commodity derivative instruments and arrangements recommended by advocates in the price insurance context. Forward contracts, including price-to-be-fixed contracts (PTBFs) and minimum price forwards, are frequently advocated along with futures and options as tools for price risk management and income stabilization for farmers and governments. (Please refer to the section above on types of derivative instruments for more information on these contracts.) Chapters 3 and 4 further discuss futures and options trading, and analyzes their success in addressing poverty among coffee farmers. In the interest of being comprehensive, below I briefly discuss commodity exchanges and commodity-linked bonds, two potential tools for price insurance suggested by derivative advocates, on which I have yet to provide detail.

A *commodity exchange* is a forum for trading agricultural commodities. In many developing countries, marketing infrastructure (e.g. roads, reliable price information) is poor and farmers, small traders, and processors often have trouble transacting effectively with one another and with larger businesses, both foreign and domestic. Commodity exchanges are designed to centralize crop marketing in one or several key locations, thereby reducing transaction costs. The exchanges help buyers and sellers meet one another, post prices regularly, establish quality and grading standards, provide warehouse (crop storage) facilities and opportunities for forward contracting, and sometimes offer futures and options contracts. Commodity exchanges are thus spot markets (cash markets), and some (but not all) offer derivative contracts on the commodities traded.

In some cases, for example the Ethiopian Commodity Exchange and Bourse Africa, exchanges first establish a spot commodity market, adding futures and options later on as the exchange and the local market mature. Even when futures and options are not offered, as in Ethiopia presently, forward contracting is commonplace on a more informal basis. In other cases, like the Kenya Agricultural Commodity Exchange, there appear to be no plans to offer futures contracts. Also, new commodity exchanges are being envisioned in Bangladesh, Jamaica, and Barbados, among other places.

There is quite a tempest brewing over commodity exchanges in mainstream development thought and practice. This is especially the case for UNCTAD and the FAO, though the institutions are also gaining some traction at the World Bank. The World Bank has tended to advocate derivatives trading on large futures exchanges that are already established, usually recommending the most liquid and heavily traded contracts in Northern financial centers like New York and London. UNCTAD, however, appears eager to facilitate the establishment of new, local derivatives exchanges housed in commodity exchanges across the South. Leonela Santana-Boado, director of the Commodity Exchanges program at UNCTAD, recently stated in a report authored jointly with the Swiss Futures and Options Association that "UNCTAD will continue actively supporting the development of commodity exchanges in interested countries, with a particular focus on the introduction of new instruments that can boost agricultural growth and reduce rural poverty."[89] As noted above, there are also a host of Southern governments that have already established commodity exchanges or are keen to do so in the future.

Moving onto *commodity-linked bonds,* governments of commodity-dependent countries often default on their debts when commodity prices fall (this is called a "sovereign" debt default). The 1980s debt crises, resulting in a "lost decade" for many countries in the South, resulted in many instances (if only partially) from falling commodity prices (e.g. cocoa in Ghana, tin in Bolivia, and copper in Peru). Since that time, it is common for governments to run into trouble financing debts and domestic expenditures during times of falling prices. Today, the Great Recession has pushed many commodity-dependent countries to the edge of another debt crisis. For example, the Jubilee Debt Campaign reports that Bangladesh, Zimbabwe, and the Philippines, among many others, are in danger of defaulting on their debts as export revenues fall due to reduced demand and falling export prices.[90]

In addition to forwards, futures, and options, commodity-linked bonds thus represent another kind of derivative that can help governments hedge risks to their revenues and expenditures posed by market volatility. These bonds are considered derivative instruments because payments to creditors (debt repayment) are linked to the prices of those commodities upon which the government in question depends. Sovereign debt obligations are dependent upon capacity to repay. In this manner, obligations to creditors fall when commodity prices fall and obligations to creditors rise when commodity prices rise. Governments are, in effect, obtaining price insurance embedded in a debt instrument such that the risk of sovereign default is reduced.[91]

The reader may want to note that some national governments are toying with commodity-linked bonds for individual farmers and businesses working in agriculture. Building off of commodity-linked sovereign debt instruments, the Government of Brazil, for example, has supported the introduction of rural product bonds for agricultural players in Brazil. Some of these instruments are designed such that repayment is linked to coffee prices.[92]

Price Discovery and Investment Decisions

As noted previously, agricultural players can benefit from derivatives markets even if they do not actually trade in derivatives. Futures markets generate prices that indicate likely future dynamics in the markets on which they are based. In other words, the "futures price can be considered as an unbiased prediction of the subsequent spot [cash] price."[93] This function of the markets is referred to as "price discovery." Fischer Black writes:

> I believe that futures markets exist because in some situations they provide an inexpensive way to transfer risk, and because many people both in the business and out like to gamble on commodity prices. Neither of these counts as a major benefit to society. The big benefit from futures markets is the side effect: the fact that participants in the futures markets can make production, storage, and processing decisions by looking at the pattern of futures prices, even if they don't take positions in that market.[94]

Speaking specifically to agriculture, Schultz elegantly noted back in 1949 that prices (cash and future) may be thought of as "production guides" from the perspective of farmers.[95] Along these lines, Herrmann writes of the benefits of price discovery for both producers and consumers in commodity markets: "Forward prices for the commodity guide sales negotiations as well as decisions about resource allocation."[96] Future prices serve as maps of sorts for producers and consumers alike, relaying information about expected future supply and demand conditions in the underlying cash market. Such information may impact farmers' decisions about planting, harvesting, marketing, and storage, among others. Indeed, future prices are thought to allow some certainty about the future to trickle down to the present, eliminating some of the uncertainty that generally characterizes farming enterprises, among other kinds of business.

Derivatives advocates argue that in an agricultural context characterized by significant uncertainty about the future, future commodity prices can serve as a kind of lighthouse, directing the path of poor farmers as they make their way through the murky and dangerous global marketplace. If farmers had more certainty about what the future holds, they could make production and marketing decisions with greater precision, resulting in higher productivity, less risk, and higher and more stable incomes.

Conclusions

Aided by policy liberalization, technological change, and explicit promotional campaigns, derivatives markets are rapidly being globalized. They are growing in size, geographic scope, and product offering, and constitute important dimension of the financialization of the global South. Further motivating financialization in the South has been the integration of derivatives and derivative-based technologies into development agendas, especially in agriculture. Drawing on the hedging and price discovery functions of these instruments, advocates suggest that the globalization of derivatives markets is providing new opportunities to address rural poverty through price discovery and innovative price and weather risk management arrangements. Whether derivatives play this role as well as advocates suggest is the subject of the next chapter.

CHAPTER 3

Coffee, Derivatives, and Income Security: Theory and Practice

To assume that the farmers, even the big farmers, can become players in these highly complicated financial markets . . . would amount to taking leave of common sense.[1]

The theoretical benefits of globalization are not always borne out in practice. This point has been painfully underscored many times over as the Great Recession unfolds and deepens. The globalization and deepening of markets for mortgage products was to have ushered in a new era of homeownership. From the United States to Hungary, individuals and communities that had previously been denied access to mortgage financing were incorporated into global capital markets, as trading in mortgage-backed securities allowed creditors to extend loans to new and different kinds of borrowers. Today, the promises of homeownership made possible by financial globalization have been swept away by foreclosure, bankruptcy, and eviction.

Speaking on the importance of credit derivatives before the crisis, then president of the New York Federal Reserve and current US Treasury secretary Timothy Geithner noted in 2006:

> Credit derivatives have contributed to dramatic changes in the process of credit intermediation, and the benefits of these changes seem compelling. They have made possible substantial improvements in the way credit risk is managed and facilitated a broad distribution of risk outside the banking system. By spreading risk more widely, by making it easier to purchase and sell protection against credit risk and to actively trade credit risk, and by facilitating the participation of a large and very diverse pool of non-bank financial institutions in the business of credit, these changes probably improve the overall efficiency and resiliency of financial markets.[2]

With the advantage of hindsight, such proclamations now appear naive, at best. The complex derivative instruments—credit default swaps—that extended and greased the secondary market for mortgage products in the lead up to 2008 have since been implicated in the deepening of the crisis. The spectacular failure of the American International Group (AIG), with the cascading train of losses its collapse set in motion, underscores the destabilizing influence of global financial innovation, in stark contrast to the assertions of Secretary Geithner.

The globalization and deepening of commodity derivatives markets is similarly envisioned by advocates in the development context as entailing far-reaching benefits for all, and specifically for small farmers in the developing world who are exposed to price volatility. As the CEO of the Ethiopian Commodity Exchange recently argued, "So a Commodity Exchange provides service to all market actors, and, by doing so, expands the range of choices and opportunities available to all, thus allowing risks to be transferred from the hedgers to the investors."[3]

Likewise, in 2006 the Government of India was considering passage of the Forward Contracts (Regulation) Amendment Act. The Bill, which was subsequently passed, reaffirmed the Government's commitment to derivatives trading and specifically allowed for the introduction of commodity options contracts on national commodity exchanges. The benefits of derivatives for farmers was among the primary rationales provided for expanding the scope of the markets, as noted in the proceedings of the Standing Committee on Food, Consumer Affairs and Public Distribution prior to the adoption of the Bill:

> The National Commodity Derivatives Exchanges Limited (NCDEX) in their memorandum submitted to the Committee favoured the passage of Bill and stated that Forward Contracts market gives advance signals of prices of commodities in future. Farmers can use this signal for hedging their price risks and also to decide which crop economically suits them . . . The State Government of Gujarat stated that besides this Commodity Futures market addresses the issues relating to smoothening price fluctuations, vulnerability of farmers to such price fluctuations on how to cope up with the prices of crop crash tomorrow. A farmer can sell his commodity at a price which is fixed today, which eliminates his risk from price fluctuations. A farmer would thus be able to lock in his future price and not be exposed to fluctuations in prices.[4]

In the ideal world pictured by derivatives advocates, farmers can thus use derivatives markets to manage risk and guide investment decisions without the inefficiencies and loss of freedom associated with government schemes. Reality, however, is somewhat less impressive. In practice, derivatives markets are inefficient part of the time, are incomplete in significant ways, and are largely inaccessible to small producers. The large gap between derivatives theory and practice, fleshed out here in the coffee context, undermines the usefulness of the markets from a development perspective. This is not to say that derivatives market fail all of the time, for there are certainly cases in which hedging can stabilize incomes, forward prices can effectively guide investment decisions, and small producers can realize these benefits. Rather, the evidence suggests that derivatives markets can address small farmer income instability in a limited and inconsistent way that counters much of the enthusiasm for the instruments in a development context. In this respect, the derivatives debate echoes broader debates about financial globalization's theoretical promises and its harsher practical realities.

The chapter proceeds as follows. In the first section, I discuss the theoretical perspectives underlying contemporary derivatives advocacy in the development context. In the second section, I provide current and historical data on the behavior of coffee prices, and set out the context for the subsequent empirical analysis, namely coffee dependence and farmer vulnerability to price risk. Third, I present empirical evidence as to the efficiency, completeness, and accessibility of derivatives markets in the coffee context. In the last section, I summarize these results and explain their significance for development policy.

Derivatives and Income Security: Theory

Derivatives advocacy in the development context is rooted in two general theoretical propositions. First, derivatives markets, as private, market-based solutions to price risk problems, occupy a *moral* high ground insofar as they undermine government paternalism and enhance individual freedom. Second, derivatives markets are thought to be more *efficient* means of managing price risk than other arrangements, particularly public ones. It is my opinion that derivatives markets are also desirable to advocates for a third, more practical, reason that is not much discussed—they are *politically* convenient. This point, about the political advantages of derivatives as development tools, is discussed at more length in Chapter 5.

Most generally, advocates of derivatives in the development context argue that the markets provide an effective income stabilization service and they do so efficiently, more efficiently than government interventions, and in a manner conducive to individual freedom and responsibility. These theoretical assumptions are deeply rooted in neoclassical economics and illustrate the decidedly neoliberal sensibilities of derivatives advocates. Neoliberalism, considered as a globally dominant (hegemonic) "theory of political economic practices," emphasizes individual commercial freedom and private property rights, the efficiency of markets in directing economic activity, and the dangers of government intervention in the economy.[5]

Neoclassical economic theory, that body of formal economic theory that underpins global neoliberalism, has been especially influential in directing agricultural, financial, and development policy since the 1970s. As discussed in chapter 1, the past 40 years have witnessed an unprecedented opening (liberalization) of agricultural and financial markets in North and South alike, with relatively free markets in agricultural goods and financial products replacing previous systems in which government played a larger role. In the context of coffee and derivatives, the influence of neoclassical theory and neoliberal policy can be seen in the collapse of the ICA, the dissolution of marketing boards and other government agricultural agencies, and the growth and expansion of derivatives exchanges, developments discussed in the previous chapter.

Neoclassical theory and neoliberalism have similarly informed the modern development orthodoxy, especially that dominant set of development ideas called the Washington Consensus. The Washington Consensus, with its mantra of "liberalize, privatize and stabilize,"[6] underpinned development policy at the World Bank and the IMF, and in many Southern governments, from the mid-1980s through the 1990s. Despite harsh criticism and systematic evidence of regular policy failure, the promarket core of the Washington Consensus remains untouched even in today's "post-Washington Consensus" development context. Contemporary derivatives advocacy is something of a reminder of this point (see Chapter 5).

As with most other areas of the economy, neoclassical theory has influenced the way in which the development establishment thinks about risk management. Critical for the discussion in this chapter is the body of neoclassical theory that prescribes commodity derivatives markets as an alternative to public commodity price stabilization. In general, neoclassical theory views free markets, if they work well, as the best vehicles for risk management. Depending on the theorist in question, this may be because free markets best preserve economic freedom or because free markets most efficiently shift risks among economic participants, or both. Government intervention—for example, in stabilizing prices or operating an insurance market—is viewed as a "second-best" solution and is usually prescribed only in instances where private markets fail or are incomplete.

Neoclassical theorist Kenneth Arrow elaborates on the idea of a second-best solution: "I propose here the view that, when the market fails to achieve an optimal state, society will, to some extent at least, recognize the gap, and nonmarket social institutions will arise attempting to bridge it."[7] Likewise, economic historian David Moss argues, "But the truth is that the markets themselves have not always proved capable of managing capitalism's inherent risks in an acceptable manner . . . it was up to the government to take up the slack, to undertake insurance in those cases where [a private market for insurance], for whatever reason, has failed to emerge."[8]

A World Bank researcher notes the logically corollary to Arrow's axiom, that free markets are the "first-best" vehicle for risk management: "In an ideal world with perfectly symmetrical information and complete and well-functioning markets, all risk management arrangements can and should be market based."[9] Robert Shiller similarly discusses "the ideal of risk sharing developed by Kenneth Arrow" as one " in which there is a market for every risk and a price for every state of nature."[10] Generally, then, neoclassical theory suggests that as private markets for risk management are completed and better structured to avoid failure they should replace public risk management arrangements. Risk privatization in this fashion will improve efficiency and give more freedom to market actors.

This broad, theoretical neoclassical position on insurance markets is replicated in miniature in the agricultural finance literature. Whereas in the past government interventions were perhaps necessary to stabilize commodity prices, today derivatives markets are better poised to do the job. For example, Milton Friedman argues that in seeking solutions to income instability among farmers "the free market should reign and government activity should be restricted to making the market freer and more effective."[11] Friedman and other neoclassical economists argue that when crafting agricultural risk management policies, the policies must be aimed at not only achieving efficiency in risk management but also ensuring the highest degree of freedom possible for producers.

Efficiency is enhanced when governments refrain from manipulating commodity prices, and instead allow the market to determine resource allocations within and across sectors of the economy. Theorist Ronald McKinnon, an early proponent of financial liberalization in the global South, writes as follows about the benefits of using derivatives to hedge price risk relative to public price stabilization schemes: "In conclusion, one can say that past attempts at commodity price stabilization have been inefficient and unsuccessful because of the preoccupation of governments with the spot price and a corresponding lack of appreciation—frequently amounting to hostility—of the benefits of futures trading. This paper, on the other hand, holds that public policy should actively encourage more futures trading . . . ."[12]

Applying McKinnon's insights to the coffee context, a host of researchers have indicted the International Coffee Agreement on the grounds that it distorted coffee prices, impeded producer freedom, encouraged overproduction, and bankrupted government agencies.[13]

Not only can derivatives markets theoretically permit efficient stabilization of farm incomes by affording opportunities to hedge, they also facilitate future price discovery. Herrmann notes, "The market's basic role is to provide rational forward prices. All new information that might affect the commodity market is embodied in both the spot (cash) and futures prices."[14] The future prices discovered in derivatives markets can also have a stabilizing impact if farmers use them to make decisions about marketing and storage. In an efficient market, theorists argue that the difference between future prices for storable commodities (like coffee) across successive contracts reflects the returns to storage. Farmers can thus use future prices to decide how much to store and how much to sell at specific times, thereby maximizing gains and potentially stabilizing incomes in markets where seasonal production patterns impact prices (as is the case with coffee). Using future prices as guides, coffee farmers might, for example, decide to store coffee during times of peak production and sell later on when prices are higher. Future prices indicate to farmers if such a strategy is profitable, that is if future coffee income will be adequate to cover the costs of storage. Peck notes, "For a storable commodity, relations among future prices of differing maturities reflect the market value of continued storage and provide a reliable guide to the returns that can be expected from that storage."[15]

In addition to enhancing efficiency, private insurance markets allow producers to freely choose the level of insurance and level of production they desire, rather than be subjected to arbitrary insurance levels and the corresponding production incentives established by government programs. In a response to Bauer and Paish's suggestion for government interventions to help stabilize farm incomes in developing countries, Friedman implores, "Is not freedom a more attractive social philosophy than paternalism, even for underdeveloped areas?"[16] Newbery and Stiglitz make a similar argument, suggesting that futures markets specifically allow for more freedom: "What we show in this chapter is that an unbiased futures market . . . provides unambiguously greater income risk insurance than perfect price stabilization. The reason is . . . that an agent does better if he is free to choose the amount of price insurance as opposed to having a predetermined amount forced on him."[17]

These theoretical arguments within the neoclassical tradition are mirrored in the policy recommendations of derivatives advocates. Claessens and Duncan echo Friedman's and McKinnon's earlier sentiments, explicitly recommending derivatives markets as superior substitutes for government schemes in the agricultural development context:

> How financial instruments fit into the broader range of stabilization mechanisms leads to the question of whether they are complements of or substitutes for other schemes. Analytically, one can conclude that financial instruments can have several advantages over traditional schemes and therefore should be substitutes . . . in general, moving toward market-based schemes is recommended.[18]

Along similar lines, Meyers writes:

> Over the years economists and policymakers have suggested a number of ways to reduce and manage the commodity price risks facing developing countries. Schemes to stabilize commodity prices—buffer stocks, buffer funds, quotas, and variable export taxes—have been the most common remedy because when credit and contingent claims markets are incomplete, stabilization schemes can reduce and redistribute risks and thereby increase economic efficiency (Newbery and Stiglitz 1981). But economists have become disillusioned with price stabilization schemes . . . One of the alternatives that has been suggested is to expand the use of market mechanisms for risk management, such as crop insurance and futures markets. These instruments allow individuals to participate at whatever level they choose and, it is argued, are more effective and efficient forms of risk management.[19]

UNCTAD puts the issue as follows:

> Admittedly, the former state monopolies were often grossly inefficient, subsidized agricultural credit schemes only reached a minority of (generally, larger) farmers, and government price stabilization often was only a way of taxing the agricultural sector, but liberalization has nevertheless left farmers in an environment with considerable gaps in support structures . . . Risk management markets, where risks can be transferred by those who cannot afford to shoulder them to those who are interested in taking on price risks, can help farmers to get more certainty about their future, at least as far as the prices that they will receive are concerned . . . .[20]

The World Bank echoes the sentiments of its colleagues at the UN:

> Governments in many countries have intervened in markets, often through state economic enterprises, to insulate producers and consumers from world prices. Most interventions have taken a nonmarket approach in the form of quota or buffer stock programs organized through state marketing boards. However, government interventions have been costly and have crowded out private sector initiatives. Price risk management that relies on market-based

products rather than government guarantees and subsidies will involve a substantially reduced overall role for government in administration.

While this may already be clear, it is important to note that, for these theorists and researchers, commodity derivatives markets complement free markets in agricultural commodities more generally. Therefore, rather than having markets structured by governments with eye toward price manipulation, commodity markets can be liberalized, prices freed to be determined by market mechanisms, and financial markets like derivatives can help agricultural players manage the risks that arise as governments retreat. In this sense, and in true neoliberal fashion, derivatives markets are institutions that *enable* and *maintain* policy liberalization in other areas of the economy by helping to manage the backlash and fallout associated with liberalization, which is in this case greater exposure to price risk and price volatility. That derivatives markets can potentially insure small farmers while simultaneously insuring neoliberalism itself confers important political advantages for advocates, a point I return to in Chapter 5.

Theorists do not, however, unequivocally recommend derivatives markets in the agricultural development context. If markets do not work well, there is cause to consider alternative methods for managing producer price risk. In order for derivatives to provide effective risk management services and appropriate guidance through the price discovery process, at least three conditions must be met.

First, the markets must be efficient; that is, forward prices must be "rational."[21] Market efficiency in this context requires that future prices are "unbiased" and that they also exhibit "predictive efficiency." Bias refers to "chronic" over- or underestimation of the future cash price. Predictability refers to the "value of the future price as a forecast."[22] If future prices are biased and/or if they generate unreliable forecasts, both hedging and price discovery are compromised. Both bias and unpredictability generate basis risk for hedgers, meaning that gains in the futures market will not cover losses in the cash market (more below in the section on market efficiency). Irrational forward prices can additionally misguide those who look to the market for assistance with marketing, storage, and production decisions.

Second, the markets must extend reasonably far into the future. McKinnon argues that futures markets must be "complete" in order to provide maximum benefits. In the case of primary producers, he suggests that there must exist long-term futures markets in order that producer incomes can be stabilized from year to year.[23] Anne Peck agrees that futures markets that offer only short-term contracts will be ineffective in stabilizing farmer incomes in the medium to long-term: "For most commodities, inter year variation in futures prices is as great as that in cash prices. Hence, reduction in income variation using a routine hedging procedure is apt to be small by these measures."[24]

Third, the markets must be accessible to those they are to help. This point, regarding barriers to entry in futures markets, is not often stated directly by theorists, but is clearly implied in their discussions of risk management for farmers.

In theory, then, derivatives markets can effectively and efficiently provide both risk management and price discovery services for farmers, thereby stabilizing incomes in volatile economic environments. However, in practice the contribution of derivatives markets to income stability among coffee producers is much less certain.

Coffee Prices, Coffee Dependence, and Vulnerability to Risk

The coffee market provides a prime example of the volatility and insecurity associated with the process of globalization, and its dangerous consequences for Southern communities. Over the past three decades, global coffee prices have become more volatile from day to day and month to month. They have also declined in real terms from year to year and across decades. Both of these price dynamics—long-run decline and short-run volatility around this trend—have made coffee farming less remunerative and have rendered the lives of coffee farmers and their families more insecure, fragile, and precarious. It is in this context that derivatives markets are thought to be able to provide some assistance.

As for so many crops, coffee price volatility has increased with liberalization in the late 1980s, when the ICA was dismantled. Jorge Cardenas, chairman of the World Coffee Conference, states in his 2001 speech, "International coffee prices have shown a fluctuation of more than 50 percent annually in recent years whereas during periods when the market was regulated prices fluctuated between 10–15 percent around their medium-term trend."[25] Likewise, "Work done by the Federación Nacional de Cafételeras de Colombia (FNC), for example, suggests that volatility of coffee prices was higher outside the periods of the international stabilization agreements."[26] Akiyama and Varangis also find that, "overall, the quota system had a stabilizing effect on world coffee prices," relative to prices since liberalization.[27]

Of particular concern in the context of volatility have been two prolonged coffee price crises since 1989. The first coffee crisis occurred immediately after the ICA's collapse, and lasted from roughly 1989 to 1992. The second coffee crisis began in early 1998 and lasted until 2002. Regarding the latter crisis, one observer wrote in 2001, "We are living through one of the most dramatic moments in the history of coffee over the last 100 years. Export prices in constant US dollars are the lowest since 1900 and are below those recorded during the Great Depression of the 1930s, which were regarded at the time as disastrous for developing countries."[28]

Volatility in the coffee market is usually linked to the weather and supply and demand mismatches, combined with some particular characteristics of coffee producers and consumers. Indeed, the global coffee market is frequently characterized by "chronic oversupply." Over the past century, coffee demand has grown slowly and constantly in concert with rising population levels in the global North, and rising population and income levels in the global South. Coffee supply, on the other hand, has grown much more quickly and, absent government intervention, tends to consistently outpace demand on world markets. Between 1990 and 2000 coffee production increased at twice the rate of consumption, resulting in rapidly falling prices during the 1998–2002 crisis.[29] Baffes and colleagues attribute recent market imbalances to major expansions in Brazilian and Vietnamese production, combined with stagnating demand in "mature consumer markets" like that of the United States.[30] Still others suggest that higher production levels in the 1990s are symbolic of the freedom producers have enjoyed since liberalization and was caused by rational responses to periods of high prices, like the high prices that followed a severe frost in Brazil in the mid-1990s.[31] Charveriat, among others, disagrees and instead attributes rising world supplies to the recommendations of the World Bank, International Coffee Organization (ICO), and other organizations, as well as the pressures of the 1980 debt crisis:

> The pressure of debt has forced countries to expand production to generate hard currency. Meanwhile, IFIs and development agencies have actively promoted production and exports, through project lending and wider macroeconomic reforms. For example, various development projects were instrumental in helping Vietnam start producing and exporting coffee. In Colombia and Bolivia, farmers were encouraged by UN-sponsored programs to switch from coca to coffee. And in Angola, the International Coffee Organization recently provided funds for the revival of the country's coffee production, which had been shut down by war.[32]

The price dynamic engendered during periods of market oversupply is exacerbated by the nature of coffee supplies. Supply is relatively price inelastic in the short to medium term largely due to the fixed nature of coffee tree investments and the time it takes for coffee plants to mature. "Elasticity" refers to the responsiveness of supply and demand to price changes. If supply is "inelastic," producers do not change their production patterns very much when prices rise or fall. David Hallam at the FAO notes:

> [F]alling prices do not necessarily prompt the expected supply response. The perennial nature of the crop means that adjustment to the scale of production through diversification and exit from the industry is slow: in the short run the price elasticity of supply appears to be very small, around 0.25. It may also be that, as is often argued for perennial crops, supply responses to price incentives are asymmetric: periods of rising prices stimulate new plantings and other fixed asset investments which are not scrapped when prices fall, but rather are simply not replaced when they reach the end of their productive life.[33]

For this reason, production increases following periods of high prices (like the rise in prices caused by frost in Brazil in 1995), but does not fall with price declines, aggravating oversupply and generating falling and volatile prices (like during the 1998–2002 coffee crisis that trailed the Brazilian frost by three years, roughly corresponding to the time it takes coffee plants to mature). Given the very high coffee prices that prevailed in 2010 and early 2011, these market dynamics imply that there may be reason to anticipate another coffee price crisis. Further, and as will be discussed at more length in the next chapter, recent increases in coffee price volatility are increasingly associated with speculative activities in coffee derivatives markets.

In addition to price volatility, real, long-run coffee prices are also falling, in absolute terms and relative to the price of manufactured goods. The decline in coffee prices relative to manufactured goods speaks to a coffee-dependent country's "terms of trade" and to coffee producers' standard of living. Terms of trade refers to the value of a country's exports relative to the value of its imports, and quantifies that country's trade "balance" (i.e. whether it is in deficit, surplus, or has balanced trade). In the presence of falling real commodity prices, commodity-dependent countries are subject to declining terms of trade in the long run, as the value of their imports (largely manufactured goods) exceeds the value of their exports (largely primary commodities like coffee). This implies trade deficits, fiscal deficits, and other macroeconomic problems, for example, more expensive external borrowing. For producers, falling relative prices may mean a declining standard of living, with increasingly meager incomes buying fewer imports. This is especially problematic for farmers who rely on imported food to feed their families and utilize imported manufactured inputs to run their farms—for example, fertilizers, fuels, and seeds.

Speaking on falling long-term commodity prices, a recent study by World Bank researchers reveals, "Over the period shown since 1970, prices have averaged a 3 percent per year price decline for arabica coffees and a 5 percent decline for robusta [sic]."[34] Analyzing the period since liberalization, Rutten and Youssef note the consequences of this trend for farmer incomes: "For some farmers, price declines have been compensated by productivity increases, but this has been the case only for a minority. By and large, coffee farmers have seen their coffee revenue falling."[35] A 1999 study of the prices of 36 commodities between 1957 and 1999 by researchers at the IMF found similar evidence of a long-run decline in commodity prices. Across many commodities, including coffee, "the magnitude of price falls in a slump is slightly larger than those of price rises in subsequent booms."[36] The researchers also found that "for the majority of commodities, price slumps last longer than price booms," suggesting the real price-related hardships producers confront.[37] Gilbert further finds that coffee prices have declined relative to those of manufactures: "Relative to the price of manufactured goods, primary commodity prices have exhibited a variable but steady downward trend over the past century."[38]

Just as there is an on-going debate on the causes of price volatility, scholars also disagree about the causes of this long-run decline in commodity prices. Raul Prebisch and Hans Singer argued that long-run price declines occurred because of differences in the income elasticities of demand for commodities relative to manufactures.[39] While income elasticities for primary agricultural products are low, meaning that rising incomes do not stimulate much rising demand, those for manufactures are high, meaning that rising incomes translate into higher consumer demand. Thus, as the world economy grows, the price of manufactures will rise proportionately more than the price of agricultural goods, generating consistent declines in terms of trade for developing countries, many of which are locked into primary product production. The global economic system, with its division of labor between the manufacturing North and agricultural South, was thus viewed as a kind of trap for developing countries who were helpless to stop the deterioration of their relative position in the global system.

By contrast, Schaeffer argues that declining commodity prices are caused by rising global commodity production in the South and declining demand from Northern countries, as new technologies allow for reduced Northern dependence on Southern crops.[40] Gilbert argues that technological innovation in manufactures in the post–World War II period resulted in higher-quality manufactured items that commanded higher market prices. By contrast, innovation in agricultural commodities did not generate a higher-quality product, but rather facilitated quantity increases and falling prices.[41]

Coffee Dependence

Ninety percent of the world's coffee is grown in the developing world.[42] The top ten coffee-producing countries worldwide in 2010 were, in descending order, Brazil (36% of world production), Vietnam (14%), Colombia (7%), Indonesia (6.5%), Ethiopia (5.5%), India (3.5%), Mexico (3.3%), Guatemala (3%), Honduras (2.9%), and Peru (2.8%), spanning four continents—North America, South America, Africa, and Asia.[43]

Despite the fact that just ten countries grow almost 85 percent of the world's coffee, coffee is an extremely important commodity, nationally speaking, for many countries that make up only a small share of world production. "For example, coffee accounts for more than half of total merchandise exports in Burundi, Rwanda, and Ethiopia and more than 20 percent in Guatemala, Honduras, and Nicaragua."[44] In Uganda, coffee exports can account for up to a third of total export earnings.[45] As discussed previously, commodity dependence is cause for concern in the development context. The FAO notes, "Such dependency means that coffee price variations have significant multiplier effects on employment and incomes beyond production itself in related upstream and downstream industries, and across the economy in general."[46] For economies such as these, economic development prospects frequently hinge upon the price of coffee on world markets.

Not only are coffee-producing countries dependent on coffee for export earnings, but so too are coffee farmers dependent on coffee for their livelihood. The World Bank estimates that some 20–25 million families produce coffee in some 50 developing countries, the vast majority of which are "smallholders," and that some 100 million people worldwide are directly affected economically by the coffee trade (Lewin et al. 2004: xi).[47] Seventy percent of the world's coffee is grown on farms of less than 25 acres in size; of these, the vast majority of coffee farms are between 2.5 and 12.5 acres.[48] Antony Wild estimates that some 25 million small farmers worldwide depend on coffee as their only source of income, and that some 125 million people depended on coffee directly or indirectly in 2002.[49] Charveriat estimates that 20 million households depend on coffee production for their primary, and sometimes only, source of income.[50] Among other things, these figures highlight the sheer size of the global community that is impacted by changes in coffee prices, with millions of small farmers and families having no other source of cash income aside from that generated via coffee sales.

Small Farmer Vulnerability to Risk

Coffee farmers, the vast majority of whom are poor smallholders, are among those most vulnerable to market shocks within the coffee industry and they tend to suffer disproportionately when a shock occurs. The International Labor Organization (ILO) notes, "In general, a poor person cannot insure to anything like the extent that a rich person can, and yet is almost certainly exposed to more risks, more uncertainty and more adverse outcomes."[51] With few or no alternatives available, poor farmers and their families often resort to reducing consumption of basic goods and expenditures on health and education in order to cope with shocks. As Rutten and Youssef put it, "Risks hit the poor hardest."[52]

Holzmann and Jorgenson note that, "The absence of efficient market-based or government provided consumption-smoothing instruments often results in the use of costly informal coping mechanisms once the adverse income shock hits, such as pulling children out of school, reducing nutritional intake, selling productive assets, or neglecting human capital accumulation."[53] Among other factors, farmers with alternative income sources, savings, sufficient productive assets (especially land and livestock) and access to credit are not negatively impacted to the same extent as are lower-income, undiversified and asset-poor farmers with bad or no credit. This is why, UNCTAD notes, "Smaller, poorer farmers are more risk-averse than larger, richer ones."[54]

Small coffee farmers, who tend to be poor for a variety of reasons discussed at length in the next chapter, often lack the assets, income, savings, and access to credit and risk management arrangements that help other coffee actors manage risk more successfully. As a consequence, price shocks hit this community very hard. Some of the most comprehensive evidence to this effect comes from the fieldwork conducted during and after the 1998–2002 coffee crisis. Sayer relates the situation of many Ugandan coffee farmers during the coffee crisis who struggled "to buy essentials like sugar, soap, salt, kerosene, tools and clothes . . . Secondary school enrollment has declined as tens of thousands of children are sent home for lack of fees."[55]

In Brazil, Watson and Anchinelli's study of coffee smallholders revealed similar results. While the *fazendas* (large coffee estates) are indeed negatively impacted by price declines, it is smallholders who are more adversely affected: "Small-scale producers in these areas are most vulnerable to instability on the world coffee market, as their incomes are precariously tied to world coffee prices."[56] Gresser and Tickell similarly find that Brazilian smallholders, like smallholders in so many other producing countries, were most negatively impacted by the crisis.[57]

In Mexico, 90 percent of the country's coffee is grown in four southern states of Veracruz, Chiapas, Oaxaca, and Puebla by small producers, many of whom are indigenous peoples. The ITF reports that some 180,000 of Mexico's 282,000 producers are indigenous with coffee being their main or only source of cash income. And, the small producers that dominate the south tend to be poorer than the rest of the country's inhabitants: "In 1996, the four main coffee producing states Chiapas, Oaxaca, Puebla and Veracruz had a per capita gross internal product that was around 43 percent of Mexico's average for Chiapas and Oaxaca, and around 64 and 67 percent for Veracruz and Puebla respectively."[58]

As in Uganda and Brazil, it was Mexico's smaller and poorer coffee farmers that experienced the most hardship during the recent coffee crisis, while wealthier, larger farmers fared much better. A recent study by Eakin, Tucker, and Castellanos of small coffee producers in Veracruz found that during the crisis almost 72 percent of producers reduced their harvest, 62 percent "reduced use of purchased inputs," almost 97 percent were "negatively affected" in their "ability to acquire basic goods," and 80 percent were less able to pay medical expenses. The study crucially finds that households with "access to market and technical information, finance and having sufficient land with which to diversify into alternative crops" were better able to deal with the crisis.[59]

Osorio makes similar findings during the coffee crisis in Vietnam, where producers were selling their meager possessions to pacify debt collectors; in Mexico, where coffee farmers abandoned their farms and died trying to migrate to the United States (the case of 14 coffee growers and laborers, the "Yuma 14," found dead in the Arizona desert made headlines in the United States); in Colombia, where coffee farmers started intercropping coca with their coffee to earn extra income; and in India, where farmers committed suicide to escape their debts.[60] Researchers have extensively documented similarly immiserating responses to price risk among smallholder farmers across a broad spectrum coffee-producing countries, including: Costa Rica[61]; El Salvador, Honduras, Guatemala, and Nicaragua[62]; Tanzania, Ethiopia, and Mexico[63]; Kenya, Uganda, Tanzania, Mexico, Ethiopia, and Guatemala[64]; and India.[65]

As noted previously, it goes without saying that falling long-term coffee prices have additional, negative consequences for coffee farmers. Short-term shocks and dangerous coping mechanisms are complemented by a gradually deteriorating standard of living associated with the long-run decline. Schaeffer notes that "falling commodity prices have made poor people poorer, creating hardship for the hundreds of millions of people who labor in fields, forests and mines across the globe."[66]

Coffee, Derivatives, and Income Security: Practice

Coffee farmers, especially small ones, are highly vulnerable to price risk and face an inhospitable market environment characterized by short-term price volatility and deteriorating long-run prices. It is in this context that derivatives markets may be of some service, protecting small farmers from the market as governments retreat from their previous role managing price risk. As noted above, for futures markets to effectively stabilize producer incomes and provide good investment advice, the markets must be efficient, complete, and accessible. Unfortunately for coffee producers and other would-be hedgers, global coffee futures and options markets are often inefficient, are incomplete in important ways, and are largely inaccessible especially for small farmers. This suggests that the theoretical advantages of derivatives markets for farmers are not consistently realized in practice. Among other policy implications, the evidence I relate in this section urges caution to policymakers considering futures for farmers and suggests the importance of considering other, viable risk management alternatives.

Coffee futures and options are traded on five exchanges globally: the Intercontinental Exchange (ICE) in New York (previously the New York Board of Trade, NYBOT), the London International Financial Futures and Options Exchange (LIFFE or Liffe) in London, the Bolsa de Mercados y Futuros (BM&F, now merged with Bovespa) in Sao Paulo, the Tokyo Grain Exchange (TGE), and the National Multi Commodity Exchange (NMCE) in Ahmedabad.

The reader should be aware that coffee derivatives have been traded sporadically over the past decade on several other exchanges. The National Commodity and Derivatives Exchange in India (NCDEX) that previously offered Robusta coffee futures no longer lists them in the exchange's product offerings. A 2009 article from the *Business Times Singapore* notes that NCDEX is working with the Singapore Commodity Exchange (Sicom) to cross-list a number of products, including Robusta coffee futures.[67] The article further notes that Sicom has offered coffee contracts for 15 years but that the market was "dormant" over this period. Further research revealed that Sicom moved its commodity derivatives trading to a platform hosted by its parent company, the Singapore Exchange (SGX), in 2010. That said, I found no evidence of consistent trading of Robusta contracts on either of these exchanges. The New York Mercantile Exchange (NYMEX, part of the CME Group) recently started offering an Arabica futures contract identical to the contract traded on ICE. Data from the exchange revealed abysmally low trading volumes, so low that there is no real need to consider them here. In the next chapter, I discuss some of the reasons exchange operators experience difficulty in offering new products that compete with established products listed on other exchanges.

Market Efficiency

Coffee derivatives markets are not always efficient and do not provide consistent, accurate forecasts of future cash prices. This presents two problems for development. First, hedging may not work to stabilize incomes as predictive inefficiency creates "basis risk" for hedgers. Second, inefficiency compromises the price discovery mechanism, generating prices that can misguide farmers who use them to make investment decisions. While this chapter is focused largely on small coffee producers, the inefficiency of coffee futures markets is significant from the perspective of any prospective hedger, be they small farmers, large farmers, commodity-dependent governments looking to hedge their revenues, or governments that have issued commodity-linked bonds indexed to future coffee prices. The reader should keep in mind that the discussion below does not completely reject coffee futures markets, but rather serves to highlight the fact that the service provided by the markets is ambiguous and inconsistent. There are a number of existing studies of futures market efficiency for several of the coffee derivatives exchanges. Unfortunately, for some of the exchanges—the BM&F in Brazil and the TGE in Tokyo—there are no existing studies of market efficiency. This represents an important avenue for future research.

Mohan and Love, recognizing the dependence of price discovery's benefits for farmers upon the efficiency of futures markets, note, "In this paper, we infer, on the basis of empirical analysis, whether producers can benefit from taking such decisions or whether such planning can result in welfare loss and misallocation of resources. In other words, we test the forecast efficiency of coffee futures and investigate the extent to which it can reduce coffee producers' price risk exposure."[68] Their 2004 study of the New York and London coffee futures markets reveals that the markets exhibit predictive *in*efficiency especially beyond three to four months. Beyond this time frame, the markets do not really predict at all, with future prices instead following cash prices.

The authors' tests result in several interesting findings. First, the results are virtually identical for both exchanges, suggesting a relatively high correlation between prices. Second, "It is difficult to establish any clear-cut relationship between futures and spot prices, except the fact that futures prices are more adaptive to the prevailing (current) spot price, rather than futures prices reflecting or predicting subsequent spot prices."[69] This implies that cash prices may be a better guide for producers than future prices because future prices simply lag behind cash prices. Third, the authors find that the markets perform even this adaptive function rather poorly, with "spot prices deviating from futures prices by about 30 percent on average."[70] Fourth, the larger the "forecast lag," or the distance into the future that coffee futures markets extend their predictions, the larger the deviation of spot from future prices. This means that futures markets do a better job predicting cash market prices in the very near future than they do as the time horizon recedes. Because of the large deviations between spot and future prices, that is, beyond three to four months, the authors argue that "futures market information does not reduce the price uncertainty faced by coffee producers" to any extent beyond this time horizon.[71] Last, Mohan and Love find that there is no systematic pattern in the bias shown in future prices—"at times the forecast price proved to be higher than the subsequent spot price and vice versa at other times."[72]

Mohan and Love thus conclude with pessimism about the benefits of using prices discovered in futures markets to guide farm-level planning: "The analysis, therefore, fails to support the price-signaling role of futures prices."[73] That the markets predict efficiently, at best, over a three-to-four-month time horizon is significant for farmers who produce over the course of a longer season, especially for coffee farmers who cultivate a perennial crop that takes several years to mature. The futures market can offer no useful guidance about these longer-term decisions.

Further, even though storage and other decisions (like how much seasonal labor to hire) might be taken on a shorter-term basis than other kinds of investment decisions, it is doubtful whether the futures market will be of help to coffee farmers even in this context. A a Mexican coffee farmer who begins harvesting in October would not, on the basis of future prices in New York or London, know with any certainty if and to what extent storing the commodity until the end of the harvest in February will be remunerative. This is because coffee farmers in many parts of the world harvest continuously for several months over the period that coffee cherries ripen on the trees, with the harvest season often extending beyond the three-to-four month period during which futures markets more accurately predict prices. The cherries ripen unevenly, with ripe and unripe cherries appearing on the same trees, meaning that coffee harvesting is both labor intensive and a longer-term process than the harvesting of many other annual crops like wheat or corn.

Predictive inefficiencies have also been found in developing country futures exchanges. While not covering coffee, the findings of Easwaran and Ramasundaram are nonetheless illustrative. The authors study future prices for cotton, castor, pepper, and soya on two Indian exchanges, the MCX and the NCDEX. They find that future prices are woefully inefficient because of very low trading volumes, among other problems. "Even though several factors attribute to the inefficient functioning of futures market, the exchange-specific problems like thin volume and low market depth, infrequent trading, lack of effective participation of trading members, non-awareness of futures market among farmers, not well-developed spot market in the vicinity of futures market, poor physical delivery in many commodity markets, absence of well-developed grading and standardization system and market imperfections are the major drawbacks retarding the growth of futures market."[74] While no specific study exists, relatively low coffee trading volumes on the NMCE in Ahmedabad indicate the likelihood of similar problems (see Chapter 4).

The inefficiency of future prices also has implications for hedging. As Loy notes, market efficiency is a "necessary condition" for effective risk management with futures.[75] Futures market inefficiencies generate "basis risk." The "basis" is defined as the cash price less the future price at a given point in time. The basis exists due to price and quality differences across markets in different locations, and also exchange rate fluctuations, among other factors. In the case of coffee farmers, prices paid to growers in local markets tend to be less than prices established on futures exchanges (i.e. the basis is negative), as transportation costs, quality differences, and other factors drive a wedge between local cash prices and future prices.

It is not the existence of a basis per se that is a source of risk for hedgers. However, the existence of a basis does indicate that the futures contract/market in question is not perfectly matched to the product a given producer is growing and selling. This suggests that the basis may not remain constant if there are factors or occurrences that impact prices in one market but not in the other. Indeed, it is *changes* in the basis over time that are a source of risk for hedgers. If the basis weakens (becomes more negative), a short hedger's gains in the futures markets will *not* cover her losses in the cash market, all else equal. If the basis strengthens (becomes less negative, or even positive), a short hedger's gains in the futures market will *more than* cover her losses in the cash market, all else equal. When one hedges she is in effect trading one risk for another—the risk that cash prices will fall is exchanged for the risk that future prices and cash prices may not fall in tandem. One commentator describes basis risk as "the risk that the insurance coverage does not exactly match actual losses."[76] In other words, one can only be certain that the price/income fixed when the contract is entered into will be the price/income actually received if the basis stays constant over the duration of the hedge (i.e. if future and cash prices move exactly together).

Mohan and Love's finding, that futures markets are most efficient within a three-to-four-month time period suggests that longer hedges that extend beyond this time frame may not be effective, and could actually increase the risk that producers face. As Teweles and Jones note, "Indeed, the trader begins to understand that in most circumstances hedging is merely a form of speculation—speculation on the basis."[77] As market inefficiencies rise, speculating on the basis becomes riskier.

A study by Fortenberry and Zapata on the relationship between prices on the New York futures market and the Guatemalan and Honduran cash coffee market also indicates that basis risk is problematic in the coffee context.

They find that when a price shock hits the futures market in New York, it is transmitted directly to these Central American cash markets. However, when a shock hits the Guatemalan and Honduran cash markets, this shock is not reflected at all in the New York price.[78] In other words, New York future prices impact local cash market prices, but local cash market prices do not impact the futures market. This suggests the likelihood of growing basis risk during local shocks, and that hedging will be less effective in the presence of such shocks.

Recent news reports from the coffee market in 2010–11 further reflect concerns about basis risk from within the industry. Two recent developments have been singled out by traders and other insiders as reducing the usefulness of coffee derivatives exchanges for hedging. First, the New York market has recently added Brazilian coffees to its lists of "origins tenderable" (see "Market Access" section for more information). While excluded in the past, Brazilian coffees will now be added into the coffee future price established in New York. Brazilian coffees have long been thought inferior to coffees grown in Colombia, for example, because they grow at lower altitudes and are often exported in "unwashed" or "natural" form. The introduction of Brazil to the futures market implies growing basis risk for producers of higher-quality coffees.[79] Second, the coffee market, along with futures markets for most primary commodities, has been subject to a rising tide of speculative activity, generating rapidly rising and volatile future coffee prices (more in Chapter 4). Many traders in the market view these higher prices as the result of a "fund-led rally" (speaking to the influence of speculating commodity index funds) that does not reflect "market fundamentals."[80] This divergence between cash market fundamentals and future prices also implies growing basis risk for hedgers.

Larger, wealthier, and more sophisticated traders have a number of tools at their disposal that help to minimize the impact of predictive inefficiencies on hedging and storage decisions, tools that for various reasons are not as widely available, if at all, to small farmers. First, wealthier and larger actors are better able to absorb the consequences of bad storage decisions and hedges gone awry simply because they are better capitalized and a single hedge or storage decision is merely one part of a much larger strategy. For many financial institutions speculating in commodity markets, these sorts of problems are further minimized as trading in coffee futures is part of a larger portfolio of commodity trades, which is itself part of a larger trading portfolio comprised of commodities, financial derivatives, stocks, bonds, real estate, and other assets.

Second, more sophisticated traders employ a technique called "rollover hedging" that enables them to minimize basis risk by trading only in those contracts where the markets are most liquid and efficient (i.e. the "nearby" contracts that expire within a month or two; as I sit and write this line in February 2012, the nearby contract on ICE is trading for delivery in March and the second nearby contract trades for delivery in May). Rollover hedging involves a continuous stream of hedges in which a position in the nearby market is "rolled" into a position in the second nearby market just before the former contract expires. For example, a rollover short hedge procedure in the coffee market might involve selling 10 September futures contracts in July, buying them back in mid-September and simultaneously selling 10 December futures contracts. The procedure would be repeated, for the duration of the hedge, as each contract approaches expiration. Based on the parameters set by Mohan's and Love's study, rollover hedging allows traders to trade contracts only within the moving three-to-four-month period during which future prices are most efficient.

Rollover hedging, while potentially profitable in the coffee context, is more difficult for traders who are not in regular contact with futures markets. This technique requires traders to more or less constantly monitor the markets to determine the optimal timing of the rollover procedure. For small producers and many other actors who do not have regular access to information the technique is more difficult to utilize. Further, rollover hedging increases transaction costs, as brokerage, clearing, and exchange fees are replicated with each rollover, another factor which may deter smaller traders from using it. This is unfortunate, especially given a recent study by Dodd that indicates that rollover hedging in the coffee market would have resulted in large gains between 1999 and 2004, a period bracketing the recent coffee crisis.[81]

To sum up, inefficiencies in futures markets interfere with the hedging mechanism and are a source of basis risk for hedgers. Predictive inefficiency in the markets further prevents effective use of future prices for decision-making. While all prospective users of the market face these risks, some have developed partial means of managing them, means that often elude smaller, poorer, and nonexpert traders.

Missing Markets

Coffee derivatives markets are not complete. The coffee derivatives markets that exist today are short-term markets. For development, this generates two major problems. First, hedging is incapable of stabilizing incomes over the long term. Second, future prices cannot provide sufficient information to guide producers of perennial crops like coffee. As with market inefficiencies, the incompleteness of coffee futures markets is significant not only for small farmers but also for other actors, like governments, seeking to hedge their exposure to price risk on derivatives markets. As with market inefficiencies, the incompleteness of coffee derivatives markets is not necessarily cause to reject them outright as development tools; instead, the discussion below illustrates the limitations of futures markets in the coffee context and thus urges caution to policymakers.

Coffee derivatives markets are short term and extend, at most, 18 to 24 months into the future. As of February 2012, ICE's most distant contract is trading for delivery in December 2014, 22 months forward. As of February 2012, LIFFE offers contracts trading for delivery as far forward as September 2013, roughly 19 months forward. On the TGE, Arabica coffee trades forward 12 months, while Robusta trades forward about 8 months.

Even for this 18–24-month period within which contracts are available, the markets tend to become thinner and less efficient as the contracts push further forward. Mohan and Love's study, discussed above, indicates that market inefficiencies grow much larger beyond three to four months. For this reason, and as mentioned above, rollover hedging is employed by many traders to avoid trading in contracts for which volumes are thin.

While the markets are short term, coffee producer price risk has some significant long-term dimensions that the markets are ill equipped to address. This implies that futures and options trading can provide at best partial coverage for farmers, and also for governments and other prospective coffee derivative traders. One of the key theoretical benefits of hedging in the development context is that it can provide farmers with a kind of income insurance that allows them to make investments in their farms under conditions of greater certainty, thereby raising productivity and long-term income. In theory, the gains from hedging can generate that stability and security required to comfortably invest, for example, in new coffee trees or new farm equipment. However, coffee trees are perennial plants, and take three to five years to mature depending on the species. Because futures and options markets are short term, producers would still be exposed to price risk for a large portion of the time over which the trees mature. Further, the benefits of looking to future prices to guide investment decisions are also diminished in this context. Future prices cannot give farmers good advice about whether or not to plant new trees or make other large investments. While prices today or three months from now may appear high enough to justify such investments, the markets are incapable of predicting the prices that will prevail in three to five years when there are coffee cherries ready to be picked and marketed. The time horizons specified in the derivatives markets mismatch the time horizons over which coffee farmers invest.

In addition, in the earlier discussion on coffee prices, the disturbing trend of long-run price declines was also highlighted. While short-term futures markets may help to lock in prices and stabilize incomes from day to day and month to month, they are ill equipped to manage steadily declining prices from year to year. Interestingly, McKinnon argues that the absence of long-term futures markets is so problematic that there is a good case for government intervention to create them. "This can be done by initiating trade in futures contracts beyond those dates in which they are now traded and being willing to take net positions in these new contracts—probably on the long side."[82] This is one of several places where it appears government intervention may be required so that derivatives work for development. The irony, of course, is that this particular solution to the coffee farmer price risk problem is generally recommended by advocates on the basis that it does *not* require significant government expenditure or participation.

There is also some evidence to suggest (ironically) that as farmers come to use derivatives for short-term risk management, long-term prices may deteriorate. In a recent article Lence outlined the possibility that hedging among rubber farmers, if this population is large enough, will encourage increased production and will inadvertently contribute to falling long-run prices.[83]

Perhaps most problematic from a development perspective is that hedging and price discovery on derivatives markets may provide a short-term incentive to stay in coffee even if the long-run trend in prices indicates that diversification of some kind is prudent, if not absolutely necessary. In other words, derivatives markets provide incentives for producers to remain commodity dependent by softening market risk. In this way, hedging on existing short-term markets may generate mixed or conflicting signals that, in some cases, may undermine long-run income growth and well-being.

Rollover hedging, mentioned in the previous section, has been suggested by some to be an adequate substitute for missing distant futures markets. The technique could in theory extend futures markets indefinitely forward and allow for continuous hedging and income smoothing from year to year. Lence and Hayenga analyze these theoretical assertions in a 2001 paper on the corn market.[84] Their findings suggest that rollover hedging is an ineffective technique for locking in high prices beyond one year. While not conclusive for coffee, the study nonetheless points out that rollover hedging is not necessarily a panacea for missing long-term markets, and that significantly more research is needed to confirm the usefulness of this technique for coffee farmers.

Whether or not rollover hedging can extend derivatives markets' time horizons, it is unlikely that poorly capitalized traders would be able to utilize the technique. If a rollover hedge is to extend beyond one crop season, as would be reasonable for producers of perennial crops, farmers must hedge several crop seasons worth of output all at once in order to adequately protect themselves from such multi-year price risk. For example, for a short rollover hedge that is to extend two crop seasons forward, farmers would have to hedge two years of expected output the first year and then one year of output the second. For the first year of the hedge, transaction fees, margin requirements, and the magnitude of margin calls double, making rollover hedging beyond one crop season very expensive.

It is also important to note that the absence of long-term futures markets is not as disadvantageous for other actors in the coffee industry as it is for producers. Coffee traders often hold coffee for only a short period, buying from exporters and large producers and reselling onto roasters and processors within weeks or months. Hedging with short-term futures markets works well in this context and is adequate to the needs of traders. The situation of roasters is even better. Roasters, along with other consumers, actually benefit from declining coffee prices in the long term, meaning that they would be unlikely to hedge against such price trends even if the necessary markets existed.

Market Access

In addition to being inefficient and short term, coffee derivatives markets are also inaccessible. Coffee farmers, along with other small, poor actors, face significant, persistent obstacles to hedging on futures and options markets, such as size, cost, information, knowledge, and so on. The information obstacles farmers face when trying to hedge also cast doubt upon the benefits of price discovery for farmers, for if farmers cannot see future prices they certainly cannot be guided by them. Over two decades of programming and experimentation, conducted by the World Bank and various national governments, to facilitate access to derivatives markets for small coffee farmers, have failed to surmount these obstacles to any great degree. In fact, the markets are so exclusive that many of the intermediaries designated to facilitate access have themselves run into the same obstacles farmers face individually. Among other key points, I ask the reader to keep in mind the sheer size and scope of these access problems, and the correspondingly difficult and extensive efforts needed to rectify them.

Size

Exchange-traded futures and options contracts specify a particular quantity of the commodity being traded and these specifications are set by the exchanges in the interests of their major clients. For example, coffee "C" futures, and options on the "C" contract, traded on ICE specify 37,500 pounds of coffee (about 17,000 kilos). The Robusta coffee contract traded on LIFFE specifies 10,000 kilograms of coffee. Smaller than ICE's Arabica contract, the BM&F

contract specifies 6,000 kilograms. The TGE specifies 5,000 kilos for the Robusta contract and 3,450 kilos for the Arabica contract, while the NMCE specifies 1,500 kilos for its Robusta contract.

If a coffee farmer grows *less* than this amount but hedges with the contract anyway, a hedging transaction becomes partly speculative and increases farmer risk. In the similar case of a put option, a farmer would be paying a higher premium for insurance than was necessary given the size of her crop. If this extra risk (or extra cost, in the option case) is viewed as a substantial one by the farmer in question, which is likely given the quantity of output that would be overhedged for most coffee farmers, small farm size will effectively exclude him from participating in derivatives markets. As it turns out, large populations of coffee farmers across the global South do not grow enough to sell even a single futures contract or buy a single option, frequently growing many times less than the quantity specified in a single contract.

Table 3.1 illustrates the mismatch between coffee derivative lot sizes and farm sizes in several coffee-producing countries. Please note that even in Brazil, which has the largest coffee farms in the world, at least 37 percent of coffee farmers are estimated to be excluded from derivatives trading on the basis of size. The Brazilian case likely represents a best case scenario—that is, because coffee farms are relatively large on average, a relatively small proportion of Brazilian farmers are excluded from futures trading. By contrast, in Ethiopia and Mexico, I estimate that at least 98 percent of coffee farmers are excluded on the basis of size. In Uganda and Ecuador, over 90 percent of coffee farmers are excluded from derivatives trading on the basis of size, and in Vietnam, roughly 85 percent of coffee farmers are excluded. The Brazilian and Indian cases also illustrate that even domestic commodity exchanges, which some have suggested are better oriented to local needs and conditions,[85] promulgate trading standards and rules exclusive of local actors. In India, though the NMCE does specify a smaller lot size than any other coffee exchange in the world, I estimate that roughly 90 percent of farmers are excluded from futures trading on the basis of size.

The far right-hand column of Table 3.1 denotes the factor by which the lot sizes specified in the futures and options contracts exceed the average output of a coffee farm of average size. (I use average yields for 2000–09 from the FAO to perform these calculations.) One way of interpreting this data is that these tables show how many coffee farmers with average-sized farms and yields would have to pool their respective crops to sell a single futures contract or buy a single put option on the exchanges. In Brazil, it would require the output of 1.3 coffee farms of average size and yield to trade a single coffee derivative on BM&FBovespa in Sao Paulo. It would require the combined

Table 3.1 Derivatives market exclusion on the basis of farm size, selected countries

Country	*Main variety of coffee grown*[1]	*Number of coffee farmers*[2]	*Average coffee farm size*[3]	*Farm breakdown by size*[4]	*Average yield/ha 2000–09*[5]	*Estimated, average, annual output for average-sized farm, 2000–09*[6]	*Derivatives exchange on which farmers would likely trade*	*Lot size specified in contract, both futures and options*[7]	*Estimated proportion of coffee farmers excluded from derivatives markets by size*[8]	*Factor by which lot sizes exceed average output for the average farm*
Brazil	Arabica (Robusta also grown)	368,961	4.91	37% < 5 ha* 13% 5 ha > 10 ha* 50% > 10 ha*	910	4,468 kg	BM&FBovespa	6,000 kg	At least 37%	1.3
Ecuador	Arabica	57,153	2.7 ha	43% < 2 ha* 6% > 50 ha*	333	899 kg	ICE	37,500 lbs (17,000 kg)	At least 94%	19
Ethiopia	Arabica	2,386,686	0.1 ha	99% < 10ha* 1% > 10 ha*	814	81 kg	ICE[9]	37,500 lbs (17,000 kg)	At least 99%	210
India	Robusta (Arabica also grown)	566,000	0.5 ha	99% < 10ha* 1% > 10 ha*	863	432 kg	NMCE[10]	1,500 kg	At least 90%	3.5
Mexico	Arabica	282,000	2.7 ha	69% < 2 ha[11] 2% > 10 ha	392	1,058 kg	ICE	37,500 lbs (17,000 kg)	At least 98%	16

Uganda	Robusta (Arabica also grown)	241,610	0.2 ha[12]	74% < 1.2 ha[13] 3% > 4 ha	645	129 kg	LIFFE /Euronext/NYSE	10,000 kg	At least 97%	78
Vietnam	Robusta	561,439	1.3 ha[14]	85% 0 ha < 2 ha 14% 2 ha < 5 ha 1%> 5 ha[15]	1992	2,590 kg	TGE	5,000 kg	About 85%	1.9

[1] Many coffee producing countries produce both major varieties of coffee. I note here the variety that accounts for the majority of exports.

[2] From national agricultural censuses, *FAO World Census of Agriculture, 2000,* www.fao.org. Data used is most recent available.

[3] Ibid.

[4] Where an asterisks appears in this category, the farm breakdown by size is for the country as whole, all crops. General farm size data are available from national agricultural censuses, *FAO World Census of Agriculture, 2000,* www.fao.org. I have used this breakdown in those country cases where specific coffee data were unavailable.

[5] From FAO's FAOSTAT database. www.fao.org

[6] Based on author's calculations.

[7] Information on contract specifications was obtained from the websites of each relevant exchange.

[8] Based on author's calculations.

[9] The Ethiopian Commodity Exchange (ECX) does not currently offer futures or options contracts.

[10] The NMCE is one of three major commodity exchanges in India, and the only exchange to offer coffee derivatives. Robusta and Arabica coffee farmers from India might also trade on LIFFE and ICE respectively, where the RC and KC contracts specify a larger lot size.

[11] Data from ITF, *Mexico: Phase 2 Report.*

[12] John Baffes, *Restructuring Uganda's Coffee Industry: Why Going Back to the Basics Matters* (Washington, D.C.: The World Bank, 2006), 2.

[13] Maurizio Bussolo, et al., *The Impact of Commodity Price Changes on Rural Households: The Case of Coffee in Uganda* (Washington, D.C.: The World Bank, 2006), 21.

[14] Anna R. Rios and Gerald R. Shively, "Farm size and nonparametric efficiency measurements for coffee farms in Vietnam," Selected Paper prepared for presentation at the American Agricultural Economics Association Annual Meeting, Providence, Rhode Island, July 24–27, 2005. Based on survey sample of coffee farmers in Dak Lak Province.

[15] Daniele Giovannucci, Bryan Lewin, and Rob Swinkels, *The Socialist Republic of Vietnam: Coffee Sector Report* (Washington, D.C.: World Bank, 2004).

Source: Author calculations based on data from the FAO and the coffee derivatives exchanges.

output of 210 Ethiopian coffee farms of average size and yield to trade a single coffee contract on ICE.

Small size further impedes farmer access to the markets for another reason. Derivatives brokers realize economies of scale in transaction costs, meaning that the costs of setting up a client account, investigating client backgrounds, and carrying out other due diligence requirements are virtually the same for clients trading one or two contracts and clients trading many contracts. This discourages brokers from working with clients whose trading needs are relatively small.

For example, Dodd notes, "Private enterprises face certain fixed costs of dealing with any one customer, and they also face increasing costs when the transactions are cross-border and involve less developed local financial markets. For instance, futures commission merchants in the U.S. (futures and options brokers) would find it very expensive to transact with customers in rural Africa, and alternatively farmers in rural Africa would find it daunting to establish accounts in the U.S. through which to trade with U.S. brokers."[86]

The Commodity Risk Management Group at the World Bank made a similar finding: "The rigorous nature of know-your-client requirements and increasingly stringent anti-money laundering initiatives require a process of due diligence, particularly for unknown clients in developing countries. Although providers view the background work and relationship with the World Bank's CRMG as a valuable addition to the due diligence process, they continue to require a lengthy list of background documentation before opening accounts to trade."[87] The CRMG later noted that such bureaucratic requirements and the costs entailed therein are an impediment to access to futures markets for small farmers.

Origins Tenderable

Every coffee exchange specifies those coffee-growing places from which deliveries will be accepted by the exchange to settle a futures or options contract—these places are called "origins tenderable" or "origins deliverable." A country's inclusion on the list of origins tenderable has mainly to do with the quality of the product and its contribution to global production (global market share).

Recent discussions at ICE about adding Brazil to the list of deliverable origins reveals the power of the exchanges and big players in the coffee industry to influence these lists. The FIA reports that ICE's coffee committee had been thinking about adding Brazil for about ten years, but that the committee (comprised of "[derivatives]dealers, coffee traders and commercial users") had previously considered Brazil's coffee to be of such inferior quality that it would degrade the usefulness of the "C" contract for hedgers. "This time though, the consensus view of the trade is that the quantity and quality being turned out from Brazil are both sufficiently large and sufficiently accepted by *roasters* that it was time to add Brazil as a deliverable origin."[88] In addition to illustrating who controls this process, the experience of Brazil also shows just how long it can take for a new deliverable origin to be added to the list. This does not bode well for those countries that are currently excluded.

Of the five coffee exchanges, only LIFFE's Robusta coffee contracts may be settled with Robusta coffee from any origin. For the exchanges on which delivery is compulsory, the TGE and the NMCE, being left off of the origins tenderable list completely precludes derivatives trading. Further, while futures and options contracts are frequently settled by offsetting trade or in cash on ICE and the BM&F, there is good reason to believe that farmers from countries other than those specified by the exchanges would not be trading on these exchanges. The ability to cash settle or settle via offsetting trade crucially requires either that domestic coffee markets are robust (specifically that demand is sufficient, which may not be the case) or that the farmer in question has access to international coffee markets (which many do not). Farmers from nonspecified countries that traded in New York or Sao Paulo may also face serious basis risk, making the transaction unattractive from a risk management perspective.

Table 3.2 shows the tenderable origins specified by each of the five coffee exchanges and those coffee-producing countries excluded therefrom. Because LIFFE allows coffee from any origin to settle its Robusta contract, I note in the "origins excluded" row only those Arabica-producing countries that are excluded from the origins tenderable lists on the three Arabica coffee exchanges (ICE, TGE, BM&F). For the reasons mentioned above, coffee farmers in the "excluded" box may be effectively precluded from trading in futures and options.

Costs

Various costs associated with futures and options trading appear prohibitive for coffee producers, especially small ones. Futures trading requires payment of an initial margin and may additionally generate frequent margin calls. Options trading requires the payment of a premium that also appears prohibitively costly in some cases. For both margin calls on futures accounts and options premiums, costs rise as future prices become more volatile. This implies that trading costs rise at precisely the same time as farm-level risk is rising. From a development perspective, this sort of procyclicality in risk management—with insurance becoming less accessible just when it is needed most—is highly problematic.

Table 3.2 Origins tenderable and excluded on coffee futures and options exchanges

Exchange	*Contract*	*Origins tenderable*[1]
ICE	Arabica coffee futures and options	Mexico, El Salvador, Guatemala, Costa Rica, Nicaragua, Kenya, New Guinea, Panama, Tanzania, Uganda, Honduras, Peru, Burundi, Venezuela, India, Rwanda, Dominican Republic, Ecuador, and Brazil[2]
LIFFE	Robusta coffee futures and options	Any and all, so long as it can be "freely exported"
BM&F	Arabica coffee futures and options	Brazil
TGE	Arabica coffee futures	Mexico, Costa Rica, El Salvador, Honduras, Nicaragua, Guatemala, Colombia, Brazil
	Robusta coffee futures	Indonesia, India, Vietnam, Thailand
NMCE	Robusta coffee futures	India
Origins excluded (all are Arabica producers)	Angola, Bolivia, Cameroon, Cuba, Democratic Republic of Congo, Haiti, Jamaica, Madagascar, Malawi, Panama, Paraguay, Philippines, Puerto Rico, Sri Lanka, Trinidad and Tobago, and Zimbabwe	

[1] This information can be found in the contract specifications documents available on every exchange's website.
[2] Brazil will officially be on the list in 2013.
Source: Author calculations based on data from the exchanges.

Clearinghouses stipulate an initial margin that must be deposited prior to the commencement of trading and maintained until the position is closed.[89] These requirements represent one of the largest, if not the largest, up-front costs for coffee producers looking to hedge on futures exchanges. The margin is collateral that the clearinghouse uses to settle a trader's losses, thereby protecting the exchange and other traders from counterparty default risk.

Some clearinghouses specify higher margins for speculators than for hedgers. Still other exchanges, such as BM&FBovespa in Brazil, LIFFE in London, and NMCE in India, employ complex formulas to determine the riskiness of a given trader's portfolio and the corresponding margin requirement (this is done using SPAN, Standard Portfolio ANalysis of risk, systems). For most coffee producers, these distinctions do not really matter. Even relatively low margin requirements are generally unaffordable for small coffee farmers.

Table 3.3 indicates the mismatch between the incomes of coffee farmers and the size of the initial margins on several coffee futures exchanges.

Table 3.3 Margin requirements relative to coffee farmer income, selected countries

Exchange	*Contract*	*Initial margin requirement*	*Average farm size*	*Average yield, 2009*[1] *(lbs/ha)*	*Average price paid to growers, 2010*[2] *(USD/lb)*	*Coffee farmer income (w/ average farm size, average yield, in USD)*
ICE	KC (Arabica)	US $5,400[3]	Mexico: 2.7 ha	Mexico: 702	Mexico: $1.06[4]	Mexico: $2,009
			Ecuador: 2.7 ha	Ecuador: 431	Ecuador: $1.62	Ecuador: $1,885
			Ethiopia: 0.1 ha	Ethiopia: 1,478	Ethiopia: $0.79	Ethiopia: $117
LIFFE	RC (Robusta)	US $1,600[5]	Uganda: 0.2 ha	Uganda: 1,346	Uganda: $0.53	Uganda: $143
BM&F	ICF (Arabica)	BR $3,000[6] (about US$2,000)	Brazil: 4.9 ha	Brazil: 2,682	Brazil: $1.34	Brazil: $17,610

[1] Average yield data were obtained from the FAOSTAT database.

[2] Historical prices paid to growers by country are available from the International Coffee Organization. www.ico.org

[3] From www.theice.com

[4] The price to growers in Mexico is from 2008, the latest year for which the ICO has this data.

[5] LIFFE employs a SPAN margining system. As of June 13, 2011, "scanning risk" was estimated at US$1600 per Robusta coffee contract. Based on LIFFE's discussion of initial margining, this $1,600 figure is a minimum estimate of initial margins. SPAN systems determine margins based on the risk of a trader's entire portfolio, even if that portfolio includes the products of multiple exchanges. Because margins are precisely tailored to a trader's individual position, it is difficult to specify a single initial margin that applies to all traders. See LIFFE's initial margin calculation methods at: http://www.lchclearnet.com/Images/LIFFE%20Commodities%20Margining%20Overview_tcm6-48592.pdf. See also LIFFE's most recent circular on Robusta coffee: http://www.lchclearnet.com/risk_management/ltd/margin_rate_circulars/liffe/2011-06-24.asp. Both files accessed on July 26, 2011.

[6] BR = Brazilian Real. According to the BM&F's margin calculator, the "maximum theoretical margin" for Arabica futures on the BM&F is between 3,032 and 3,188 Brazilian reals, depending on the delivery month. The US dollar amount specified is based on the 1.5 reals: US$1 exchange rate prevailing on July 26, 2011.

Source: Author's calculations based on data from the FAO, ICO, and the exchanges.

Specifically, I compare initial margins for a single coffee future traded on ICE, LIFFE, and the BM&F with estimated annual incomes for coffee farmers in 2010. To calculate coffee farmer incomes, I multiply the size of the average farm in the appropriate country by the average yields in that country for 2009 (the latest year for which data are available from the FAO). I then multiply this output level by the average coffee prices paid to growers for 2010 (available from the ICO).

Please keep in mind that the income calculations represent estimated farm income from coffee only. As coffee is frequently the only source of cash income, especially for small coffee farmers, this is not an unreasonable assumption, though there are certainly many farm families who earn income from producing other crops and/or working off farm. Please further note that in each country a majority of farmers are often smaller than average, have lower than average yields, receive lower than average prices, and, thus, face margin requirements that are more unaffordable than indicated in the figure. Please also keep in mind that these income comparisons represent something of a best-case scenario. Like food prices in general, coffee prices reached incredible heights in 2010, meaning that the farmer income estimates I make for 2010 will be higher than average. This makes margin requirements appear more affordable than they might be in other years.

Table 3.3 estimates the affordability of initial margin requirements for coffee farmers having farms of average size, producing at average yields, and receiving the average price paid to growers in that country. In Brazil, where farms are very large and yields relatively high, the initial margin is most affordable. To trade a single coffee future on the BM&F, an average farmer would have to post as margin roughly 11 percent of her estimated income from coffee for 2010. Turning to the other cases, the situation becomes gloomier. The margin required of Mexican coffee farmers looking to trade a single future on ICE is about 270 percent of average coffee farm income in 2010. In Ecuador, posting margin to trade one future on ICE would require 286 percent of average income in 2010. For Ugandan farmers, the margin required to sell a single Robusta future on LIFFE is 1,119 percent of average coffee income for 2010. In Ethiopia, farmers would have had to make 4,615 percent of the average income from coffee to post margin on a single contract on ICE.

It is not only initial margins that exclude farmers from participation in the coffee derivative market. Clearinghouses additionally employ an accounting method called "marking to market," and they do this *daily*. Market gains and losses are tallied daily, that is, "marked-to-market," meaning that farmers are required to post additional margins every trading day if the market moves against them. Investors must maintain their margins to keep their positions open.

Given significant day-to-day fluctuations in future prices, accounting practices like these can be devastating for would-be hedgers, precluding effective participation. Anderson and Danthine note that "the day to day fluctuations of the futures price will generate a series of random cash flows over the period during which a futures position is held. This is due to the requirement that futures accounts 'mark to market' daily." [90] Even if the general trend in future prices is downward, short hedgers (like coffee farmers) could still face serious, temporary income losses due to the day-to-day volatility of future prices. Put differently, a hedge that is profitable over a period of a year or so may be very unprofitable from day to day or month to month depending on market behavior.

As an example, consider the period between 1998 and 1999, the first year of the recent coffee price crisis. Hedging with futures during the first year of the crisis would generally have been profitable for short hedgers, given the steep decline in coffee future prices. Figure 3.1 illustrates coffee future prices for the March 1999 Arabica contract on NYBOT (this exchange was purchased by ICE in 2006, but the specifications for its coffee contract remained the same). Note that the trend line shows a decline in future prices over this period. Please also note the significant interday price volatility, around the downward trend.

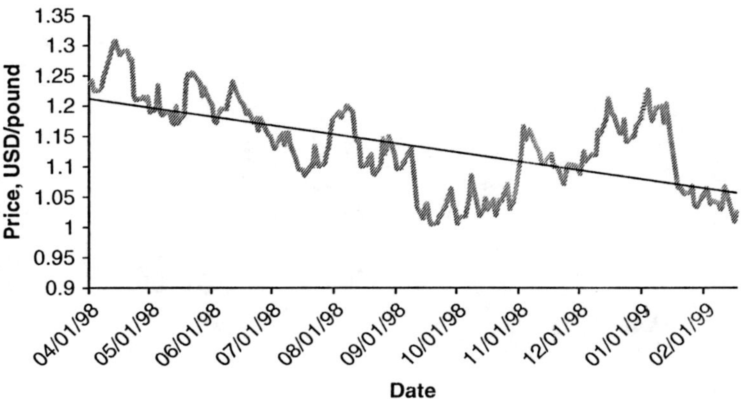

Figure 3.1 Daily settlement prices for March 1999 coffee "C" contract (USD/pound)
Source: New York Board of Trade.

If a coffee farmer put in place a simple hedge over this period, the hedge would have been a profitable one. Let's say, as an example, that a coffee farmer sees prices falling in early 1998 (as they did). On April 1, 1998, our farmer says, "Enough! I need some protection!" So, she sells her not-yet-harvested crop forward for delivery in March 1999 using NYBOT's coffee "C" Arabica futures contract, locking in a price of US$1.2375 per pound. When our farmer decides to unwind her hedge (get out of it) in mid-February 1999, the prevailing future price is US$1.0255 per pound. This represents a gain of US$0.212 per pound for each of the 37,500 pounds hedged (this is the standard lot size), or a total US$7,950 profit.

However, it is far from certain that our hypothetical farmer would have made it this far. One potential, or even likely, scenario is that she would have been "blown out" of her hedge before this time. Because future prices are so volatile over the course of the hedge, the farmer would have had to make daily margin calls to settle losses when they occurred. This is the consequence of marking to market daily. Absent sufficient cash reserves, liquid assets, or access to credit, the margin calls are unaffordable and the trader's account would be closed by the clearinghouse. Figure 3.2 depicts our hypothetical farmer's cumulative margin account balance at the end of each trading day, assuming, for simplicity, that there is no initial margin requirement (please note from above that these are really quite high).

Unfortunately for our coffee farmer, the margin account dips significantly below zero early on in the hedge. Daily margin calls during the first month of the hedge range from just under US$40 to almost US$1,700. While future prices move unfavorably later in the hedge as well, by this point (assuming the

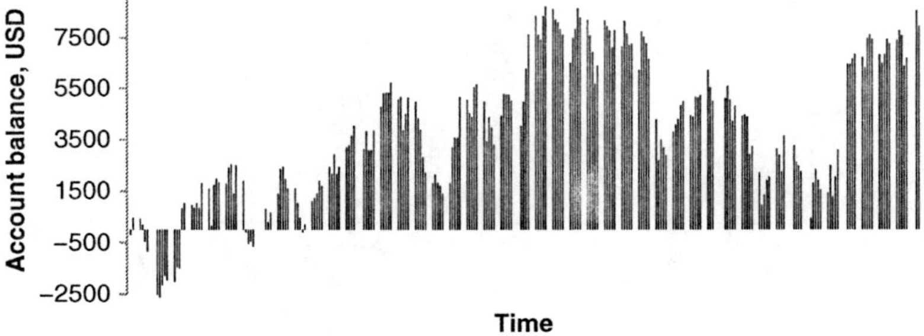

Figure 3.2 Margin account balance for hypothetical short hedge, April 1, 1998–February 17, 1999 (in USD)

Source: Author's calculations based on data from NYBOT.

farmer makes it this long) our hypothetical farmer made sufficient gains from the hedge earlier on to cover later margin calls. As mentioned previously, some derivatives advocates have recommended extending lines of credit to hedgers for margin calls in this context.

The high costs of margin calls have led other derivatives advocates to suggest that options trading may be best from a development perspective. Options purchasers are not required to post margin or make margin calls. Yet, options premiums are expensive and actually increase as future prices become more volatile. From the perspective of the option writer, this makes perfect sense. As uncertainty about the future grows, so does the cost of insurance. Yet, from a development perspective, insurance costs rise just when they are needed most, potentially depriving farmers in their time of greatest need.

Interestingly, Rutten and Youssef suggest the potential for farmers, or the cooperatives of which they are a part, to use what are called "zero-cost" options, which require no margin nor the payment of an options premium.[91] "Zero cost options combine the purchase of put options with the sale of call options, which implies that the producer is paying for the price insurance by giving up their potential gain from price increases above a certain level."[92] However, Rutten and Youssef note that these sorts of products are currently sold only over the counter, and that accessing these markets is difficult for large companies in the South, let alone individual farmers, suggesting another bias in derivatives markets toward the largest players. Because "know your client" requirements have become so stringent since 9/11, transaction costs have risen enormously for derivatives market intermediaries:

> They [brokers] can never recuperate this [cost] for a client that will trade less than a few million dollars a year. So while in the mid-1990s, a coffee trader from Burundi was able to deposit £5,000 with a London broker and start managing the risks of his operation, now only the large companies in developing countries have access to developed country brokers. And for a number of reasons (including, until fairly recently, currency controls in most developing countries) there are not many brokers based in developing countries that can offer access to western exchanges.[93]

Generally, then, many of the costs associated with coffee futures and options trading are prohibitive for smaller Southern actors. Perversely, the costs of trading in some cases rise as future prices become more volatile, suggesting the likelihood that insurance will become more expensive and less accessible just when it is needed most.

Information and Knowledge

Of all the access issues discussed so far, information and knowledge are the most difficult to systematically quantify. What is discussed in this section is largely anecdotal evidence from a variety of international organizations about how information and knowledge issues pose obstacles to farmer use of futures and options markets.

Beginning with information obstacles to effective futures trading, Mohan notes in a recent article that, "making reasonable decisions based on fine-tuned hedging instruments (futures and options) requires permanent access to information and processing of the various data."[94] Gibbon agrees that "users need to be in daily contact with financial markets in order to use them optimally."[95] The references here to "permanent access" and "daily contact" suggest both the significance of market information for farmers as well as the scale and intensity of the information-gathering effort.

At the same time, acquiring the necessary information to trade in futures is difficult for many coffee producers, especially those with little access to information and communications technologies (ICT) and lower incomes. Indeed, these two factors—availability and affordability—are linked, with income levels often determining an individual's ability to acquire and use ICT. National income is also an important determinant of the level of infrastructure development. This is the general message of Roberts' (2008) statistical report on global ICT for the United Nations.[96] The findings indicated an increase in the use of ICT of virtually all types across all countries that were part of the study (a fairly broad global contingent). That said, across the developed world ICT usage is highest, and usage declines as country incomes decline, with the "least developed" countries using ICT less than any other country category.

Confirming this broad global trend in the agricultural context and also making the explicit link between farm size and information access, UNCTAD notes, "Small farmers in developing countries often suffer from lack of information on market conditions at different locations or different points in the marketing chain."[97] Potts discusses this same general problem in the coffee context: "Producers, policy makers, roasters and even consumers are constantly faced with asymmetric information on the actions of other players within the coffee market.... [There is a] persistent context of imperfect information within the coffee sector...."[98]

Please keep in mind that these authors are discussing problems faced by producers in obtaining information about the *coffee market.* That producers also need information about the futures market only adds to the difficulty they confront in gathering the relevant information. Fafchamps and Hill's

2006 study on price risk management in Uganda suggests that potential hedgers lack even the most basic information about futures—indeed, many had not even considered hedging because they did not know that futures and options instruments existed at all.[99]

Further, information costs exhibit considerable economies of scale. The information required to effectively trade one futures contract is the same as that required to trade 10 or 100 contracts. A bias toward larger farmers trading in multiple contracts can thus be seen in this context as well (recall that this was also one conclusion of the earlier discussion of broker transaction costs).

The existence of a domestic futures exchange may permit easier information gathering for traders in that country. Mohan argues, "The price discovery information in a local exchange will be more transparent to producers and local traders. They can access historical information with no restrictions . . . ."[100] UNCTAD agrees: "In many parts of the developing world, a new breed of commodity exchanges are proactively expanding market access—both to the exchange markets but also crucially to the exchange's pricing information."[101]

The ability of domestic exchanges to reach rural producers with price information largely depends on the manner in which the information is delivered. While the information provided by the BM&F is free of charge, it is provided over the Internet, which requires connectivity and a computer. In Uganda, the government has been working to create a "market information system" (MIS) that will eventually provide farmers around the country with regular price information via text message over mobile phones, radio, newspaper and other media outlets. The project, funded in part by the Common Fund for Commodities and administered via the United Nations Office for Project Services, has plans to expand its data coverage to additionally include "quantities produced and traded, potential buyers, quality standards and other requirements."[102] These plans do not include future price information, nor does it seem currently possible for the quantity of data required to hedge effectively to be delivered and processed adequately via mobile phone and radio. The reader should be aware that there are a large variety of ongoing efforts in various countries to ensure timely delivery of market information to people in rural areas. As these efforts continue, information obstacles to futures trading may diminish accordingly.

Last, knowledge of derivatives markets and trading further presents a final access obstacle for many prospective traders, including small coffee farmers. While information accessibility is problematic for a variety of reasons discussed above, knowledge gaps appear to be a qualitatively different problem.

"Knowledge" here refers to those skills, capacities, aptitudes, and technical capabilities required to make good use of derivatives markets.

Some scholars discuss knowledge-related capabilities in the financial context in terms of "financial sophistication" or "financial literacy." However, I think this phrase confuses the matter if only because there are many financially sophisticated and literate individuals who nonetheless find it difficult to understand derivatives, let alone make good use of them. Tickell argues that as far as financial sophistication is concerned derivative instruments are in a class of their own—he notes that in some high-profile financial firms there is only one person who understands how the firm's assets have been leveraged with derivatives. The untimely death of this one person, Tickell writes, has thrown firm operations into turmoil as there is no one left who understands the complexity of the instruments and how they were used.[103]

Indeed, the terms "quantum finance" and "nuclear financial engineering," invoked to describe the work of those entrenched in this growing corner of finance, are another testament to their opacity and frustrating complexity for potential users. Figlewski argues, "[T]he large derivatives losses experienced by major financial institutions in recent years suggest that even sophisticated investors are capable of making big mistakes about derivatives."[104] For example, both recipients of the 1997 Nobel Prize in Economics, Myron Scholes and Robert Merton, who, along with Fischer Black (who died in 1995), developed the Black-Scholes options pricing formula (discussed in Chapter 2), went on to form a derivatives-trading hedge fund—a fund called Long Term Capital Management (LTCM). LTCM found itself in serious derivatives-related financial trouble in 1994 and was ultimately bailed out by the US Government. Thus the two Nobel Prize winners Myron Scholes and Robert Merton—who figured out how to price an option by drawing on the differential equation for heat diffusion employed in physics—were not able to avoid large derivatives losses. Few would argue that Myron Scholes and Robert Merton are not financially literate or sophisticated—again, derivatives are perhaps in a class of their own.

The World Bank's ITF and CRMG consistently regard lack of "technical capacity" as among the largest obstacles to effective derivatives trading in the developing country agricultural context. The ITF reports that "lack of knowledge of such market-based price insurance instruments" and "lack of understanding of how to use the tools available" are among the foremost obstacles for accessing derivatives markets for small farmers in particular.[105] The CRMG writes, "Training by the CRMG at the farmer and even the cooperative level has proven to be a lengthy exercise and may not be the most efficient way to build capacity."[106]

In the Mexican coffee context, the ITF has found that "there is a need for specific training and technical assistance."[107] The need for technical assistance in Mexico is compounded by the socioeconomic characteristics of residents of Chiapas, Veracruz, Puebla, and Oaxaca, states that collectively account for the majority of Mexican coffee production: "The majority of Mexico's illiterate and poorly educated adults can be found in the states of Chiapas, Oaxaca, Guerrero, Hidalgo, Veracruz, Puebla, and Michoacan. Children in these states leave school out of economic necessity to support their families".[108]

Similarly, working in the coffee and cotton sectors in Uganda, the CRMG recognizes the "high needs for capacity."[109] In Uganda where 70 percent of the population is involved in agriculture (over 40 percent of whom live in poverty), illiteracy and low educational levels are the norm particularly among women and girls.[110] In Brazil, Watson and Anchinelli's study on a community of small coffee farmers in the Brazilian state of Minas Gerais revealed that literacy rates are the lowest in the state and only 66 percent of farmers have completed *primary* school.[111]

Intermediation

That futures markets exclude small- and even medium-sized farmers has not gone unnoticed. Over the past decade, and even earlier in the case of Brazil, institutions have been erected to *intermediate* between farmers and futures markets. These institutions aim to bridge access problems encountered by smallholders, or otherwise deliver market-based price insurance to them. In this section I focus on the experiences of Mexico, Brazil and Uganda in setting up futures market intermediaries. In Mexico, both the federal government and farmer cooperatives are engaged as derivatives market intermediaries. In Brazil, the federal government and private investors have devised two different means of addressing access difficulties. In Uganda, both farmer associations and a local bank are filling similar roles. While intermediation efforts are ongoing in other countries as well, the experiences of these three countries serve to highlight some of the critical issues that have arisen in this context.

Among other key points, please bear in mind that derivatives market intermediation efforts have been ongoing since the early 1990s in some places, with very little success in systematically incorporating small producers. Among the primary impediments to successful intermediation have been small lot size, and lack of information and technical capacity(knowledge), some of the very same obstacles that impede direct farmer access. In terms of policy, a kind of false optimism prevails among many researchers evaluating futures market intermediaries. By my reckoning, not once has a researcher from the World Bank, UNCTAD, the FAO, or the UNDP questioned whether futures market intermediation should be on policymakers' agendas at all. This question is important. Is facilitating futures market intermediation a good use of the limited time, energy, and resources of those involved in such efforts? The evidence below suggests that policymakers might fruitfully pursue altogether different policy options.

Beginning in Mexico, at least two distinct institutional solutions to derivatives market access problems have been developed. First, marketing cooperatives in Mexico often guarantee coffee farmers a minimum price for their crop. In this way the cooperative provides a service to its members that approximates the service offered by futures markets, with the risk of volatile or low coffee prices being transferred from the farmer to the cooperative. For example, the *Union Regional de Pequeños Productores de Café Forestak y de Agroindustrias de la Zona de Huatusco,* in Veracruz, is a cooperative union with almost 2,000 members (it also markets the coffee of an additional 2,000 nonmember farmers). The average member farm size is 2.3 hectares, and members are required to market at least 80 percent of their crop through the union.

Members have several options when marketing their crop. The most popular is the *anticipo,* in which farmers deliver their crop to the union after harvest and receive a portion (usually 60–70%) of the final expected value of the coffee. After all of the coffee is sold by the union several months later, the farmer receives an additional payment equal to the difference between *anticipo* price and the final price if the latter is larger. "This system exposes the Union to significant price risk. If the final price turns out to be lower than the first payment (the *anticipo*), the Union stands to lose as it cannot recover money from the farmers."[112] Of course, the union could simply pay out a smaller initial *anticipo,* the level of which would reflect the risk of prices falling until final sales are made. However, in doing so the union risks losing its business especially when coffee prices are very low. "A smaller *anticipo* may encourage farmers to market their coffee elsewhere, or, even worse, be small enough that farmers will decide not to harvest their crop at all."[113]

On the one hand, such a payment system shifts the risk that prices will fall from the time of harvest through the subsequent marketing period from the producer to the cooperative itself. The cooperative is essentially giving producers a put option—farmers do not bear the risk of prices falling below the *anticipo* price, but they are able to take advantages of rising prices (see Chapter 3 for an explanation of options). On the other hand, one of the foremost advantages of trading in futures is that farmers have some certainty of the price they will get for their crop *before* the harvest, such that the application of inputs and technologies as well as family expenditures over the preharvest period could be managed and capital rationing avoided. Thus, while the cooperative union does indeed provide an important price risk management service, preventing falling prices during the marketing period, it is not the same service that is provided by futures hedging.

Putting this point aside for the moment, from a market access perspective, such an arrangement appears ideal for the individual farmer. Obstacles pertaining to size, cost, yield, information, and knowledge are shifted from the farmer to an actor that is arguably more capable of effective derivatives market use—the union deals in larger lot sizes, has larger revenues, is more creditworthy (i.e. can potentially finance various costs), and likely has superior means and expertise to effectively gather and utilize market information. So long as the cooperative is itself able to lay off its own risk via derivatives markets, thereby ensuring the organization's financial viability, the farmer will gain at least some of the income benefits of derivatives trading (depending on how the cooperative structures and times its price guarantees). The only potential obstacle that remains for the individual farmer is the cost of joining such a cooperative.

The price guarantees offered to many Mexican coffee farmers by cooperative associations are complemented by an ongoing governmental effort to more directly intermediate between farmers and derivatives markets. A government program called *Apoyos y Servicios a la Comercialización Agropecuaria* (ASERCA) assists farmers via direct income support, financial and technical support for agricultural commercialization, and a relatively new program to facilitate farmer hedging of price risk via options markets. The new program, *la Subprograma de Apoyos para la Adquisición de Coberturas de Precios Agropecuarios* (la Subprograma), subsidizes the purchase of put and call options by farmers, cooperatives, and processors producing maize, wheat, sorghum, soybeans, cartamo (an oil seed), rice, cotton, livestock, porkmeat, orange juice, and coffee. The program first got started in 1996, with coffee options available for subsidy by the late 1990s. The government pays for one-half of the option premium, which is repaid only if the transaction is profitable. The options for coffee available to Mexican farmers through this program are options on the coffee "C" (Arabica) futures contract.

From the perspective of farmer access, ASERCA addresses many of the obstacles discussed above. The program subsidizes the costs of trading, provides information on the coffee and options markets, offers technical assistance on strategy and the like, and operates a brokerage account on behalf of participating farmers. That said, farm size remains problematic, and even subsidized premiums may be too expensive for some producers. While there has been talk of ASERCA allowing farmers to buy "shares" of an option, such that small farmers with smaller lot sizes could participate individually, the ITF notes that the "typical user" of the program is currently either a large individual producer or associations of small- and mid-sized producers.[114] That Mexican producer associations utilize ASERCA to purchase price insurance for their members is an interesting phenomenon—double derivative intermediation.

Indeed, farmer associations frequently face similar access obstacles to derivatives trading as do farmers themselves. In terms of broker transaction costs, the CRMG recently remarked that fulfilling due diligence and "know your client" requirements "is more complicated for producer groups and cooperatives than for local banks." Additionally, and depending on the cooperative in question, lack of technical expertise is still a large obstacle. The CRMG notes, "For intermediaries lacking basic business skills, the benefit of education about price risk management instruments will be marginal. Additionally, attempts to build risk management capacity in organizations that have more critical problems such as poor communications infrastructure, institutional instability, underdeveloped marketing/financial skills, and weak managerial authority are likely to be ineffective and inefficient."[115] The ITF's work in Mexico also focused squarely on the need to improve the technical capacities of producer organizations themselves such that they may be able to hedge effectively.[116] The fact that intermediaries might also need intermediaries to address access obstacles comes to the fore in the Ugandan case as well (more below). Absent such second-tier intermediation, cooperatives may have a difficult time sustaining price guarantees to their members.

While determining precisely how many small- and medium-sized producers are able to indirectly acquire some price insurance via their cooperative (or other producer association) was not possible for lack of data I was able to estimate participation in the ASERCA program. ASERCA made available the lists of *la Subprograma's* participants for 2004 and 2005 on its website.[117] Included in these records are the names of the participating individuals and/or entities, the product they were hedging, the number of contracts purchased, and the quantity of the commodity hedged. In the case of farmer cooperatives and groups, I have estimated the number of farmers represented by these organizations based upon the quantity of coffee hedged (provided by ASERCA), average yields for 2004–05,[118] and the average coffee farm size in Mexico.[119]

Please also note that it is uncertain whether all individual participants are farmers, and whether all participating groups are farmer cooperatives or other farmer organizations. *La Subprograma* is also open to agribusinesses that can demonstrate that they purchase coffee from farmers and that that they are using hedging instruments to protect prices paid to farmers.[120] It is possible, then, that processors, exporters, or other middlemen may be participating in the program. However, I am assuming, for the purpose of my calculations, that all individuals and groups participating are individual farmers or farmer groups. This can only bias the results in favor of presenting derivatives markets as more inclusive.

The data suggest that, of Mexico's roughly 282,500 coffee farmers, only 0.03 percent participated in the program in 2004. In 2005, the figure increased slightly, with 0.4 percent of coffee farmers participating in the program in 2005. By any measure, these are very low participation levels.

The Mexican case generally illustrates not only how intermediaries may bridge access problems (e.g. through cost subsidization, opening up brokerage accounts, and providing technical assistance, or indirectly via price guarantees to members of cooperatives), but also how the access obstacles that confront individual farmers are sometimes reproduced at the level of the intermediary. In Mexico, coffee cooperatives often face the same access difficulties as individual farmers. In instances such as these, two intermediaries, or perhaps even more, might be required to effectively link farmers to derivatives markets. From a policy perspective, this suggests that efforts to facilitate futures market intermediation are likely to be ongoing commitments that require frequent monitoring, experimenting, and reconfiguration. For example, the ITF, as noted above, has had to significantly widen its search for appropriate intermediaries and rethink the role of cooperatives in response to difficulties on the ground in training cooperative leadership. Further, low participation rates in ASERCA's Subprograma suggest that intermediaries may be almost as exclusive as derivatives markets themselves. While erected ostensibly to provide farmers with much needed risk management services, la Subprograma fails to deliver price insurance to that population of Mexican coffee farmers that needs assistance most. Indeed, the mere existence of an intermediary does not ensure that smallholder communities are able to participate.

Similar to Mexico's ASERCA program, the Brazilian government has also intermediated between farmers and options markets in the past. Further, an innovative Brazilian financial product, the Cedula de Producto Rural (CPR), combines price risk management with a debt instrument in a model of futures market intermediation that the World Bank (among others) is very excited about. These are each discussed in turn.

The World Bank briefly describes a program developed by the Brazilian government during the coffee crisis. "According to BM&F management, the government has decided to support coffee producers in light of the falling coffee prices by selling coffee put options dated March 2004."[121] Contributing authors to a 2005 World Bank book on commodity markets note that the Brazilian government "has been auctioning put options to farmers at well below fair value; these options are exercisable as sales of coffee to the government."[122] Leao de Sousa and Pimentel describe the program as follows: "[T]he government takes 'short positions'—and, therefore, assumes the obligation to buy the production at the target price. The buyers, in turn, are the farmers; while government has the 'obligation' to buy, farmers get the 'right' to sell their production to the government at the target price, if the market price is not more attractive at the period of delivery. For that, farmers pay a premium established by electronic auctions at the Commodity Exchanges throughout the country, which guarantees the required transparency."[123]

The 2004 World Bank report makes note of the fact that small producers were excluded from the program, as they were too small to meet the lot specifications in the options contracts.[124] That said, the program seems to have addressed other access obstacles, namely difficulties in finding a broker and the costs of options premiums. Baffes et. al., in the statement above, indicates that the options were sold at below market value, meaning that the government subsidized their purchase by farmers. Leao de Sousa, however, writes that the premiums were established by electronic auction, indicating that premiums may not have actually been subsidized.

A recent proposal from derivatives expert Randall Dodd bears some resemblance to the Brazilian government's program. Calling the plan "Puts for People First," Dodd suggests that governments issue nontransferrable put options to farmers with a strike price equal to that day's market price.[125] The options would expire about two months after the harvest, and the output level specified in the contract would be based upon past or expected future yields.[126]

Dodd's suggestion fundamentally differs from the Brazilian program in several important respects. The author suggests that the provision of put options could be accompanied by environmental requirements, such as requiring that producers work on soil conservancy as a condition of receiving the option. Also interesting is Dodd's suggestion that governments could issue the options based on current market prices for subsequent crop years (not just the current one) "so that producers could invest in their farming activity based on some assurance of future crop prices."[127] Critical as well is the manner in which Dodd's proposal addresses the size constraints that producers face, by tailoring the contracts to individual farmer yields.

On the one hand, such a program could conceivably address many of the concerns that I have raised throughout. Dodd's program, if executed properly, could be expected to address the following access issues: the costs of futures trading, problems finding a broker, and farm size. That said, making good use of the put option (i.e. exercising it appropriately) likely requires access to market information and knowledge of the instruments and how they work.

All of this is to say that policymakers must look carefully at the capacity of each program and intermediary to address the broad range of obstacles farmers face. While some of these issues may be given policy priority over others, it is likely that no single intermediary or government program will be sufficient to address all of the issues raised thus far.

A different sort of intermediation is also ongoing in Brazil. In 1994, rural agricultural bonds—las Cedulas de Producto Rural (CPR)—were introduced in Brazil with the primary goal of ensuring that farmers had the financing and inputs required for production.[128] The CPR may be settled in three different ways, with each method of settlement implying a different kind of relationship to coffee prices.

The "physical" CPR works as follows: "The producer receives cash (or inputs) upon the issuance and selling of the bond for their physical product and has the obligation of delivering an agreed amount of rural production at an agreed location and future date . . . In this way, the physical CPR provides crop financing for the production of the crop—or livestock—and also manages the producer's price risk by linking the debt to the physical product."[129] In other words, debts are repaid in actual coffee (or whatever the crop might be) such that if prices fall farmers are still able to repay. This is a form of price insurance, as the value of the debt decreases in tandem with coffee prices.[130] This system does have a big drawback, however: Farmers are reluctant to repay the bond when coffee prices are on the rise, as their coffee is valued higher on the open market than it is for CPR repayment (i.e. total value of the coffee on the open market is greater than the amount of credit that was extended initially when the CPR was issued).

The "cash settled" or "financial" CPR does not appear to offer price protection for farmers at all, and is in fact a source of new risk. Because the prospect of future delivery discouraged many investors from buying the physically settled bonds, cash settlement was seen as a way of making the CPR market more liquid. At the time the bond is issued, a price at which the contract will be settled after harvest is determined. Depending on whether coffee prices rise or fall between the time of the bond issue and repayment, the farmer or association will gain or lose, respectively. The World Bank notes that "this new contract is more advantageous to the buyers as it leaves market price risk of the underlying commodity with the supplier" (2005a, 15).[131] Leao de Sousa and Pimentel suggest that the cash-settled CPR is more of a tool for speculation than for risk management, as farmers tend to prefer the cash-settled CPR when they think that coffee prices will rise in the future.[132]

The "indexed to futures" CPR is the final type of bond.

> Contract settlement is based on a local or foreign futures market reference price or the price calculated by a reliable source, such as a university. In this case, the settlement is based on the amount of production established on the bond, multiplied by the agreed upon reference price at the time of settlement. The indexed CPR, like the physical CPR, brings benefit to the seller because it transfers the price risk to the buyer while at the same time allows the buyer of the CPR to settle the contract financially, the key element of the Financial CPR.[133]

Indeed, the lower the settlement price the lower the amount that issuers have to repay, a system that reduces the likelihood of producer default during times of falling prices.

As was the case with the minimum price guarantees offered by cooperatives in Mexico, in Brazil the nature of the intermediation alters the specific price risk management service that is being provided. In the case of the CPR, price risk management is linked to debt repayment, with income benefits accruing to farmers indirectly. The ability to repay debts may indirectly smooth consumption by opening channels for new extensions of credit during future income shocks. Further, the ability to obtain preharvest financing and the certainty of repayment may allow producers to make investments in production technologies that increase future income. That said, issuing a CPR still leaves farmers exposed to the potentially harmful effects of price-induced income shocks in terms of lower consumption, malnutrition, and reduced expenditures on education and health.

Moreover, the cash-settled CPR is not a risk management instrument at all—it is a debt instrument that exposes producers to price risk from the time of issuance to the time of settlement. Unfortunately, this particular CPR is currently the most popular. Of the almost 130,000 CPRs issued between 1994 and 2004, almost 70 percent were of the cash-settled variety; only 1–2 percent were indexed to futures, while roughly 25 percent are physically settled.[134] A minority of bonds issued were embedded with any sort of price insurance, while the majority serve to insure investors with producers bearing added price risk.

One could raise other concerns about the model employed here by the Brazilian government—the linking of price risk management to producer credit. While on the one hand, credit (especially short-term, preharvest financing) is crucial for sustaining a farming enterprise, on the other debt can be a source of financial hardship and insecurity. Oxfam's 2005 report, *The Coffee Crisis Continues,* clearly describes the manner in which debt acts as a double-edged sword particularly for small coffee producers: "Many small-scale farmers entered into the coffee crisis shouldering significant debt at above market rates. Those who survived through the lowest prices continue to bear the heavy burden of this obligation. Unable to refinance debt taken on before and during the crisis, many farmers risk losing their land and lack pre-harvest working capital to invest in their crop—all despite higher coffee prices."[135] Oxfam points crucially to several factors that help to determine whether extension of credit to coffee farmers will broadly be beneficial or harmful—lending terms, existing debt levels, and prospects for repayment. While innovative means of making financial markets work for small coffee farmers are exceptionally important, credit is not a cure-all.

In any case, it is doubtful that the CPR is reaching small Brazilian producers. The World Bank notes, "The instrument has become a relevant financing and commercialization mechanism for producers of various sizes in Brazil, especially for medium and large-sized producers."[136] It goes on: "Tracking the total number of operations by value of CPR contracts, the value from US$3,000 to US$10,000 is found to be most commonly used, which is typically a sufficient fund to finance medium-size producers."[137] Like the futures markets themselves, the Brazilian debt-linked price risk management instrument appears to bypass smallholders.

In Uganda, the World Bank's CRMG along with the ITF have focused upon two different intermediaries, both of which have delved into derivatives markets in a limited fashion: a local bank and an umbrella farmer cooperative.

Centenary Rural Development Bank recently worked with the ITF on incorporating price risk management into its lending operations, an idea not unlike the Brazilian CPR. The ITF and CRMG generally have high hopes for the use of local banks as intermediaries across the developing world, as opposed to other actors like cooperatives, traders, and exporters. According to a 2005 CRMG report on the "lessons learned" in its price risk management work thus far, banks have several advantages over other actors. Banks have more technical expertise, are usually sufficiently financially sophisticated, have sufficient communications channels to work with brokers in other countries, can achieve economies of scale in certain costs (e.g. information costs), and can increase lending (or reduce the costs of lending) via its facilitation of hedging.[138] Further, banks can potentially extend credit to producers to finance initial margin requirements and subsequent margin calls.

Perhaps most importantly, banks have the proper "commercial incentive" to offer price risk management services.[139] The incentives of banks are (arguably) such that they are willing, without any further inducement, to provide price insurance to farmers (for a fee of course) because price insurance directly benefits the bank itself by reducing the risk of loan default. Other actors in the coffee industry that are positioned sufficiently close to producers either have the wrong incentive or no incentive at all (e.g. domestic traders who are only marginally exposed to price risk over the short time that they actually hold coffee would need some financial inducement to hedge and pass on the savings to producers). Although marketing cooperatives might have a similar commercial incentive (as in the case of the Mexican cooperative union that was itself exposed to price risk), their expertise, communications infrastructure, and unfamiliarity with brokers in developed countries render them less viable in this context.

While these World Bank organs seem keen on discouraging developing country governments from providing such financial inducements, others have suggested that subsidies may be absolutely necessary to bridge the gap between farmers and futures markets. This is yet another place where government intervention may be required to make derivatives workable in a development context. Rabobank International, a private firm that has worked extensively with the Government of the Netherlands on farm-level price risk management, states:

> Presumably, it was considerations concerning entry barriers and economies of scale which led the World Bank in the direction of sold-on price insurance rather than first-hand futures trading when it came to smallholder producers. But whether even this model can be operationalized without subsidies both to international traders and credit institutions is unclear. Certainly the transaction costs of such schemes will be high and there seems no incentive for international traders or credit institutions to assume them for third parties without a subsidy.[140]

Aside from the subsidy issue, local banks also encounter obstacles to derivatives trading. Centenary Rural Development Bank in Uganda did not conform to the broader expectations of the CRMG regarding local banks as intermediaries. In fact, the bank fell prey to one of the very same obstacles that confronts producers trying to access futures markets directly. "After an extensive capacity building effort, implementation was frustrated by a high level managerial decision at the bank that the account-opening requirements of the providers (in particular, request for copies of passports) were too stringent for Board members to comply."[141]

Just as the World Bank noted in regard to producer cooperatives, UNCTAD remarks that local banks in developing countries may lack the skills and expertise necessary to offer price insurance to their clients.[142] The Ugandan case illustrates that additional access obstacles also confront local banks. As was the case in Mexico, access problems are reproduced at the level of the intermediary, perhaps indicating the need for double (or triple) intermediation. To reiterate, that intermediaries might also require intermediation to effectively use futures markets is a serious policy concern.

Fostering each layer of intermediation will require significant time, energy, and resources on the part of governments and private actors. Depending on the types of intermediaries favored in a particular country context (private, public, cooperative), each layer of intermediation can also add an additional layer of cost for farmers.

Union Export Services Ltd. (UNEX), an umbrella organization of Ugandan farmer cooperatives created to facilitate coffee exports, also delved into derivatives trading on behalf of its membership. In 2002, UNEX successfully purchased an "over-the-counter NYBOT-based put option." The CRMG reports that this initial transaction was successful but that, three years later, it had yet to be "replicated." Among the issues that frustrated the CRMG's plans was the fact that "UNEX [faced] strong demands from its farmers for more training on the subject of price risk management . . . The original concept was to have UNEX purchase the contract on behalf of farmers who would share in the costs and benefits. That idea has been very difficult to replicate, because of the high capacity building needs for farmers, who, when directly involved, request more and more training."[143]

Conclusions

In theory, derivatives markets can allow producers to hedge risk and make good investment decisions in a manner that eliminates the need for government interference in commodity markets. Coffee futures and options markets that are efficient, sufficiently long-term, and accessible may make important contributions to the welfare of the some 25 million small farmers who produce the world's coffee.

In practice, however, coffee derivatives markets are sometimes inefficient, extend at most 18–24 months forward, and systematically exclude small actors like farmers from participating. From a policy perspective, these empirical findings are alarming and urge caution to policymakers interested in pursuing derivatives for development. This is not to say that futures trading cannot be beneficial for some actors—there is a hefty empirical and anecdotal record of large companies in agriculture and finance benefiting extensively from such trading—but, rather to say that there are numerous factors that cast doubt upon their usefulness for smallholders. That said, the inefficient and short-term nature of the markets suggest that even for larger entities, like the governments of coffee-dependent countries, the markets will be of only limited use. Governments that trade will also have to contend with basis risk (though they may have access to superior instruments for managing it), and will still be heavily exposed to falling long-term prices.

There are three specific findings that are especially salient for policy and deserve to be repeated. First, the scale of the access problems that small farmers face in accessing derivatives suggests that policy efforts to intermediate between farmers and derivatives markets will be time-consuming and resource intensive. The experiences of various countries and international organizations with intermediation efforts confirm that many would-be intermediaries confront the very same obstacles to trading as do farmers themselves.

Second, futures and options markets may sometimes work at cross-purposes with development goals. For example, futures and options trading becomes more expensive—in the case of both margin calls and options premiums—when prices become more volatile. This suggests that farmers will be deprived of insurance services precisely when they need them most. A similar problem arises in the context of the short-term nature of derivatives markets. Short-term insurance may provide an incentive to continue producing coffee or even increase production when long-term price trends suggest that gradual exit from coffee production might be prudent.

Third, there are several indications that making derivatives markets work for development will require extensive support from government, in contrast to the theoretical claims of advocates. McKinnon argues that for futures and options markets to effectively stabilize farmer incomes, they must extend sufficiently far into the future. If they do not, government will have to position itself as a "market-maker," creating and sustaining the long-term market. There is additional evidence that governments may need to subsidize and otherwise support intermediation efforts. Potential intermediaries may not only require a financial incentive to provide insurance to farmers, but also will probably need training and other services. It further goes without saying that futures and options exchanges have to be regulated and monitored, suggesting even greater public costs as commodity exchanges proliferate across the South.

Again, while the evidence does suggest that the coffee derivatives market may be of some limited use, it also suggests that the theoretical benefits stipulated by advocates are seriously undermined in practice. For this reason, a cautious policy approach is warranted.

CHAPTER 4

Coffee, Derivatives, and Poverty: A Global Commodity Chain Approach

Modern bourgeois society with its relations of production . . . is like the sorcerer who is no longer able to control the powers of the nether world that he has called up by his spells.[1]

In many respects, today's global agricultural and financial systems are object lessons in the law of unintended consequences.[2] The global economy is a complex system in which seemingly innocuous or beneficial innovations and policy reforms often result in significant and overwhelming changes that were largely unforeseen at the time the reforms were made. Hidden channels and complex feedback loops, always more visible in hindsight, can frustrate even the most well-intended researchers and policymakers.

Technological innovation is one of the most obvious sources of unintended consequences in both finance and agriculture today. It is often the case that technological innovations, initially promising great gains for early adopters, generate significant costs that are only apparent long after their initial introduction. Indeed, it was largely unforeseen in 1970 that the new practice of mortgage "securitization," then being pioneered by a newly created US government agency called Ginnie Mae (Government National Mortgage Association), would be so widely adopted by the private sector and would eventually contribute to the most severe global financial crisis since the 1930s. Securitization, in this context, is the process by which large numbers of mortgages were pooled and then sliced up into small financial pieces, each of which represented a claim on a tiny piece of every mortgage in the underlying pool. As the 1970s unfolded, Fannie Mae and Freddie Mac, the other quasi-governmental mortgage agencies, began financing large segments of their mortgage-lending operations via the sale of mortgage-backed securities to global investors. By the 1990s, private lenders had adopted the practice and were rapidly securitizing subprime and Alt-A mortgages (these are loans made to less creditworthy borrowers).[3] As the financial crisis developed in 2007, it became clear that securitization had permitted the diffusion of default risk among US homeowners across a huge array of investors worldwide, such that the US housing crisis was quickly transmitted in a domino-like effect to the balance sheets of hedge funds, pension funds, sovereign wealth funds, insurance companies, banks, and endowments of various types. Securitization surely worked to deepen the US mortgage market and extend mortgage financing to individuals previously overlooked by these markets, but it also provided a vehicle for the spread of financial contagion, allowed for the diffusion of risk throughout the global economy, and heightened global financial fragility. Today, securitization is commonly implicated as a leading contributor to the Great Recession that began in 2007.[4]

Another illustration of the unintended consequences that stem from rapid technological innovation can be found in the case of genetically modified seeds for several popular cash crops. When the US agribusiness giant Monsanto introduced Roundup-Ready seeds for soy, corn, cotton, alfalfa, and canola over the course of the 1990s and early 2000s, they were hailed as a means to increase farm yields and profits. Roundup-Ready seeds are genetically modified (GM) such that the plants that grow from them can resist continued applications of the herbicide Roundup. Farmers can apply the herbicide without killing the main crop, and do not have to excessively till their land to get rid of weeds, thus reducing fuel costs and soil erosion. Monsanto's website promises "maximum profit opportunity," "efficiency," and "convenience" to the farmers that adopt this cutting-edge technology.[5] While debate rages about the costs and benefits of GM seeds, there is growing evidence that heavy applications of Roundup have given birth to a new generation of "superweeds." Resistant to Roundup, superweeds are becoming problematic for farmers who now have to apply even more herbicide, reintroduce extensive tilling, and even pull weeds by hand in some cases. Costs for farmers are rising as superweeds reproduce and multiply. Andrew Wargo III, the president of the Arkansas Association of Conservation Districts, was recently quoted in the *New York Times* as saying, "It is the single largest threat to production agriculture that we have ever seen."[6] There are concerns that Indian farmers, who have also recently adopted GM seeds en masse, will face a similar threat in the future.

This chapter engages the problem of unintended consequences in the context of derivatives and development. The previous chapter provided a variety of empirical evidence illustrating that derivatives markets do not consistently meet the expectations of advocates. While certain actors may use the markets to their advantage at various times, coffee futures markets are often inefficient, always short term, and largely inaccessible for most coffee farmers, even with intermediation efforts. These findings urge caution to policymakers who might rely on derivatives markets as risk management instruments in the agricultural context.

However, the problem for policy is not only that derivatives markets fall short of their theoretical promise but also that the markets may actually work at cross-purposes with development and poverty alleviation goals. Considering "poverty" from a broad, historical perspective, this chapter presents evidence that derivatives markets may, despite the good intentions of policymakers, actually be aggravating poverty and insecurity in coffee-farming communities in the developing world.

First, and perhaps most disconcerting, derivatives markets are price risk management institutions that leave the structure and operation of the underlying coffee economy untouched. Indeed, this is partly what recommends derivatives to advocates. In this manner, derivatives address the symptoms of coffee farmer poverty—vulnerability to price risk—without addressing underlying causes. Problems of chronic oversupply in the coffee market, commodity dependence, and inequalities in wealth and power along the coffee commodity chain, which connects primary producers to final consumers, are simply not addressed with the application of derivative instruments. Second, derivatives markets, as they come to be relied upon by policymakers as tools for risk management for small growers, may deepen inequalities among farmers, and between farmers and other actors in the global coffee commodity chain (GCCC). Third, derivatives markets also provide a conduit for the transmission of price volatility into local markets. These negative spillovers have especially severe consequences for poor smallholders without access to viable risk management arrangements.

In this chapter, I first discuss the perspective on coffee farmer poverty prevalent among derivatives advocates, a vision that precludes anticipation and consideration of the unintended consequences I discuss subsequently. In the second section, I present the GCCC and focus on the relationship between poverty among small producers and structural inequalities in wealth and power in the global coffee economy. In the third section, I present the coffee derivative commodity chain and analyze the implications of this structure for poverty and insecurity among smallholder coffee farmers. Specifically, I address the manner in which derivatives markets maintain the status quo in the coffee economy, enhance inequalities along the coffee chain, and contribute to increased cash price volatility. In the last section, I conclude with summary remarks and discussion of the implications of these findings for policymakers.

Debating Poverty

The work of the World Bank and other development organizations generally reflects a relatively narrow and ahistorical conception of poverty. It is an economic vision of poverty that ignores the manner in which distributions of power in the global political economy undermine the well-being of coffee farmers. It is an insular vision of poverty that takes coffee price volatility and commodity dependence as "given" or "natural," without questioning the sources of these trends. It is an ahistorical vision of poverty that fails to capture the manner in which long-standing cleavages between empires and colonies, governments and farmers, agriculture and industry, and agribusiness and the peasantry have contributed to the position of coffee smallholders today. As such, this vision of poverty forecloses consideration of some of the dangers associated with the globalization of derivatives markets in the developing country context, dangers that I elaborate in subsequent sections.

That said, and in the interests of fairness, derivatives advocates do not offer a single, uniform understanding of poverty among smallholder farmers. Depending on the source, peasant poverty is variously rooted in one or some combination of the following: poor national policymaking that overtaxed agriculture and deprived it of the appropriate investments[7]; the disintegration, with liberalization, of social arrangements that used to support farmers[8]; rising levels of price volatility and uncertainty[9]; the "handicaps" that plague small producers in trying to access global markets for commodities, credit, and risk management[10]; and commodity dependence, supply capacity constraints and inadequate diversification.[11]

A 2007 Expert Meeting at UNCTAD about the impact of globalized commodity markets on small producers illustrates a typical formulation of smallholder poverty. From this perspective, to be revisited in Chapter 5, poverty in small farming communities is rooted in the inabilities of smallholders to effectively access markets for global commodities. Access problems are, in turn, based in a combination of infrastructure issues (physical, information, and financial), farm-level capability deficits (like quality problems), and inadequate public policy (such as regional trade barriers). The experts write:

> Poverty was linked to the inability of small producers in developing countries to effectively integrate into a more global economy. The withdrawal of Governments from markets as a result of adjustment and market liberalization had

> confronted small producers with new challenges. To sell their products, small producers needed, inter alia, to get goods to market, find buyers, obtain market information, secure finance and meet standards.[12]

In this document, UNCTAD does indeed recognize, for example, the power that large agro-food multinationals (MNCs). that process and sell food items have in determining who participates in production and who does not. For example, "Retailers such as supermarkets have launched voluntary standards initiatives or adhere to existing standards. Non-compliance with private standards, although they are voluntary, excludes producers from retailers' markets."[13] This issue of standard-setting, one that I also find problematic, is discussed at more length below. Yet, the problem here for UNCTAD is not the inequalities of wealth and power that allow Northern MNCs to exercise such an outsized influence on the lives of smallholders. Rather, the problem lies with smallholders and their governments who have not adapted to these new global realities. Further, there is virtually no recognition of the power-related problems that arise for small producers once they actually come to participate in global commodities markets. As will be seen below, coffee producers are subject to the market power of large traders and roasters who use their dominance to exacerbate competition among farmers and put downward pressure on prices paid to growers. Ironically, while exclusion from the global coffee economy consigns smallholders to poverty, so does participating in it.

The ahistorical nature of these sorts of formulations is also problematic, and results in the conflation of effects with causes. The same document from the UNCTAD Expert Meeting notes: "The Director of the Division on International Trade in Goods and Services, and Commodities, made a statement on the commodity problematique, in which she highlighted the recurrent problem of developing countries' commodity dependence. She emphasized the need for commodity-dependent countries to derive remunerative returns from the commodity sector."[14] As formulated here, commodity dependence is conceived as an independent variable, a naturally "recurring" contributor to smallholder poverty.

Historically, however, commodity dependence is an expression of longstanding, pervasive inequalities in wealth and power on the global stage. Indeed, the colonizing powers deliberately *created* colonial economies such that they would be subservient to the needs of the empires, that is, supply them with raw commodities and depend on them for income, food, and manufactured goods. The resulting legacy of commodity dependence has been further reinforced more recently by trade liberalization, which traps some countries in those few endeavors, like coffee production, in which they hold a competitive advantage. It has also been reinforced by export promotion by national governments and international development agencies, with specialization in commercial export crops still broadly recommended to rectify trade imbalances and finance government debt repayment. As many critics have noted, development policy recommendations for agricultural liberalization and increasing primary commodity exports themselves reflect global power inequalities, particularly the dominance of the United States and US-trained economists in the global development establishment.[15]

All of this is to say that global inequalities in wealth and power have significant explanatory power in thinking about the plight of the 25 million families worldwide who grow coffee. I do not mean to say that there are not other factors and dynamics important to understanding poverty—poverty is a very complex, socially constructed problem that differs enormously in content across time and space and may be attributable to a variety of causes that interact in unique and unpredictable ways. Rather, what I argue here is that considering inequalities in wealth and power, historically and at present, is important for thinking about poverty in the global coffee economy, and for devising and analyzing price risk management arrangements.

In the next section I present the GCCC and a brief, stylized overview of the chain's history. The chain helps to visualize the changing structure of the global coffee economy over time, especially changing distributions of wealth and power and how these structures contribute to the impoverishment of smallholder farmers.

Small Farmer Poverty and the Global Coffee Commodity Chain

Chains and networks are wonderful tools for understanding how the global economy operates and the relationships that characterize it in a world where national borders are increasingly insignificant. A commodity chain is an analytical framework that sees the global economy as a messy complex of production processes, processes that link individuals and communities across the globe to one another by virtue of their participation in the production of a particular good or service. Among other advantages, chains and networks allow us to see and investigate the geographic scope and scale of production processes, the socioeconomic and political conditions that frame each stage of the process, and the relationships between actors at various stages, especially distributions of wealth and power. As will be seen, the historical and contemporary distributions of wealth and power along the global coffee chain figure importantly in explaining poverty among small farmers.

The GCCC connects producers in the global South to final consumers who live mainly in the global North. In between primary production and final consumption, there are a host of additional "nodes" or stages in the coffee production process. Green (unroasted) coffee flows from producers (mostly small farmers, but also some large estates) to exporters, often via small traders and hullers who act as middlemen and basic processors. Hullers remove the flesh and inner parchment layer from the coffee cherry, exposing the green beans. Exporters aggregate large quantities of coffee from many producers and sell their lots to international traders. International traders pass the green beans downstream to coffee roasters, who roast, process, and package the beans such that they are appropriate for final consumers. Roasters sell their products to supermarkets, cafés, and other retailers, who pass on the finished product to the final consumer.

Not all nodes on the coffee chain are created equal. According to Hopkins and Wallerstein, most global commodity chains are comprised of core, semiperipheral, and peripheral "nodes" or stages that are linked together in a variety of complex and dynamic ways.[16] "Core" production processes are characterized by high use of technology and capital relative to labor, low levels of competition, and high profits. By contrast, "peripheral" production process tends to be more labor intensive, more competitive, and less profitable. "Semiperipheral" production processes fall in between, representing a transitional category in global economic relations and production processes. As Wallerstein notes, "What we mean by core-periphery is the degree of profitability of the production process. Since profitability is directly related to the degree of monopolization, what we essentially mean by core-like production processes is those that are controlled by quasi-monopolies. Peripheral processes are those that are truly competitive."[17] In other words, commodity chains link together a variety of people and firms from around the world that are each producing in different environments and under different constraints.

While certainly not a uniform or universal one, there is nonetheless a tendency for peripheral production processes to accumulate in peripheral regions of the world—the Third World or global South—and for core production processes to accumulate in core regions of the world—the First World or global North.

> Core-like processes tend to group themselves in a few states and to constitute the bulk of the production activity in such states. Peripheral processes tend to be scattered among a large number of states and to constitute the bulk of the production activity in these states. Thus, for shorthand purposes we can talk of core states and peripheral states, so long as we remember that we are really talking of a relationship between production processes.[18]

When linked together in a chain, periphery, semiperiphery, and core describe the division of labor, power, wealth, and well-being in the context of a single production process. Because core nodes enjoy monopoly power in the markets in which they operate, firms in these nodes reap monopoly profits and have the power to direct and organize the entire chain in their own interest.[19] Peripheral nodes, by contrast, represent the most marginalized and least powerful nodes of a commodity chain, and are generally subjugated to the core. Being "peripheral" to a production process consigns one to low living standards, insecurity, and fierce competition. In an important sense, to be "peripheral" in the global political economy is to be poor.

Some nodes on the coffee chain, like the small farmer node, are peripheral, characterized by fierce competition, virtually no market power, relatively poor technology, and low profits. Other nodes on the coffee chain, like the roaster and international trader node, are core nodes. Firms engaged in core production processes enjoy low levels of competition, employ lots of capital and high technology, and reap substantial profits. Semiperipheral nodes on the chain, for example, exporting and retailing, incorporate firms that are more profitable than peripheral ones, employ relatively sophisticated technologies, and are moderately profitable, but are still dominated by the core.

Please keep in mind that these categories are not fixed over time and that certain nodes may contain actors from more than one category. For example, while many cafés are subordinated by large roasters, other retailers, for example, the multinational giant Starbucks, enjoy significant market and negotiating power with the larger retailers and final consumers. Gresser and Tickell note, for example, that Starbucks enjoys significant market power relative to consumers, and can maintain high final consumer prices even when green coffee prices are falling.[20] As another example, consumers may have more power in the context of specialty coffees, where demand for ethically traded, organic, and special origin coffees have influenced the strategies of retailers.

Figure 4.1 depicts the global coffee commodity chain. Each box on the chain is shaded according to its designation of core, peripheral, or semiperipheral.

The monopolies enjoyed by firms in core stages of the coffee production process give them the market and political power to extract "surplus" (profit) from the periphery and channel it to the core in an exploitative process called "unequal exchange." Unequal exchange refers to the process by which surplus value (profit) is moved from periphery to core, and involves the exchange of commodities containing "unequal amounts of social labor."[21] A classic example of this relationship is the production of primary agricultural commodities (e.g. cotton or green coffee) by the periphery that are then sold to the core at prices often below the cost of production (or, in the colonial period, at prices that reflected the use of slave labor), and the production of sophisticated

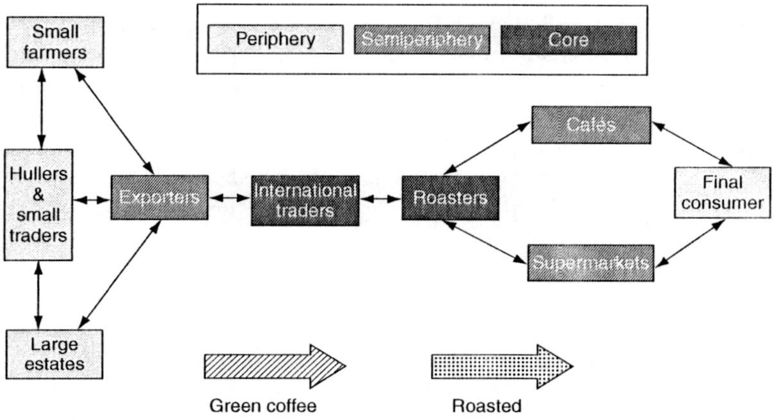

Figure 4.1 The global coffee commodity chain
Source: Author's depiction, partly drawn from illustration by Stefano Ponte (2002).

processed goods in the core that are sold back to the periphery (e.g. finished clothing or instant coffee). The powerful monopolies in the core further have the power to exclude other actors along the chain from participation, picking and choosing among a host of competitive suppliers, searching for the highest quality at the lowest price.

The processes of unequal exchange and exclusion, enabled by and reinforcing growing inequalities along the coffee chain, have been in the past and remain today leading contributors to the impoverishment of small Southern coffee farmers. Historically, those who labor to grow and tend the green beans have always been subordinated to the interests of more powerful, wealthier actors from the core who consume the product, resulting in the marginalization, disempowerment, and impoverishment of Southern coffee communities. Indeed, many scholars of coffee in the colonial era see colonialism as the process by which "core" and "periphery" were created, as capitalist economic systems were forced upon colonized peoples in Latin America, Africa, and Asia.

As will be seen, imperial powers frequently utilized export commodities like coffee as mechanisms of colonial control and subjugation. Forced dependence on single export crops helped to maintain a system in which the colonies remained dependent upon the empires for survival, with this dependence paradoxically surviving after independence in many cases. While the International Coffee Agreement softened to some degree the processes of unequal exchange and exclusion, even in this era coffee farmers represented the weakest and poorest links on the coffee commodity chain, and were often exploited by their own governments. With liberalization, unequal exchange has intensified as the now-deregulated coffee economy has further disempowered producers, resulted in lower prices, increased coffee production and competition, and opened up space for continued consolidation of monopoly power in the core. Indeed, liberalization has exacerbated inequalities along the coffee commodity chain and provided the context within which exploitation and exclusion of the periphery by the core has intensified.

The Colonial Coffee Chain

Coffee trading dates to the Yemeni port of Mocha in the sixteenth century, but Wild finds coffee's origin in the Ethiopian highlands perhaps thousands of years earlier.[22] He posits that Sufi missionaries, who traveled extensively over the Middle East and northern Africa during the fifteenth and sixteenth centuries, ultimately brought coffee from Ethiopia to Yemen, where it was grown to feed demand from the Ottoman Empire. At Mocha, coffee was "discovered" by Dutch and British traders, who brought the new commodity back to Europe and to their tropical colonies. The Dutch brought coffee to Java and Sumatra in Indonesia. Topik notes that in 1721, Amsterdam imported 90 percent of its coffee from Mocha, but that by 1726 a full 90 percent was sourced from Java.[23]

The British brought it to East African colonies like Kenya and Uganda. Legend has it that a Dutch diplomat brought coffee to the court of French emperor Louis XIV, who cultivated several trees in his private greenhouse. From this private cache, a couple of trees were taken to the French colony of Martinique. From the Caribbean, coffee cultivation spread throughout Latin America, with the Spanish and Portuguese empires encouraging coffee cultivation in their colonies as well. The French also introduced coffee to their African colonies, like Cameroon, Madagascar, and Cote D'Ivoire; and in the 1850s, they brought coffee seeds to Indochina (now Vietnam).

As with other tropical export crops like sugar, tea, cocoa, cotton, and tobacco, from the very beginning coffee was deployed by the empires as a tool for the subjugation of the colonies. Introducing coffee and encouraging its commercial cultivation (often by force) met several imperial needs. The empires required raw materials to finance and feed global exploration and expansion, growing populations at home, and, later, industrialization. Metals like silver and gold, precious gems like diamonds, and the "precious vegetables" (as they were known) like coffee each filled this role in various colonies at different times. Further, encouraging coffee production was a means of creating a colonial economy that would be entirely dependent upon, and thus wholly subordinate to, the empire. To this end, the colonial powers destroyed native industries such that manufactured goods and processed commodities would have to be imported from the North. As native food production was also often destroyed, the colonies had to rely on imported temperate food crops (e.g. wheat) for survival. According to Magdoff:

> The world capitalist system which evolved in the process of forcibly transforming noncapitalist societies and adapting the weaker to the needs of the stronger nations, had two historically new features: a) the institution of an international division of labor between manufacturing nations and those that mainly supplied raw materials and food, and b) the creation of a hierarchy in which the overwhelming majority of nations and people were, to a greater or lesser degree, economically and financially dependent on a few centers of industry and banking.[24]

The GCCC was thus a colonial creation, and power dynamics along the chain took their character from the broader global inequalities that characterized the nascent capitalist economic system. Green coffee, for most coffee was roasted at home in cast iron frying pans until the late nineteenth century, flowed from colonies to empires in a manner that exemplifies the concept of unequal exchange. Cheap coffee flowed out of the colonies to the core, and relatively more expensive temperate agricultural goods and manufactured items flowed from the empires to their colonies in the periphery, effectively redistributing wealth toward the imperial centers. For instance, with reference to colonial Latin America, it was noted that: "The mines, haciendas and plantations of Latin America were the envy of Northern Europe and Anglo America. Yet it was Latin America that ended up as a dependent Third World region, and the root reason was that the profits from the mines, haciendas and plantations enriched northern Europe and Anglo America far more than they did Latin America."[25]

The highly unequal division of labor, power, and wealth along the colonial coffee chain was mirrored in miniature at the farm level. Like most tropical crops in the colonial era, coffee was grown on large plantations owned by white settlers and worked by indigenous slaves, those imported from Africa and/or by indentured laborers. This was especially the case in Latin America and Indonesia. In Brazil, the world's largest coffee producer historically and presently, slave labor on coffee plantations continued long after independence:

> Romance aside, the harsh reality was that the world's greatest coffee economy was founded on the continuation of slavery long after it had been banned in Europe. Brazil only definitively banned slavery only in 1888. The impact on

> the coffee economy was enormous. As one Member of Parliament was to say in 1880: "Brazil is coffee, and coffee is the negro."[26]

While Topik disagrees with the picture of "agricultural producers as servants or as providers of brute labor-power, willingly serving up their produce to thirsty European buyers," he nonetheless attributes Brazil's "caffeinated dominance" during the nineteenth century in part to the Brazilian government's commitment to "guaranteed property (especially in slaves until 1888)." On some level Topik's clarification of the matter is even more horrible, for, in the Brazilian case, some of the oppressed became the oppressors after independence from the Portuguese in 1822. Indeed, it was "native born or African or Portuguese immigrants" who dominated coffee production and used slave labor after national emancipation.[27] Indeed, across much of Latin America, independence did not eliminate the use of forced labor to produce coffee. "Spanish American *fincas* rapidly expanded exports after the 1870s using domestic labor, though often peasants were coerced into work through debt peonage."[28]

In parts of Africa, where colonization efforts were ratcheted up following the end of the slave trade, coffee was produced by both native peasant farmers and by settler-farmers who "coerced native labor into working on their farms."[29] Stavrianos emphasizes the way in which coffee production was subordinated to the interests of the colonial powers: "[T]he British and the French encouraged the peasants to grow export crops because this not only met the need for such crops in the home markets but also provided income for the peasants with which they could pay the head tax that was the main financial prop of colonial administrations."[30] Critically, West African peasant coffee producers at the turn of the twentieth century encountered the very same power inequities along the commodity chain that plague the industry today:

> This West African trade in agricultural produce was dominated by a hierarchical trade network.... The most powerful by all odds were the European companies, which enjoyed monopolistic advantages. They controlled warehousing, shipping and marketing, and therefore were able to dictate prices to the unorganized small farmers.... These firms enjoyed a double advantage in dealing with West African farmers. The firms could set low prices on the produce they bought, knowing that the farm families grew a large proportion of what they needed, and that they had to sell in order to obtain cash for the head tax. Conversely, the foreign companies could charge high prices on their imported goods such as tools, clothing and bicycles, because they had no competitors.[31]

In some cases in East Africa, as in Uganda, independent coffee production by native peasants was forbidden in the earlier colonial period and reserved only for settler farmers. For much the same reason that native African cultivation had been banned in Kenya, another British colony, peasant cultivation was banned in Uganda on quality grounds—the bigoted fear was that black planters would "degrade quality and spread disease."[32] The exclusion of peasant farmers from coffee production by colonial administrations in the core presages the similarly exclusionary practices of multinational traders and roasters, who today wield quality and quantity standards in much the same way that the colonizers brandished race.

Turning to the relation between coffee and finance, in Magdoff's reading of the imperial age, between the sixteenth and early twentieth centuries the colonies were transformed from sites for plunder and pillage into fully functioning capitalist satellites that provided the empires with raw materials for industrialization. Over this period global financial interests came to play a large and growing role in the exploitation of the colonies. With Lenin, Magdoff argues that this latter period of imperial expansion was a period of "monopoly capital" in which "the giant corporation is in ascendency and there is a high degree of economic concentration." In this period, there was a sharp rise in the "export of capital" abroad, a manifestation of the "obvious need on the part of investors of capital for a safe and friendly environment."[33] Indeed, finance is portrayed as both dominant and parasitic during this period, subjugating colonial economies to its profit logic. Hobson discusses the mass movement of American finance capital into the Third World in the early twentieth century:

> The adventurous enthusiasm of President Roosevelt and his "manifest destiny" and "mission of civilization" party must not deceive us. It is Messrs. Rockefeller, Pierpont Morgan, Hanna, Schwab and their associates who need Imperialism and who are fastening it upon the shoulders of the great Republic of the West. They need Imperialism because of the desire to use the public resources of their country to find profitable employment for the capital which otherwise would be superfluous.[34]

The expansion of Northern finance into Southern economies, including agriculture, would continue over the course of the twentieth century. The case of coffee and derivatives under examination here provides a fine modern-day example of this process.

The Coffee Chain from Independence to 1989

Over the course of the late nineteenth and twentieth centuries, the coffee-growing slaves, indentured laborers, and dispossessed peasants of the colonial era would become today's small coffee farmers. The largely plantation-based coffee economy in Latin America transformed into a more peasant-dominated affair through a variety of mechanisms.

Topik notes that as high coffee prices stimulated increased production in Costa Rica, Venezuela, and Colombia in the early twentieth century, it became common for plantation owners to pay now-free laborers in "usufruct rights," giving them the right to work estate lands and claim the produce for their own.[35] Watson and Achinelli write that the high coffee prices of the 1950s motivated the Brazilian government to offer financial concessions to up-start coffee farms, many of which were smallholdings, as a means of boosting production and export revenues.[36] In Mexico, Rice notes that land redistribution efforts and government promotion of coffee production both figured into the rise of smallholder coffee production. Prior to colonization, farming in Mexico involved the *ejido* system, where agricultural activities took place on communally owned lands. Following the 1917 revolution, the system was reinstated and contributed strongly to the growth of the peasant farming community.[37]

While peasant coffee production for export was encouraged during the colonial period in West and East Africa at different times and to varying degrees, after independence land redistribution and export promotion efforts further peasantized the coffee sector. Stavrianos writes regarding tropical crop production in "neocolonial" Africa:

> A basic feature of the neocolonial society was its emphasis on producing for foreign markets as the prerequisite for getting started on the way to economic growth. This led to the encouragement of cash crops at the expense of traditional food production. Cash crops were stimulated by the allotment of the best arable lands, by supporting road and railway systems, by government-sponsored irrigation schemes and by a wide range of scientific inputs, including fertilizers, pesticides and high-yield seeds.[38]

According to Davis, the unequal core—periphery division of labor in the late nineteenth and early twentieth centuries was reflected in prevailing global price dynamics. Characteristic of the process of unequal exchange, the agricultural products produced in the core commanded higher prices globally relative to the gradually declining prices of tropical crops produced in the periphery: "With the exception of sugar, all the commodities whose price was lower in 1913 than in 1883 were commodities produced almost wholly in the tropics. All the commodities whose prices rose over this thirty-year period were commodities in which the temperate countries produced a substantial part of total supplies."[39]

As the production node of the coffee chain in the mid-twentieth century changed and became more peasant dominated, other features of the coffee commodity chain were retained basically intact. On the one hand, it is true that the governments of the independent Third World states came to have a growing role in coffee production and trade, replacing the colonial administrations that had existed previously. The International Coffee Agreement (ICA), agreed in 1962, exemplifies the active orientation of Southern governments in the post–Great Depression period. Southern governments, via international quotas, marketing boards, and the like, inserted themselves into the coffee production chain such that they counterbalanced to a degree the power of large Northern consumers. Instead of selling their crops to private merchants as in the past, farmers sold their coffee to government agencies. These agencies frequently guaranteed minimum prices to farmers, and also limited the supply of coffee that made it to the world market, in accordance with ICA quotas. In this manner, farmers received generally higher and more stable prices as global coffee supplies were maintained at a lower, more stable level (see Chapter 3 for discussion of historical trends in coffee prices).

On the other hand, while farmers were perhaps less subordinate to the needs of Northern colonizers, merchants, and roasters than in the past, they were in many cases subjugated to new development and industrialization projects at home. The post–World War II period witnessed unprecedented economic intervention by governments into the economic development process. The governments of Southern states from Argentina to Ghana undertook to foster industrialization by erecting heavy trade barriers around new industries, channeling investment capital into industry and away from agriculture, and maintaining overvalued exchange rates that made capital imports cheap while penalizing agricultural exports. Such policies led to now well-known critiques of the notorious "bias against agriculture" in development policy. As Bello notes, "A third force destabilizing peasants was the industry-first policies adopted by many countries. The agricultural surplus was commandeered for rapid industrialization through taxes on the peasantry and differential pricing."[40] In the coffee context, differential pricing was a common method of taxing coffee farmers to feed industrial projects in urban areas. Government marketing boards, like that in Uganda, would set producer prices at one level, and then export coffee to the world market at a higher level. The government captured the difference between farmgate and export prices, an implicit tax on coffee farmers.

This is not to say that the ICA era didn't bring some relief to smallholders who had previously farmed without much, if any, government support at all. In some cases, as in Mexico, the ICA regime often meant better treatment for smallholder farmers as INMECAFE (*Instituto Mexicano de Café*/

Mexican Coffee Institute), the government's coffee marketing board, facilitated higher prices, and provided fertilizers, coffee seedlings, and other forms of assistance. In most coffee-producing countries, comprehensive agricultural extension systems were erected in the post–World War II period, providing farmers with instruction and training in the use of new technologies, among other services. Agricultural development banks, since dismantled with liberalization, were also critical pieces of this support system, directing credit to smallholders who were generally ignored by private global capital markets.

For all the new powers exercised by Southern governments in the global coffee economy during this period, in important respects the domination of coffee production in the South by powerful actors in the North remained a persistent feature of the coffee chain between World War II and the collapse of the ICA in 1989. As Wild notes, "With the dieback of former European imperialism, and the increasing assertion of the hegemony of the USA over the western hemisphere, the many coffee-producing countries of Central and South America have found themselves overtaken by US neocolonialism."[41] Data in the subsection directly below on income distributions in the coffee economy show that even during this period farmers received a paltry portion of the wealth generated along the coffee chain, with Northern actors capturing the lion's share. While the period of global coffee stabilization was thus certainly an improvement over colonial times, when those who produced often received only meager food and shelter, it was nonetheless marked by severe inequalities in wealth and power.

The dominance of the core over the post–World War II global coffee economy is arguably best exemplified in the rise and fall of the ICA. While Brazil had attempted to stabilize volatile global coffee prices as early as 1906, with Colombia among other producing countries joining the effort during the Great Depression, it was not until the United States agreed to be party to an international agreement in the late 1950s that stabilization efforts were broadly successful.[42] The United States agreed to the ICA largely as a Cold War gambit.[43] Following the Cuban Revolution in 1959, US officials were concerned about the spread of communism among poorly-compensated Latin American coffee farmers. The ICA was a means of alleviating some of the economic hardships associated with coffee farming, thus stemming the appeal of communism. It is no coincidence that the ICA collapsed in 1989, as the Berlin Wall fell and the communist threat diminished. Without US cooperation, other consuming countries also failed to reduce their commitments. Without the participation of the consuming countries, producing countries were powerless to control supplies.

As in the later colonial period, the coffee chain in the post–World War II period was largely controlled by powerful Northern corporations that were trading coffee and beginning to process it on a broad scale. New processing techniques developed in the postwar years conferred growing power upon trading and roasting companies, as centralized purchasing and manufacture became more viable. Wild writes, "Historically, vacuum packing was the system that effectively delivered coffee from the tyranny of the here-and-now. An exclusively industrial process, it allowed the development of advertised coffee brands, lengthy distribution chains, and centralized buying and production."[44] Talbot further explains that advancements in instant coffee production generated an enormous new market for processed coffee products, a market almost wholly dominated by large corporates from the core. Speaking on the rise of instant coffee production in the United States, he notes:

> The capital-intensiveness of instant-coffee production led to a high concentration of market shares in these major markets. Only the largest coffee-processing firms possessed enough capital to compete in developing new technologies and building more modern production facilities. In addition, only the largest firms could afford the advertising and promotional expenditures necessary to compete in the national market.[45]

Thus, the continuing (though somewhat diluted) importance of multinational coffee merchants (carried right through from the colonial period) and the growing importance of technologically sophisticated roasting and processing companies in the postwar period reflect a changing coffee chain to be sure, but one in which small producers remain disempowered, marginalized, and impoverished relative to other actors downstream in the production and distribution process. While the ICA to some degree counterbalanced the power of the large corporates (though this managed coffee economy was still dominated by Northern interests), Southern governments too subjected the needs of coffee farmers to the interests of urban development and industrialization. As will be seen, liberalization has intensified and exacerbated inequality along the coffee chain, to the detriment of especially small producers.

The Coffee Chain from 1989

Liberalization of the global coffee market began with the 1989 collapse of the International Coffee Agreement and continued over the next decade as Southern governments dismantled their national systems of coffee support. As noted previously, the collapse of the ICA resulted in both lower and more volatile global coffee prices. As recognized by some derivatives advocates, chronic oversupply and heightened competition among producers since 1989 have contributed to these price trends. However, oversupply and competition are themselves rooted, if only partially, in policies for market liberalization encouraged by the North and the development establishment, as well as global inequalities in wealth and power. Further, these conditions have provided an environment conducive to the continued consolidation of wealth and power among large Northern MNCs who trade and process green coffee. Small producers have not fared well under these conditions.

Oversupply has been a periodic, though serious, problem in the global coffee market since 1989, the low global stocks of 2010–11 notwithstanding. Oversupply can be traced to a variety of factors, including investment in productive capacity in the ICA era, stagnating demand in the core, and asymmetric producer responses to prices. That said, liberalization and the widespread adoption of market-oriented development policies in the South are also important explanatory factors. When the ICA collapsed, national governments released the buffer stocks they had accumulated under the quota system. The world market was flooded with cheap coffee and coffee prices fell precipitously between 1989 and 1992. Also over the course of the 1990s, many producing countries increased their production levels, encouraged by high prices in the mid-1990s and rising levels of competition between producing countries, each of which had an incentive to increase production to capture a larger market share. According to Bates, the ICA succeeded in limiting competition among producers, as the agreement fixed the global market share enjoyed by each producing member country. With its collapse, producers and producing countries rushed to gain market share by raising production levels and employing competitive price setting practices.[46]

Oversupply and competition have also been aggravated by organizations like the World Bank, which has, for several decades now, been recommending commodity specialization and increased export crop production as a means of raising export revenues, paying off debts, and "jump-starting" the development process.[47] Much of the new coffee produced since liberalization has been of the poorer quality Robusta variety. Because roasters and traders can now more easily substitute cheap beans for higher-quality ones (more on this below), the prices of higher-quality coffees, and indeed of coffee in general, have fallen. Encouraged by the international development organizations, "African producers such as the Ivory Coast, and Asian growers, especially in Vietnam and Indonesia, flooded the world market with Robusta.... This undercut the price of Arabica beans, lowered the overall quality of coffee consumed, and increased returns to ever-larger processors rather than to growers."[48]

Liberalization of the coffee market additionally entailed the dismantlement of extensive systems of social support that farmers had relied upon previously. The "developmentalist" agricultural state in the South frequently provided subsidized credit, seeds, fertilizers, and fuel, among other kinds of direct assistance.[49] Agricultural extension networks were relatively robust and regularly assisted farmers in adopting new technologies and adapting to new climatic realities. With liberalization and encouragement from the development establishment to "reorder" fiscal priorities, most of the funding for these sorts of programs were cut and farmers were left to fend for themselves.[50]

The disappearance of the state from the coffee chain, combined with oversupply and rising competition, has significantly altered the balance of power between coffee farmers and the large consumers they confront downstream along the chain. Ponte writes, "From a fairly balanced contest between producers and consumers within the politics of the commodity agreement, market relations shifted to a dominance of consuming country based operators (including their agents based in producing countries) over farmers, local traders and producing country governments."[51] Gresser and Tickell note that coffee farmers are less able to negotiate for better prices with traders and roasters: "There is a vast imbalance of power in the global coffee supply chain. Farmers face a whole series of obstacles, starting with the very low international price for coffee. But some farmers Oxfam spoke with also complained of having to accept the price offered by the trader and of having very little, if any, power to negotiate."[52]

Liberalization not only disempowered and marginalized producers but also empowered multinational coffee roasting and trading firms in the core, resulting in increased monopolization of the chain and rising levels of inequality in wealth and power. As Wild puts it, "By effectively tying coffee farmers to a small number of transnational buyers and creating, through institutions such as the World Bank, trading conditions that demolish any international controls on the trade, the corporations have profited hugely while the farmers' share of the revenue pie has diminished."[53]

Regarding monopolization of international coffee trading, Newman reports:

> In 1998, the two largest coffee traders (Neumann Kaffee Gruppe (NKG) and Volcafé) controlled 29 percent of total market share, and the top six companies 50 percent. In 2006, Volcafé (now part of ED&F Man) and the NKG have maintained their dominant positions in the market, and control over 30 percent of world trade in green coffee. Concentration of the top 5 companies has also increased since 1998, and now accounts for a market share of over 55 percent.[54]

Ponte describes similar trends in the roasting node: "[T]he top two [roaster] groups combined (Nestlé and Philip Morris) control 49% of the world market share for roasted and instant coffees. The top five groups control 69% of the market. Nestlé dominates the soluble market with a market share of 56%."[55] Topik writes that following the 1989 collapse of the ICA, "The nature of the buyer... changed. Giant food conglomerates such as Nestlé, General Foods, Coca-Cola, Ralston Purina, and Kraft began to take advantage of their growing market power to buy up smaller successful coffee companies."[56]

Monopolization feeds into falling coffee prices since liberalization. Because of their market power and new processing technologies (like steam-cleaning the beans), roasters and traders have been able to source more "flexibly" from a variety of origins, substituting different kinds of coffee for one another in various blends.[57] In this manner, competitive sourcing strategies place downward pressure on prices and foster competition between producers of very different quality coffee beans.[58] Bates confirms that prices across different varieties of coffee have both fallen and converged on one another since liberalization, partly in response to the sourcing behavior of these core consumers.[59]

As a consequence of growing inequalities and the enabling environment provided by liberalization, small coffee producers face both exploitation via unequal exchange and exclusion from coffee production altogether, and sometimes both occur in tandem. Not only have absolute incomes fallen as coffee prices fall, but Ponte notes that the distribution of profits along the coffee chain has become more unequal since liberalization. The exploitative process of unequal exchange has intensified. Preliberalization, about 20 percent of profits generated along the coffee chain were retained by coffee-producing (peripheral) countries, while 53 percent was retained by consuming (core) countries. Since liberalization, the producer share has dropped to 13 percent, while the share retained by consumers has risen to 78 percent.[60] Others present a still grimmer picture: "Ten years ago, producer countries earned $10bn from a coffee market worth around $30bn. A decade later, they receive less than $6bn of export earnings from a market that has more than doubled in size. That's a drop in their share from over 30 percent of the market to under 10 percent."[61]

Exclusion is also readily apparent, and, combined with low prices for green beans and cutthroat competition among producers, also appears to be at least partly a consequence of the dominance of monopolistic traders and roasters over the coffee chain. Increasingly, roasters utilize a tiered supply network in which certain suppliers are given preference over others. Specifically, producers must be able to guarantee sufficient quantities and qualities of coffee in order to supply the big roasters. "Most roasters tend not to accept coffee for their blends from countries that cannot guarantee a minimum reliable supply.

As a result . . . minor producers may become increasingly marginalized in the future."[62] Smaller Southern exporters are also being swallowed up by large multinational traders aiming to ensure steady supplies of quality coffee to the big roasters.[63]

The prerogatives of big roasters—that is, the need for large supplies of cheap coffee of acceptable qualities—have also encouraged vertical integration by traders into coffee farming. Neumann Kaffe Gruppe, one of the two largest global coffee traders, notes on its website that it now owns and leases coffee farms across the developing world in an effort to more effectively supply its clients.[64] Consolidation at the farm level has also been aided in some cases by the large debts that small coffee farmers accumulated during the 1998–2002 coffee crisis. For example, in the Mexican state of Veracruz, one researcher notes that indebted small- and medium-sized coffee farmers have sold their plots in large numbers to newly established coffee plantations in an effort to escape their debt burdens.[65]

One observer concludes as follows about the contemporary plight of coffee growers:

> It would be tempting to assume that coffee cultivation had somehow emerged from the shadow of colonialism and empire into the sunshine of a more enlightened era. However, it is becoming increasingly clear that, although the players have changed, the orchestra is producing the same tune. Local labor on subsistence wages produces coffee at the lowest possible cost for markets in the developed world. The main difference is that instead of living by the old maxim that "Trade follows the Flag," powerful corporations have realized that it is easier to dispense with the burdensome responsibilities of actual colonization, and use modern transnational institutions such as the WTO, the World Bank and the IMF to impose their will from the boardrooms of Manhattan, Paris and Berlin. For the impoverished farmer whose national politics bend to the needs of these transnational institutions and the corporations they serve, the notion of democracy is a spurious validation of the yoke under which they are forced to work.[66]

Indeed, the global coffee economy is a stratified and hierarchical economy, marked by severe inequalities in wealth and power that date to the creation of the chain during the colonial period. With some respite during the ICA era (albeit brief, spotty, and insufficient), globalization and liberalization of the coffee commodity chain has been accompanied by falling coffee prices, growing supplies, heightened competition among producers, and reduced public support for coffee farmers (in risk management and other social supports). This environment has set the stage for rising levels of concentration in core nodes of the chain, with these inequalities reinforcing low prices and exacerbating competition. As in the colonial era, competition and disempowerment in the periphery and monopoly and dominance in the core have set the stage for unequal exchange, producer exclusion from the production process, and an intensification of coffee farmer poverty, insecurity, and marginalization.

The next sections discuss the troubling likelihood that derivatives markets, as they globalize and are integrated into development agendas, may make the plight of small producers more dire still.

The Coffee Derivative Commodity Chain, Poverty, and Insecurity

The coffee derivative commodity chain exhibits at least three characteristics of real concern in considering the negative, unintended consequences of integrating derivatives into agricultural development agendas. These characteristics shape the derivative chain such that, when overlaid atop the coffee chain itself, derivatives are transformed from instruments for poverty alleviation into generators of poverty and insecurity for small farmers.

First, the coffee derivatives chain is an ancillary, service chain that does not fundamentally alter the structure of the underlying coffee chain that it serves. It relates to the mother chain *symbiotically*, with the structure of one supporting the structure of the other and vice versa. Whether or not this symbiosis is, as a biologist might ask, an example of mutualism or parasitism is a matter I leave to the reader. Second, the coffee derivative chain is an *exclusive* chain that permits neither broad participation nor a wide diffusion of its services. High barriers to entry exist at each and every node of the chain. Third, the coffee derivative chain is increasingly characterized by high levels of *speculative participation* in trading. As the character of traders moves decisively toward speculation, derivatives markets become engines of cash market volatility.

The Symbiosis between the Coffee and Coffee Derivative Chains

This first point is a simple one. Liberalized markets are required for derivatives to work, and derivatives for their part may enhance the longevity of liberalization programs. Derivatives markets require and thrive upon underlying markets where prices are determined by private forces instead of governments, where trading is relatively strong globally and where prices are relatively volatile. This relationship explains, for example, the explosion of commodity and financial derivatives trading, as markets for commodities and financial products were pushed open in the 1970s and 1980s (see Chapter 2).

As derivatives markets expand their reach, they, in turn, generate forces that would maintain liberalized and globalized markets in the underliers. As indicated in the sections that follow, derivatives markets, even in coffee, are populated by very powerful financial and agricultural interests who are daily more invested in derivatives transactions. It will not be an easy feat to undo national policies for agricultural and financial liberalization given pressures from these quarters. Insofar as commodity derivatives trading requires liberalized and globally oriented commodities markets, the derivatives community will likely be a powerful oppositional force to altering the structure of the underlying coffee chain. Further, as policymakers become more invested in derivatives-based programs, they too may be reluctant to reverse their positions, for political or ideological reasons.

There is evidence that some derivatives advocates recognize the synergy between derivatives and the status quo. The World Bank's ITF notes, "A market-based approach to risk management may serve as a catalyst for reform and enhance the sustainability of liberalization programs in some commodity sectors."[67] Because derivatives markets function well only in liberalized policy environments, committing to derivatives entails a secondary commitment to maintaining liberalized coffee markets, a commendable relation according to the ITF.

Similarly, an official from UNCTAD noted recently, "Nowadays, and contrary to the situation in the late 1990s, many of the world's largest commodity exchanges (in terms of trading volumes) are located in developing countries. These exchanges have proved to be an important corollary to efficient domestic liberalization of the commodity sector, and an important contributor to the competitiveness of a country's agricultural industry."[68] The founder of Agricultural Commodity Exchange for Africa likewise implores governments to liberalize their commodity sectors to make way for new exchanges. Governments must "remove remaining tariff and nontariff barriers as soon as possible" and "de-regulate markets, to allow the free movement of agricultural produce between countries, to expand marketing opportunities and encourage production."[69]

In the coffee context, the likelihood that derivatives expansion will help maintain the existing state of affairs is alarming. Global coffee supplies are, over the medium to long term, far too high, and long-term prices are steadily falling. Commodity-dependent coffee farmers have few alternatives when coffee prices are volatile or low. The global coffee economy is riddled with pervasive inequalities in wealth and power. As discussed in the next chapter, most risk management solutions for coffee farmers that do propose ways to mitigate oversupply, address commodity dependence, and counterbalance inequalities require structural changes in the coffee commodity chain, in one way or another. Derivatives markets thus support the status quo *and* undermine the viability of alternatives that may work better for small coffee farmers.

Derivatives: Exclusion and Speculation

Like derivatives chains in general, the coffee derivative chain is an exclusive commodity chain. It does not permit for broad participation nor for a wide diffusion of its services. At every stage of derivatives production, the chain is dominated by large, sophisticated, and relatively wealthy corporate actors, mostly from the North or with connections to Northern MNCs. As Rabach and Kim argue more generally, large size is critical for participation in sophisticated services sectors: "The barriers to entry represented by high-end service activities in core niches can be overcome only by the largest of economic actors. Although 'big' is not enough, it is certainly necessary. High capital investment capabilities (to cover costly service overhead such as marketing and telecommunications networks) and other start-up costs are essential to enter or survive the competition."[70] Indeed, the derivatives chain is dominated by actors from the core, resulting in a reinforcement of the core–periphery inequality along the underlying coffee chain.

Even within specific nodes of the chain, for example, the trading node, the dominance of large Northern financial interests is more apparent daily. Of special concern is the growing influence of "index speculators" in coffee derivatives trading—for example, hedge funds, pension funds, insurance companies, and university endowments—as well as the large Northern multinational commercial and investment banks that intermediate these speculative activities. I argue below that the exclusiveness of the coffee derivatives chain as well as dominance in trading by speculators have important, negative consequences for the well-being of small coffee farmers.

The Coffee Derivative Commodity Chain

Geographically, the coffee derivative chain spans a broad area, though it is dominated by core regions, namely the United States and the United Kingdom. The major Arabica coffee exchange, the Intercontinental Exchange (ICE), is located in New York. Two other exchanges also trade Arabica coffees of more limited origins, the BM&FBovespa in São Paulo, Brazil, and the Tokyo Grain Exchange (TGE). ICE and the BM&F offer both futures and options, while the TGE offers only futures. Robusta coffee trading occurs mostly in London, and is dominated by the London International Financial Futures and Options Exchange (LIFFE or Liffe, pronounced "life"), now merged with Euronext and the New York Stock Exchange (NYSE). Robusta coffee of more limited origin is also traded on the TGE and the National Multi Commodity Exchange (NMCE) in Ahmedabad, India. LIFFE is the only Robusta coffee exchange to offer options contracts in addition to futures. The reader should know that all of these exchanges offer multiple derivative products in addition to contracts on coffee. As will be seen, exchanges in the core countries represent the vast majority of coffee traded on global futures exchanges.

The clearinghouses associated with the exchanges are usually located in close proximity to the exchanges they serve. Traders and brokerage houses involved in coffee derivatives trading may, at least in theory, be located anywhere in the world where there is access to the Internet, thanks to recently and widely adopted electronic trading platforms by most exchanges. In reality, however, trading and brokerage require access to information, technologies, and financial resources that put participation out of reach for many individuals and firms, particularly those in the periphery.

As the reader may have already noted, despite the fact that all of them offer coffee derivatives, the precise nature of the product differs across the exchanges. Robusta coffee is traded in London, Tokyo, and Ahmedabad, while Arabica is traded New York, São Paulo, and Tokyo. The London, New York, and São Paulo exchanges offer both futures and options,[71] while Tokyo and Ahmedabad offer only futures. Trades may be settled without delivery in London, New York, and São Paulo, while delivery is compulsory in Tokyo and Ahmedabad. In São Paulo and Ahmedabad, the only future coffee traded is local future coffee (from Brazil and India, respectively), while the New York, London, and Tokyo exchanges trade future coffee from multiple origins. Each exchange further specifies different contract sizes, among other varying specifications.

While the general service provided in derivatives markets might be deemed a "risk transfer" service (see Chapter 2), the derivatives commodity chain is actually comprised of several discrete steps (or nodes), each of which contributes a more specialized service that contributes to the overall goal of risk shifting. As the reader will see, the coffee derivatives chain is something of a marvel of financial intermediation.

Exchanges. Derivatives exchanges sell the forum required to shift risks (today these are usually very sophisticated electronic platforms), gather and sell market information, and establish and enforce rules and standards for orderly mass trading. Exchanges may also offer commodity storage (warehousing) and grading (quality determination) facilities. Teweles and Jones write, "It is important to note that the exchanges themselves do not trade contracts, nor do they set the prices at which contracts are traded. They merely furnish a place where people in the commodity business, speculators, or their representatives can meet to buy and sell futures contracts and also establish rules and procedures designed to make such trading fair and orderly."[72] Exchanges charge for their services by levying a fee on every trade made on the exchange.

The exchange node of the chain is highly concentrated among relatively few actors, with the exchange in New York capturing the vast majority of coffee derivatives trading, followed by the London exchange. To illustrate, Tables 4.1 and 4.2 show concentration in coffee futures and options markets in 2009. I calculated concentration in futures trading with two different measures: the proportion of contract volume captured by each exchange and the proportion of future coffee volume captured by each exchange. While Southern commodity exchanges often post high trading volumes, they do not usually trade as much future coffee as the Northern exchanges because the contract sizes are smaller.

The data in the figures illustrate several important points. First, the coffee derivatives market is huge, with over six million futures contracts, representing over 80 billion kilograms of coffee, traded in 2009, along with almost 1.5 million options (puts and calls combined) traded the same year. To put these volume figures into perspective, the ICO reports that in 2009 total world coffee production was about 7.4 billion kilograms, less than a tenth of the amount traded in the futures markets the same year. While part of the discrepancy stems from the fact that a single kilogram of coffee may be hedged several times over, it is also due to the growing presence of speculators in the markets. Speculators, who generally do not participate in the underlying coffee chain and are not hedging, are not bound by actual production levels in their derivative trading activities (more below in the section on speculative commodity derivatives trading).

Second, the coffee derivatives market is highly concentrated, with ICE's coffee "C" contract representing 70 percent of all futures contracts traded and 88 percent of all future coffee volume traded in 2009 (future coffee volumes represent the aggregate quantity of coffee traded via futures contracts). The next closest competitors to ICE are the NMCE with about 11.5 percent of coffee contracts, and LIFFE with just over 6 percent of coffee volume in 2009. While it may be surprising that a developing country commodity exchange like the NMCE contends with the London-based LIFFE, the reader should be aware that NMCE's market share has been waning since 2009. According to the exchange, contract volumes dropped precipitously in 2010 and through mid-year 2011. Further, NMCE accounts for only a small proportion (1.3%) of coffee futures trading by coffee volumes because of the small lot size specified in its coffee contract. In the coffee options market, ICE holds a near monopoly, facilitating 96 percent of all coffee options traded in 2009.

Table 4.1 Concentration in coffee futures markets, 2009

Exchange	Coffee variety	Contract volume	% of all contracts	% of Robusta futures	% of Arabica futures	Future Coffee Volume	units	% of total coffee traded in fut. mkt.	% of Arabica coffee traded in fut. mkt.	% of Robusta coffee traded in fut. mkt.
Liffe	R	519,324	8.51	42.51	n/a	5,128,260,000	kilos	6.26	n/a	82.87
ICE US	A	4,235,349	69.44	n/a	86.82	71,947,991,138	kilos	87.88	95.06	n/a
TGE	A	46,281	0.76	n/a	0.95	159,669,450	kilos	0.20	0.21	n/a
TGE	R	1,860	0.03	0.15	n/a	9,300,000	kilos	0.01	n/a	0.15
BM&F	A	596,435	9.78	n/a	12.23	3,578,610,000	kilos	4.37	4.73	n/a
NMCE	R	700,352	11.48	57.33	n/a	1,050,528,000	kilos	1.28	n/a	16.98
Total		6,099,601	100.00	100.00	100.00	81,874,358,588	kilos	100.00	100.00	100.00

Source: Author's calculations based on exchange data.

Table 4.2 Concentration in coffee options markets, 2009

Exchange	Coffee variety	Contract volume	% Total	% Total Arabica options	% Total Robusta options
Liffe	R	51,894	3.49	n/a	100
ICE US	A	1,427,032	95.94	99.41	n/a
BM&F	A	8459	0.57	0.59	n/a
Total		1,487,385	100.00	100.00	100.00

Note: I do not calculate the % of total coffee traded via coffee options contracts because data is not available as to how many of these contracts were exercised.
Source: Author's calculations based on exchange data.

Disaggregating the data by variety of coffee, Arabica or Robusta, the markets grow more concentrated still. ICE controls 87 percent of the Arabica futures market by contract volume and 95 percent by coffee volume, and facilitates 99 percent of Arabica coffee options trading. The Robusta market is split relatively evenly between LIFFE and the NMCE when looking to contract volumes; however, measured by coffee volume LIFFE completely dominates the Robusta futures market, facilitating 83 percent of future Robusta coffee traded worldwide. LIFFE has a true monopoly in the Robusta options market as no other exchange in the world offers this product. Overall, the ICE coffee exchange in New York has monopolized the global coffee derivatives market, with LIFFE representing the second-largest contender. The BM&F, the TGE, and the NMCE appear relatively marginal at the global level, though certainly are more important locally and regionally.

There are several factors that explain why the market for coffee derivative exchange services tend toward monopoly. First, according to "network market" research, financial markets like derivatives markets display characteristics that make concentration among one or a few lead firms inevitable. Network markets, including telecommunications, railroads, and many financial markets, are characterized by the presence of "network externalities," particularly size externalities. "In a typical network, the addition of a new customer (or network node) increases the willingness to pay for network services by all participants."[73] As new participants enter a network market they make the product appear more desirable to new potential entrants who, once they also enter, encourage still more new entrants. In the financial market context, this means that market liquidity is "self-reinforcing"—liquidity builds upon itself, giving ever-larger advantages to the operators of the most liquid markets. In derivatives markets, high liquidity (trading volumes) is critical for effective price discovery, hedging, and speculation. Network effects help to explain why derivatives exchanges in particular invest so heavily in new trading technologies that expand their client bases.

Economides crucially notes that network effects have important implications for market structures and the size of typical firms: "As a direct consequence of their self-reinforcing nature, networks frequently exhibit *positive critical mass*. This means that no network of size smaller than this positive size, called critical mass, is ever observed, at any price."[74] Financial markets thus tend toward concentration, specifically "monopoly" according to Economides and "cartel" according to Domowitz and Steil.[75] These findings also help to explain why the largest coffee derivatives exchange is so much larger, in terms of contract and/or coffee volumes, than its next-closest competitor. With trading volumes increasing in a self-reinforcing manner, even a small initial difference in the popularity of the exchanges can translate into larger discrepancies as time proceeds. Critically, network dynamics suggest that upstart commodity exchanges may have a difficult time competing independently with the large exchanges, as they struggle to generate the contract volumes necessary for effective trading.

Second, exchanges incur large up-front capital and technology costs, for example, expenditures on trading platforms and related technologies, information, staff, and marketing. Simon notes that "no self respecting exchange operator could be expected to be taken seriously if they were not sporting a fully integrated cutting edge electronic trading platform."[76] While it is true that setting up a financial or commodity exchange is cheaper today than it used to be, due to the advent of electronic trading and regular reductions in the cost of these technologies since their debut, UNCTAD notes that it is still an expensive undertaking particularly in new markets where initial trading volumes are relatively small.[77] Speaking on the financial barriers to entry experienced by upstart commodity exchanges, UNCTAD notes:

> Given the nature of its business, there is a serious risk that an exchange will run out of cash to manage its operations properly before it reaches break-even. And even before that, cash flow constraints can lead to cuts in critical expenditures, in particular on marketing, which is the key tool for attracting users to the exchange. After a short preparatory period, considerable expenses have to be made in equipment, systems and training. Then, when the exchange starts trading, the number of staff in the exchange is gradually increased—most of the staff will need further training, and the absorption capacity of the exchange is initially quite limited. In terms of cumulative expenditure, this implies that the major part of the expenditures for the exchange will have to be made before the exchange actually starts operating.[78]

Third, exchanges utilize merger and partnership arrangements to reduce global competition and enlarge their client bases. The FIA notes that several factors have contributed to the "merger fever" among derivatives exchanges since 2008. Most important from the perspective of monopoly, exchanges are looking to capitalize on "scale": "The cost structure of a typical exchange is mostly fixed, so revenues from additional volume go almost entirely to the bottom line. That's a powerful incentive to acquire another exchange and consolidate both sets of products on a single technology platform."[79] Combined with the self-reinforcing effects of network markets (where liquidity begets more liquidity to the detriment of less-liquid and relatively poorly networked markets), these economies of scale suggest that mergers are a powerful tool for reducing competition.

Notable mergers in the coffee derivatives context include the merger of NYSE and Euronext/LIFFE to form NYSE LIFFE in 2006. The Intercontinental Exchange acquired the New York Board of Trade (NYBOT) in 2006, resulting in the formation of ICE Futures US and the acquisition by ICE of NYBOT's clearinghouse (now ICE Clear US). Perhaps most interesting is the recent partial merger of the CME Group and the BM&F. The CME Group is the largest derivatives exchange in the world, and, a product of merger mania itself, actually incorporates four separate exchanges under the CME Group umbrella (the Chicago Mercantile Exchange-CME, The Chicago Board of Trade-CBOT, the New York Mercantile Exchange-NYMEX, and the Commodity Exchange-COMEX). In 2008, the CME Group acquired a 10 percent minority stake in the BM&F (for about US$631 million). Critically, the acquisition also included a new "order-routing" agreement designed to increase trading volumes on both exchanges. The agreement allows CME clients to access the BM&F directly through electronic platforms and permits BM&F customers direct access to the CME Group's exchanges. Merger mania continues today as regulators consider a merger between NYSE/Euronext and Deutsche Boerse that would create the leading derivatives exchange in Europe. The trend toward merger, acquisition, and client-sharing agreements between Northern and Southern exchanges has potentially detrimental consequences in the development context, as I will discuss in more detail below in the section on derivatives, exclusion and inequality.

Clearinghouses. Clearinghouses provide trading settlement services such that gains and losses among traders are settled in a reliable and timely fashion, and generally serve to mitigate the risk of counterparty default present in the marketplace. Clearinghouses levy a fee on each trade cleared. Loader writes, "In general terms the role of the clearing house is to act as a counterparty to both sides of the trade thereby breaking the direct counterparty relationship between the two trading counterparties. It is fundamental to the integrity and credibility of the market for which it operates, as its purpose is to guarantee the performance of each and every transaction."[80] Clearinghouses employ different measures to ensure that timely payment is made, including requiring margin payments from futures traders and collateral from option writers. They also generally employ very high-tech monitoring and settlement systems, such as SPAN margining systems that involve complex, algorithmic determination of appropriate, individual trader margins.

Clearinghouses may be associated with a particular exchange or they may be independent firms. For example, on the BM&F, clearing is performed by the BM&F Derivatives Clearinghouse, a division of the exchange. Similarly, trades on ICE in the US are cleared by ICE Clear US, also a division of the exchange. Clearing for the TGE is conducted by the Japan Commodity Clearing House (JCCH), a firm that is collectively owned by and clears trades for all of Japan's commodity exchanges. By contrast, trades on NYSE LIFFE are cleared by an independent firm, LCH Clearnet, which also performs clearing operations for other London-based derivatives exchanges. Likewise, clearing for the NMCE in India is outsourced to HDFC Bank.

Like the market for coffee derivatives exchange services, the market for coffee derivatives clearing services is also highly concentrated. For each of the coffee derivatives exchanges noted above, there is only one designated clearinghouse. It is not possible, for example, to clear a coffee future purchased on ICE via the BM&F's Derivatives Clearinghouse. Each clearinghouse is matched specifically to each exchange.

Concentration in clearing is attributable to several factors. Like exchange services, clearing requires sizable capital and technology investment on the part of the clearing entity. Clearinghouses must be capable of drawing on large financial resources if they are to do their job effectively and maintain the confidence of market participants. "Clearing houses must be financially robust," says Loader, "in order to sustain a default in the market in which they operate. The financial standing of the clearing house is a very important consideration for brokers when they are contemplating becoming clearing members of an exchange. It is also an important issue for companies researching the potential of trading in the market . . . ."[81] Speaking on the financial capacity of the CME Clearing House, the clearinghouse responsible for settling trades across the four derivatives exchanges that make up the CME Group, Melamed notes, "The Clearing House system's aggregate financial resources are today over $100 billion, including its $8 billion guaranty fund. In 2008, it handled 3.3 billion contracts with a notional value of $1.2 quadrillion."[82] While these figures misrepresent the issue slightly, for surely not all derivatives clearinghouses need to be this well capitalized to enjoy some success, it certainly does circumscribe the outer limits of the financial ballpark within which clearinghouses operate.

Like the exchanges, Turbeville discusses the proliferation of mergers and acquisitions in the clearing node of the chain. He notes that clearing has become more concentrated of late, following a period of intense competition around the time that electronic trading was popularized in the 1990s:

> Clearinghouses, which had for more than a century been sleepy enterprises, run like utilities for the benefit of their members, were now intensely competitive businesses. Clearinghouses curried the favor of the dealer banks, who controlled volume on which revenues depended. They pushed to broaden product lines and lower transaction costs in the form of fees and margin intended to protect them from risks. The clearing business became highly concentrated as the acquisitions piled up.[83]

Also key here is the control over clearinghouses exercised by its member banks. "Clearing membership" is discussed in more detail below, yet it is important to note that the large banks that dominate the brokerage node of the chain also exert their influence on the clearinghouses and their practices. For example, Turbeville notes that member banks can influence the manner in which prices are relayed to the public, the products for which clearing is offered, the fees collected by the clearinghouses, and the size of margin requirements.[84]

Brokerage. Moving to the next node, brokers "sell" market access, and sometimes intermediate clearing services, trading advice and market information. Brokers are also frequently traders themselves, trading for the benefit of the brokerage house itself as well as for its clients.

Coffee derivatives brokers are sometimes members of the exchanges and clearinghouses on which they trade. Exchanges and clearinghouses extend their "memberships" to other financial firms who meet specific requirements, generating another level of intermediation in the derivatives chain. Exchanges offer "trading" or "broker" memberships, while clearinghouses offer "clearing" memberships.[85] The general idea behind membership is the same in each case: Membership establishes a smaller, elite group of firms who are permitted to deal directly with the exchanges and clearinghouses, limiting risk exposures, due diligence obligations, and other related administrative costs for the latter parties. The members are "pass-thru" points on the derivatives chain, passing the services of exchanges and clearinghouses through to traders, for a fee of course. Members are frequently large traders in their own right.

However, many smaller brokerage houses are not exchange and clearing members (they are "non-member traders"), instead placing orders through a larger member brokerage firm. Exchange and clearing memberships are expensive, precluding many smaller or poorly capitalized brokerage firms from joining. Clearing members, because they take on the credit risk for all of the trades executed by nonmember clients, must also be capable of drawing on large pools of capital in the event of client default. In the United States, the CFTC designates and monitors "futures commission merchants" or FCMs. FCMs are brokerage firms that trade on behalf of clients and must meet minimum capital requirements in order to operate legally in US markets. The CFTC notes that designation as an FCM requires minimum net capital reserves of US$1 million or more.

Also contributing to market concentration in the brokerage node, the most sophisticated brokerage firms employ state-of-the-art, often proprietary, trading technologies. Indeed, the technologies employed at each level of derivative production, along with their expense, contribute strongly to the exclusiveness of the chain. Melamed notes:

> Hugely successful proprietary trading enterprises have sprung up in all parts of the globe with jealously guarded algorithms (trading programs) that have achieved a new generation of analytics. These programs, operating at unimaginable speeds, apply advanced mathematical models in order to capture countless sophisticated trading strategies based on price correlations and associations between markets that were never before possible.[86]

There is additional evidence that the biggest clearing members on some exchanges, all enormous multinational banks, use their power to exclude potential rivals and competitors. In an interesting report from the *New York Times*, journalist Louise Story explains how several big banks—including JP Morgan, Goldman Sachs, Morgan Stanley, Citigroup, and Deutsche Bank—have colluded with one another to prevent other banks from joining the ranks of "clearing membership" on ICE and the CME. In the wake of the 2008 financial crisis, US regulators pushed strongly for the creation of new and better clearinghouses for certain financial derivatives, recognizing that OTC trading posed systemic risks (e.g. AIG's foray into credit default swaps) and that moving OTC trading onto exchanges with clearinghouses would prevent some of this instability. In order to entice big banks to collaborate, ICE and CME offered potential clearing members—the big banks noted above—memberships on their "risk committees." These committees are responsible for approving new clearing memberships, among other responsibilities.

Stanford professor Darrel Duffe is quoted in the report as saying, "The revenue these dealers make on derivatives is very large and so the incentive they have to protect those revenues is extremely large. It will be hard for the dealers to keep their market share if everybody who can prove their creditworthiness is allowed into the clearinghouses. So they are making arguments, thus far very successful ones, that others shouldn't be allowed in."[87] The report further intimates the considerable influence that big banks in the derivatives business have on other aspects of market operations and on national legislation: "Under the Dodd-Frank bill [passed in the wake of the Great Recession], the clearinghouses were given broad authority. The risk committees there will help decide what prices will be charged for clearing trades, on top of fees banks collect for matching buyers and sellers, and how much money customers must put up as collateral to cover potential losses."[88]

The market for coffee derivatives brokerage is generally less monopolized than exchange and clearing, but still relatively concentrated and dominated by large multinational financial firms. As noted above, trading and clearing "members" are an elite group of brokerage firms who have met the stringent membership requirements established by the exchanges and clearinghouses, as well as the capital adequacy requirements of regulators. Depending on the exchange in question, there may be as many as 100 or more trading and clearing members. Some firms are both clearing and trading members, and a few firms are members of all of the coffee exchanges and clearinghouses. This suggests a relatively high degree of horizontal integration within the brokerage node, across the various coffee exchanges.

For example, according to membership directories available on LCH Clearnet's website, there are 50 firms that are "clearing members" of NYSE LIFFE's coffee market, meaning that these firms are permitted to trade and clear for themselves and for their clients.[89] Among these are some familiar financial giants: Barclay's, Citigroup, JP Morgan, Goldman Sachs, Merrill Lynch, The Royal Bank of Scotland, Deutsche Bank, and UBS, among others. There are by my calculation an additional 184 nonclearing members of the exchange.[90] The data further reveal that in some cases the same firms are clearing members of multiple coffee exchanges. Of the roughly 65 broker members and close to 70 clearing members on the BM&F, there are significantly fewer firms that hold both memberships.[91] Many of these joint broker and clearing member firms are the same clearing members that we see on other coffee exchanges. For example, Goldman Sachs, JP Morgan, Citigroup, Deutsche Bank, and Merrill Lynch are broker and clearing members on both LIFFE and the BM&F.

There is also evidence that large firms dominant in the underlying coffee chain, for example, the international coffee trading giant ED&F Man, are diversifying horizontally into coffee financial services. ED&F Man is a clearing member of LIFFE, among other exchanges, and offers derivatives services in addition to coffee services to its clients. Likewise, the world's other largest coffee trader—Neumann Kaffee Gruppe (NKG)—is also involved in derivatives trading. TRX Futures Ltd., a subsidiary of NKG, is a clearing member on ICE and LIFFE and offers "brokerage, trade facilitation and clearing services in many commodities, financial and energy futures and options."[92] As will be discussed in more detail below, the exclusiveness of the derivatives brokerage node, particularly at the "member level," may be problematic in the development context.

Trading. Traders constitute the final node on the chain; they "buy" and "sell" risk exposure from one another to speculate and hedge. These smaller "traders" may be nonmember brokerage houses and also individual traders (corporate or individual investors). Coffee derivatives traders are the actors that are actually producing and consuming coffee futures and options. For every short position a coffee derivative trader takes, there must be an equal and opposite long position taken by another trader. As indicated above, these trades pass through several levels of intermediation, first through brokers (maybe several of them), then through the exchanges and associated clearinghouses.

Traders are usually categorized as being either "commercial"—which means they trade to hedge their exposure in the cash market—or "noncommercial"—meaning they are speculators. Speculative traders are generally multinational financial companies like investment and commercial banks, hedge funds, commodity index funds, and derivatives brokerage houses. Hedgers in coffee futures and options markets tend to be corporations invested in the underlying coffee market itself. Exporters, international traders, roasters and processors, and large retailers regularly trade in coffee derivatives to manage risks to their inventories, revenues, and profits, and also sometimes for speculative purposes.[93]

While the trading node is the least exclusive of all the steps on the coffee derivative chain, here too there are signs of concentration. Although important differences exist among coffee derivatives traders, the common factor across most of them is that they are generally relatively wealthy, large, and sophisticated firms, even if their ranks are more numerous than in other nodes. Indeed, most coffee hedgers come from the core-like nodes of the underlying coffee chain. Some of the best evidence available to support this observation can be gleaned from the exchanges themselves. For example, NYSE LIFFE notes that large multinational firms, both commercial and noncommercial, are the main traders of its Robusta coffee products: "The main contract users are coffee exporters, international trade houses, European and U.S. coffee roasters, managed futures funds, institutional investors and options specialists."[94]

Commodity futures trading among financial firms, like hedge funds, pension funds, and commodity index funds, using the markets to speculate, represent a growing proportion of coffee derivatives traders globally. Newman reports that the share of speculative interest in total interest in ICE's coffee "C" market has risen from between roughly 10–30 percent in 1986 to between 40–65 percent in 2007.[95] Although these shares are volatile, these figures do illustrate dramatic changes in the typical coffee futures trader and the growing dominance of the coffee derivatives market by firms entirely outside of agriculture.

The last few years have witnessed especially large influxes of institutional financial speculators into global commodities markets. As will be discussed in more detail below, the Great Recession, like the 2001 dot.com crash, reduced returns on many traditional financial assets, not least stocks and real estate, with the latter more important in the context of the recent crisis. Responding to their shrinking portfolios, financial investors have entered commodity derivatives markets en masse over the past decade, with their numbers rising further in 2007–2011.

Particularly important is the growing presence of "commodity index speculators" in agricultural derivatives markets. Commodity index speculators profit by placing bets on the movement of a commodity index. An index is a weighted, moving average of commodity prices, and the indices are based entirely upon future prices established in derivatives markets. Among the most popular indices are the Standard & Poors Goldman Sachs Commodity Index (S&P GSCI) and the Dow Jones AIG Commodity Index (DJ AIGCI), both of which include coffee. Index speculators do not actually trade the index, but rather try to "replicate" the movement of the index, and profit on its upward movement, by trading in a spectrum of separate futures contracts. Large institutional investors engaged in commodity index speculation, like pension funds, insurance companies, sovereign wealth funds, and university endowments, traditionally outsource the management of their trades to large banks who specialize in these kinds of transactions. "Reportedly, 85% to 90% of Institutional Investors seeking to allocate money to commodities choose to do so by entering into over-the-counter (OTC) commodity index swaps with Wall Street Banks. Once an institution has entered into the swap agreement, it becomes the Bank's responsibility to trade the futures correctly in order to replicate the index on the investor's behalf."[96]

Speaking on the rise of "index speculation" in commodity futures markets, Masters and White write, "Index speculators have bought more commodities futures contracts in the last five years than any other group of market participant. They are now the single most dominant force in the commodities futures markets."[97] Wise notes that trading has become significantly more concentrated among index speculators since 2007: "index fund purchases from 2003–7 already were higher than the futures market purchases of physical hedgers and traditional speculators combined. *Then they doubled in the first half of 2008.*"[98] And, while index speculators are increasingly dominating the commodity derivatives market, trading is further concentrated in the handful of firms that handle the business of the speculating pension funds and other investors. "The four largest commodity swaps dealers—Goldman Sachs, Morgan Stanley, J.P. Morgan and Barclays Bank—are reported to control 70% of the commodity index swaps positions."[99]

Partly explaining concentration among very large, wealthy, and sophisticated investors, the analysis of market access obstacles in the previous chapter indicates that derivative trading is near impossible for a variety of coffee actors like small farmers who in theory might use the markets to hedge. These obstacles are partly caused by the rules and standards set by the exchanges and clearinghouses in the interests of their major clients. Lot sizes are skewed toward larger traders, as are margin requirements and practices like "marking to market," as discussed in the previous chapter. Exchanges further limit those origins from which coffee can be delivered to settle contracts, with "origins tenderable" generating additional obstacles to trading by hedgers. Other obstacles, like lack of information and knowledge, also restrict the access of non-experts in remote rural areas to derivatives markets. This suggests that among hedgers and speculators alike, derivatives trading activity is monopolized by larger, wealthier actors with access to the requisite infrastructure, information, and expertise.

The coffee derivative commodity chain appears below as figure 4.2. I have noted the relevant flows of futures and options and fees and services that characterize the chain, in addition to indicating the level of concentration apparent along the various stages of derivative production.

Derivatives: Exclusion and Inequality

The exclusiveness of the coffee derivative commodity chain has several concrete implications for poverty in coffee communities, particularly for the distribution of wealth and power along the coffee commodity chain.

First, the exclusiveness of the chain at the trading level suggests that, despite policymakers' good intentions, the actors who need price risk management most are those most likely to be deprived of hedging services. While serious obstacles to trading exist for growers, more powerful actors along the chain, such as roasters and traders, can and do easily trade in derivatives for risk management purposes. In the presence of price risk, uneven access to risk management instruments is a mechanism for increasing inequalities along the chain. As noted previously, growing disparities in wealth and power in

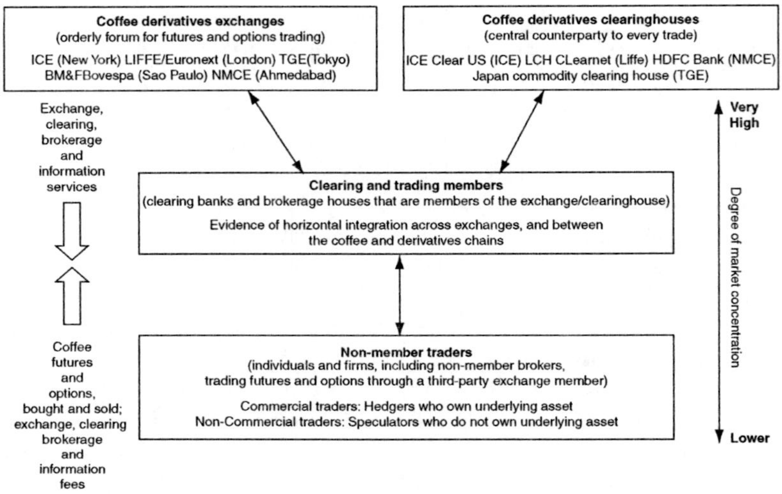

Figure 4.2 The coffee derivative commodity chain
Source: Author's depiction.

coffee production and distribution are important contributors to low prices, high levels of competition, and exclusion of small growers from production. As trader and roaster power continues to concentrate, these effects may well be aggravated, with negative implications for the well-being of coffee farmers. To the extent that the operators of large coffee estates—for example, international trading companies that now own or lease farms in the South—can and do hedge, this will also drive a wedge between larger and smaller farmers, to the detriment of the latter, and will drive consolidation in coffee production.

There is some evidence that uneven risk management capabilities are having precisely this impact on the distribution of wealth and power along the chain. Crucially, Ponte notes that the ability of some international traders to manage price risk with derivatives has allowed them to remain competitive and even acquire firms that do not hedge. "International traders went through considerable restructuring in the last two decades. Mid-sized traders with unhedged positions suffered major losses. They also found themselves too small to compete with larger ones. As a result, they either went bankrupt, merged with others, or were taken over by the majors."[100] The profitability gap between those who hedge and those who do not in this way results in greater monopolization of the chain, to the detriment of small- and medium-sized traders who could not compete and growers who now have to market their products to these trading behemoths.

The effects of uneven derivatives usage upon the distribution of income and power across different actors along the coffee chain is magnified by the fact that the poor are already disproportionately impacted by exposure to market shocks. Wealthier actors along the coffee chain already command sizable resources, have regular access to credit and other means of effectively weathering shocks, means largely unavailable to poor, small producers. That derivatives markets are also out of reach for small coffee farmers implies that income and power gaps may widen considerably in the presence of price risk, and especially during price crises. Indeed, the coffee actors that need risk management most—those who are poor and small—are precisely those who are excluded from futures markets. Yet, those actors that need such arrangements least—larger, wealthier actors (roasters, traders, large coffee estates) that have other ways to successfully deal with shocks—are those who are best positioned to reap the benefits of hedging.

For example, Davis' study of *ejido* producers in Mexico since liberalization in the 1980s reveals that wealthier producers were able to respond to increased risk and uncertainty more effectively than poorer producers. Specifically, producers with larger plots of land, greater levels of assets (like livestock), and more "human capital assets" have been better able to adjust to the risks associated with economic liberalization than producers with less land, less human capital, and few to no assets. While the former group has invested in more cattle as well as fruit and vegetable production (which is less prone to low prices than corn, which was farmed almost exclusively before liberalization), poorer producers continue to struggle. "These households, with less land, livestock, migration and human capital assets, have significantly lower household incomes than the households referred to above that have been able to adjust successfully. Without access to adequate levels of assets, these households will continue to struggle in the current austere macroeconomic environment."[101]

The risk that uneven risk management capabilities will worsen inequality along the chain grows greater as derivatives markets substitute for other price risk management arrangements in the minds and agendas of policymakers. This risk also grows greater as prices become more volatile, which increases the premium to effective risk management. Small producers require some kind of effective price risk management arrangement if they are to maintain or improve their position along the coffee chain. As indicated in the previous chapter, derivatives markets are not structured so as to be easily accessible to small traders like coffee smallholders, nor have intermediation efforts been very successful thus far.

Second, the exclusiveness of the derivatives chain at the brokerage and trading nodes implies that some actors along the coffee chain will be able to expand their businesses in new directions and obtain new sources of profit, while others will be denied these opportunities. As mentioned previously, coffee traders are expanding their businesses to include financial intermediation services for clients that want to utilize derivatives markets. The biggest international coffee trading firms—ED&F Man and Neumann Kaffee Gruppe—operate derivatives divisions and are members of the biggest coffee exchanges. Coffee actors without the necessary memberships, financing, and technologies are effectively excluded from similarly diversifying their businesses. This also has negative implications for the distribution of wealth and power along the coffee chain. The firms that are already dominant and can also use derivatives markets for insurance are given yet another advantage in the form of new revenue opportunities at the intersection of derivatives and coffee markets.

Newman additionally notes that firms previously involved in coffee hedging only—generally larger roasting and trading companies—are now integrating speculative derivatives trading into their business plans, fueling further concentration of trading among speculative interests and generating large additional profits in the core nodes of the coffee chain:

> This speculative element of futures trading by commodity trading companies has been increasingly built into the corporate strategies of the large international trading companies. Increasingly, physical traders take into account the influence on prices of financial investors on the exchanges. Coffee trading at the international level has become a financialized business. "There are some very savvy physical traders that know exactly what the speculators do, how they think and what they will do next and they play the game. They make it part of their own game."[102]

Third, it must be noted that the exclusiveness of the coffee derivatives chain at the exchange level may have implications for the ability of upstart coffee derivatives exchanges in the global South to better meet the needs of small, local farmers. While it is true that not all (or even most) local, Southern commodity exchanges will offer futures and options, the exclusiveness of the derivatives chain at the exchange level should be of concern to those exchange operators (and their sponsors from government and the development establishment) who would try to break into this market.

The presence of network effects in the coffee derivatives market suggests that expanding trading volumes at upstart exchanges will not be easy as the new exchanges compete with more liquid and popular established exchanges. As mentioned in the previous chapter, trading volumes on some of the new exchanges in India, for example, are abysmally low and have contributed to price distortions and market inefficiency. Further, upstart exchanges face large financial and technological barriers to market entry, which may be eased in practice by partnering with larger exchanges. Gross, writing for the UNCTAD Secretariat, notes, "For smaller exchanges facing far tighter resource constraints, the development of close, collaborative partnerships with technology developers will be the key to surviving—and thriving—in the technology era."[103] The rapid pace at which derivatives trading and clearing technologies change augments the likelihood of such partnerships and alliances.

To the extent that local exchanges need to partner with Northern exchanges to meet these volume and cost constraints, or are absorbed by them, it is unlikely that derivatives products will be tailored to better meet the needs of smaller traders. Not surprisingly, exchanges create and change products in accordance with the needs of major customers, generally not smallholder farmers. LIFFE, for example, in 2009 altered the specifications to its Robusta coffee contract, doubling the standard lot size from 5,000 to 10,000 kilograms. Spokespeople for the exchange noted that the change "better [reflects] activity in the physical market and [reduces] costs for customers."[104] In other words, the major users of the Robusta contract were interested in a larger contract and the exchange complied. As local Southern exchanges partner with Northern exchanges, to bridge financing gaps, share technologies, and increase volumes by sharing clients, it is likely that they will be similarly oriented toward the needs of major international clients.

There is some evidence that this process of merger, partnership, and acquisition between Northern and Southern exchanges is already happening and that it is changing the orientations of the local exchanges, propelling them outward toward serving the global marketplace. As mentioned above, the BM&F in Brazil has partnered with the CME Group in the United States (New York and Chicago) for financial, technology-sharing, and client-sharing purposes, a partnership thought to make both exchanges more "competitive" (the irony here is palpable).[105] The BM&F notes that the merger assists in its "consolidation as a global player."[106] In India, the Multi Commodity Exchange (MCX) is partly owned by the NYSE, which purchased a 5 percent stake in the MCX in 2008. Then CEO and Managing Director Jignesh Shah said, "This strategic partnership is an excellent case study and example of how we plan to work together with global partners, like NYSE Euronext, to execute our vision of creating one of the largest global exchange networks across the fast growing economies of Africa, Central Asia, Middle East, and India, China."[107]

As indicated by the experience of ICE and LIFFE, a more global orientation does not bode well for the ability of Southern exchanges to accommodate the trading constraints of small growers. ICE and LIFFE, as globally oriented exchanges, promulgate rules and standards that while beneficial to major clients do not serve small farmers very well. As such, the establishment of new exchanges, while beneficial to the financial interests involved and potentially also to larger hedgers from agribusiness and governments (who may gain new sources of tax revenues and relief from balance of payments pressures), may not work to better accommodate small producers to the extent that the new exchanges are increasingly globally oriented and connected to the big global exchanges in the North.

There is also the risk here, to the extent that upstart exchanges require public assistance to function properly, that a bias against peasant agriculture may be reinforced in national policies. Public resources spent on setting up new exchanges (capital, technology), advertising new exchanges, and monitoring and regulating exchanges will potentially "leak" out of agriculture to the financial sector, out of peasant agriculture toward agribusiness, and out of the South toward the North. This latter possibility—of Southern governments subsidizing the financial activities of Northern firms—is more likely as upstart commodity exchanges in the South partner with Northern exchanges to share clients, and if they come to allow speculative trading by foreign entities as a means to increase trading volumes and turnover on the exchange. Indeed, the Indian government is today debating the merits of allowing foreign speculators to trade on the country's national commodity exchanges.[108]

To sum up, exclusiveness along the coffee derivative chain is a mechanism for increasing inequalities along the coffee chain, to the detriment of smallholders. Rabach and Kim put this point neatly, though not in the financial services context:

> The astonishing fact is that despite the dramatic proliferation of production processes and service activities, the international economy is not "freer" in any sense. Rather, this fragmentation is accompanied by a marked consolidation and centralization of the number of economic agents exerting a dominant influence over the governance of global commodity chains because of their command of high end services.[109]

Exclusion of growers from hedging under conditions of price risk exacerbates inequalities between roaster and traders on the one hand and growers on the other. Even within the grower node of the coffee chain, uneven risk management capabilities across farmers of various kinds may lead to further concentration at this stage of production. Exclusion of producers and other small participants in the coffee chain from brokerage and trading creates an additional disadvantage. While derivatives markets provide opportunities for large coffee multinationals to expand their business and profit, these new opportunities are systematically denied to smaller actors. Exclusionary forces at the exchange level suggest that upstart commodity exchanges may need to partner with Northern exchanges in order to survive, indicating the potential inability of local exchanges to tailor their products and rules to meet the needs of small farmers. The encroachment of Northern actors upon Southern exchanges also creates the potential for resource "leakage," reinforcing bias against peasant farmers.

Derivatives Markets: Speculation, Insecurity, and Inequality

Derivatives markets may also contribute to insecurity for producers and inequalities along the coffee chain for a different reason. The previous section discussed the likelihood of growing disparities in wealth and power as derivatives come to be relied upon by policymakers as risk management arrangements for smallholders. Because the markets are largely inaccessible for small coffee farmers, policymaker reliance on derivatives in the presence of price risk dangerously disadvantages small producers relative to other powerful and wealthy actors along the chain.

There is additional evidence to suggest that the activities of those who *can* trade in derivatives may actually make coffee prices more unstable, generating further hardships for small producers. A growing body of new research argues that rising levels of speculative activity in commodity derivatives markets are generating volatility in future prices, and this volatility is spilling over into the cash markets. As if coffee prices are not already volatile enough, derivatives markets, by facilitating speculative trading, may make prices more volatile even as they deny risk management services to those who need them most. Further, the activities of speculators drive inefficiencies in the futures markets such that basis risk for hedgers increases.[110] These inefficiencies also distort the price discovery role of the markets and may misdirect producers and others who use them for marketing and investment decisions. Please recall that the problems associated with market inefficiencies were detailed at length in the previous chapter.

As mentioned in the previous section, speculation in commodity markets has grown tremendously over the past decade, with the Great Recession further contributing to this trend. Among other kinds of speculators, "commodity index speculation" by pension funds, insurance companies, sovereign wealth funds, and university endowments (among others) has grown in tandem with the declining value of traditional assets like stocks and real estate. Between mid-2003 and mid-2008, the amount of funds allocated toward commodity indices rose from US$13 billion to US$317 billion.[111] A number of researchers now attribute the exceptional recent volatility of commodity prices—i.e. the global food price crisis—to the growing presence of these actors in futures markets.

When index speculators enter into a commodity swap agreement with a financial institution, in the interests of replicating the movement of a commodity index, they are usually "swapping" the rate of return on three-month US Treasury bills (plus management fees) for the return generated by the movement of the commodity index. In other words, index speculators are betting on the differential between short-term interest rates and commodity future prices (as tabulated in the index). Financial institutions who take these bets, and are obligated to pay the speculators returns on the index, hedge their own positions by trading in commodity futures markets. In order to minimize their risk, these institutions must trade in such a way so as to replicate the movement of the index perfectly.[112]

Because the operators of the index, as well as the financial institutions entering into commodity swap agreements, do not want to make delivery of all of the different commodities that make up the index, they perform a "rollover" near the expiration of the futures contracts. Recall that rollovers allow traders to stay in the nearest contract month and avoid having to make delivery; the technique involves selling the contract that is about to expire at the same time as one buys the second nearby contract. Of critical importance in the context of index speculation is the fact that all of these financial institutions and index operators roll their positions all at once over the course of a few days near a contract's expiration. This means that there is a large movement of funds out of the nearest contract and into the subsequent one, as these speculators trade in tandem. "When all Index Speculators roll their positions in unison, it impacts the markets significantly."[113]

Because commodity index speculators are "long-only," meaning they bet only that prices will rise, when these parties enter the commodity futures markets they can cause prices to rise rapidly. Conversely, when speculators exit the futures markets, prices can fall equally rapidly. Ghosh notes that the role of financial speculation in causing the rapid food price increases of 2007–08 and the equally rapid fall in prices over mid-year to year-end 2008 is widely agreed: "It is now quite widely acknowledged that financial speculation was the major factor behind the sharp price rise of many primary commodities, including agricultural items over the past year . . . . Similarly, the subsequent sharp declines in prices were also related to changes in financial markets, in particular the need for liquidity to cover losses."[114] As the housing crisis became apparent in the United States, investors began redirecting their funds toward the commodity sector, resulting in rising future prices; however, as losses were sustained on real estate and other assets, these commodity positions were liquidated, resulting in falling future prices. "These sharp spikes are historically unprecedented even in the volatile price history of primary commodities. Such wild swings in prices obviously cannot be explained by short term supply and demand factors or any other 'real economy' tendencies. Instead, these acute price movements are clearly the result of speculative activity in these markets."[115]

Masters and White, hedge fund manager and financial accountant (respectively) who have recently testified on these issues before the US Congress, argue that the clearest evidence of the influence of commodity index speculators on future prices can be gleaned from the fact that those commodities that feature in the most prominent commodity indexes (e.g. the S&P GSCI, DJ-AIGCI) have witnessed very rapid and towering price hikes over the past several years. Table 4.3 shows these trends.

In the coffee futures market (these data are for the ICE Arabica market), the volume of coffee held by index speculators in the form of long positions in the coffee futures market increased from about 195 million pounds in July 2003 to over 2.1 billion pounds in July 2008, an 11-fold increase in the coffee "futures stockpile" in just five years. Table 4.3 indicates that this increase in artificial coffee demand contributed to a 160 percent increase in coffee future prices over this period. It is also important to note that between 2003 and 2008, the purchases of coffee futures by index speculators outweighed the purchases of traditional speculators and hedgers almost 2 to 1, further illustrating the outsized influence of speculators on the market.[116] Likewise, as investors pulled out of commodity markets while the financial crisis deepened in the second half of 2008, coffee prices fell precipitously. The executive director of the ICO wrote in October 2008: "Coffee prices fell sharply during the month of October in the context of the financial crisis, which seems to be exerting downward pressures on virtually all commodity prices . . . in the last two months coffee prices have declined by over 17%."[117]

All by itself, the volatility of future prices gives reason for concern. As mentioned previously, as future prices become more volatile hedging becomes more difficult for futures traders facing frequent margin calls and more expensive for options traders who must pay higher premiums. Further, future price volatility can give mixed or wrong signals to those looking to the market for investment and marketing guidance (i.e. price discovery). For example, as coffee prices rise with index speculation, farmers may be encouraged to plant more coffee despite the fact that underlying demand for coffee in the cash market does not justify the new plantings. In this manner, speculators may be further undermining the usefulness of derivatives markets for actors in the commodity sector, like farmers and other (prospective) commercial market users. This scenario may, depending on the precise conditions, also portend a severe coffee price decline as new (unwarranted) coffee trees come on line.

Table 4.3 Commodity futures price increases, July 2003–July 2008

Agricultural	Cocoa	+101%
	Coffee	+160%
	Corn	+214%
	Cotton	+18%
	Soybean oil	+196%
	Soybeans	+160%
	Sugar	+121%
	Wheat	+177%
	Wheat KC	+190%
Livestock	Feed cattle	+30%
	Lean hogs	+11%
	Live cattle	+48%
Energy	Brent crude oil	+397%
	WTI crude oil	+364%
	Gasoil	+448%
	Heating oil	+399%
	Unleaded gas	+298%
	Natural gas	+154%
Base metals	Aluminum	+124%
	Lead	+265%
	Nickel	+157%
	Zinc	+141%
	Copper	+433%
Precious metals	Gold	+169%
	Silver	+298%
Average		+203%

Source: Masters and White (2008).

In a similar vein, additional problems arise from the fact that index speculators place their bets without regard to price or supply and demand fundamentals in the underlying markets. Instead, index speculators look for a place to "park" their funds and generate a return, irrespective of the actual trends in a particular commodity.[118] This means that rising prices are not necessarily justified by the conditions prevailing in the underlying cash market. In some cases, this may lead to a growing basis, as future price increases are not paralleled in the cash market. Of course, these inefficiencies also have implications for price discovery. Future prices are not only volatile, but they may also be wrong in their predictions. To the extent that future price volatility is passed through to cash markets the impact of speculation on basis risk will be diminished, as cash and future prices move more in tandem.

Along these lines, and as indicated by Ghosh above, there is evidence that volatility in futures markets, partly caused by speculative activity, is "spilling over" into cash markets. Speculator-driven price increases in futures markets caused cash prices to increase as well, while speculator-driven price declines caused cash prices to fall. This is an interesting dynamic in itself, particularly because the relationship between futures and cash markets is traditionally theorized to work in reverse. Bryan and Rafferty elaborate, "By the 1980s research started to produce evidence that in many markets, even in agricultural markets, pricing was running in the opposite direction to the intuition informing traditional understanding of derivatives. Instead of derivative markets reflecting spot or cash markets, prices were being formed in derivative markets and were then running to cash markets."[119]

There are at least two ways in which rising future prices translate into higher cash prices, and falling future prices translate into lower cash prices. First, future prices are used to make storage decisions by participants in the cash market.[120] If futures markets predict a return to storage (i.e. when future prices are sufficiently above cash prices), there is an incentive for cash market participants to store the commodity and wait to sell it until cash prices rise in the future. The process is largely self-fulfilling. High future prices encourage storage, which takes commodities out of the market, thereby reducing supplies and putting upward pressure on prices. Conversely, falling future prices relative to cash prices will induce cash market participants to sell now, avoiding losses as prices fall. As these sales occur they increase supplies in the market and place downward pressures on prices. Because of the relation between future prices and storage decisions, future price changes often translate into parallel cash price changes.

Second, there is evidence that the growing use of future prices as "benchmarks" for cash market transactions has generated another conduit for the transmission of future price volatility to the cash markets, in defiance of theoretical expectations. Roasters use future prices to guide their purchasing negotiations, as do international traders and exporters. In some cases, and this practice is becoming ever-more popular, an increase in the future price by one cent results in a one cent increase in the price paid to farmers and vice versa with falling future prices.[121] In other cases, as Newman's recent study of coffee marketing in Uganda suggests, local coffee traders protect themselves from international price volatility by offering low prices to farmers. Rather than purchasing at different prices as dictated by the futures markets, local traders instead protect their margins by offering a sufficiently low price to farmers, a price low enough to take into account the risk of a sudden fall in international prices. In Tanzania, Newman reports that farmers sell directly to exporters at weekly auctions, meaning that they are exposed to weekly, but not daily or intraday, price volatility on futures markets.[122]

Thus, while different marketing practices in different countries suggest that future price volatility impacts cash prices and farmers via different mechanisms, there is nonetheless evidence that volatile global coffee future prices are transmitted to farmers in some way or another. This is alarming given that small farmers are generally unable to hedge, and have very few if any substantive price risk management alternatives, yet are hit harder by price risk than most other actors along the chain. While derivatives markets increasingly provide a place for large multinational financial firms and funds to earn large profits, they simultaneously make farming and life more difficult still for smallholders. For the same reasons specified in the previous section on exclusion and inequality, the presence of severe price risk combined with ineffective risk management arrangements at the farm level is an engine for inequality along the coffee chain. Newman further adds that even as volatility makes farming harder, it may increase the profits of international traders and other coffee actors speculating in the derivatives market.

Conclusions

To conclude, not only do derivatives markets not work as well as advocates might like but the markets also, as they globalize and are integrated into development agendas, work to actively disadvantage small coffee farmers and undermine their livelihoods. From the perspective provided by commodity chain frameworks, poverty in smallholder coffee farming communities is strongly connected to historical and contemporary inequalities in wealth and power along the commodity chain. Historically, those in the South who grow coffee beans have been consistently subordinated to the interests of Northern actors trading and processing them. Today, roasters and international traders both exert downward price pressures and work to exclude some small producers from coffee production. The consolidation of power among these coffee actors has been aided by market liberalization and helps to maintain market liberalization, reduced public support for smallholders, falling long-term coffee prices, market oversupply, and fierce competition among producers, to the detriment of smallholders.

Derivatives markets work to maintain and worsen these inequalities in three distinct ways. First, derivatives markets relate to the underlying coffee chain symbiotically. Liberalization and consolidation along the coffee chain have provided an enabling environment for derivative market growth. Derivatives markets, for their part, generate a constellation of interests (financial and political) intent on maintaining the structure of the underlying chain. In this way, derivatives markets may work to buttress a global coffee system that is consistently undermining the well-being of smallholders. Indeed, derivatives address symptoms of coffee farmer poverty without really addressing underlying causes—i.e. inequalities in wealth and power, market liberalization, reduced expenditures on smallholders and agriculture in general, oversupply, low and volatile prices, and too-fierce competition.

Second, the coffee derivatives chain is a highly exclusive chain, largely populated by elite financial and agricultural firms from the North or with extensive Northern connections. The exclusiveness of the chain at the exchange, brokerage, and trading levels has concrete implications for coffee smallholders who are excluded from participation. While the derivatives chain provides some actors with an opportunity to hedge and to embark on new and profitable business strategies, smallholders are denied these opportunities. Unevenness in the ability to use derivatives markets in this way works to widen the already-large inequalities along the coffee chain. The relative disadvantage of smallholders is only worsened by the fact that price risk is already more harmful for this community, relative to other actors along the chain who have more wealth, better access to credit, and more assets. The exclusiveness of the coffee derivatives chain at the exchange level also hints at the serious difficulties local Southern commodity exchanges may have in catering to smallholder farmers. In this context, it may be the case that public and donor resources dedicated to establishing and promoting new exchanges may inadvertently "leak" into the pockets of Northern firms.

Finally, there is a large and growing body of evidence to suggest that derivatives markets are a forum for speculative trading and that they provide a conduit for the transmission of price volatility into cash markets. The big gains of speculators thus come at the expense of smallholder farmers who are most hurt by volatility and least able to manage it. As with the second point above, volatility combined with the poverty of smallholder risk management contributes to widening gaps in the coffee economy between those who can manage and profit from risk and those who cannot. Speculative trading in derivatives markets also generates inefficiencies in the price discovery and hedging mechanisms, while future price volatility makes futures and options hedging more difficult and expensive.

From the perspective of policy, these findings again urge extreme caution to policymakers. The exclusiveness of the derivatives chain implies that policymakers may not want to rely on derivatives as risk management vehicles for smallholders, lest they inadvertently contribute to a deterioration of the position of farmers and the empowerment of those actors who already capture the lion's share of wealth and power along the coffee and derivatives chains. The evidence also suggests, in direct contravention of the claims of advocates, that erecting new commodity exchanges in the South may not be an effective solution to smallholder access problems. Even further, policymakers may be unwittingly supporting a forum for speculative activity that erodes the functionality of derivatives markets and introduces volatility into cash markets, with both of these forces working against small farmers in a number of ways.

CHAPTER 5

Derivatives and the Politics of Alternatives

A single, one-dimensional way of thinking has created a monoculture of the mind. And the monoculture of the mind has become a self-fulfilling prophecy.[1]

Some have suggested that the global financial and food crises have motivated policymakers and international organizations to rethink their perspectives on globalized and liberalized markets. While critiques of modern financial and commodities markets have been mounting for decades, if not centuries, the twin crises have perhaps provided an opportunity to revisit these issues. The crises have created the "space" necessary for considering alternative economic policies and structures.®

One of the more memorable moments in the recent history of the Great Recession was when former chairman of the US Federal Reserve Alan Greenspan publicly admitted before the US Congress, "I was wrong". When asked by Representative Waxman (D-CA), "Do you feel that your ideology pushed you to make decisions that you wish you had not made?," Greenspan replied: "Yes, I've found a flaw. I don't know how significant or permanent it is. But I've been very distressed by that fact."[2] Krugman argues that the financial crisis will push economists to rethink their models and assumptions, and "this will translate into more cautious policy advice—and a reduced willingness to dismantle economic safeguards in the faith that markets will solve all problems."[3] Grabel cautiously contends that the financial crisis has induced new thinking on capital market regulation at the IMF, where officials are now talking more earnestly about capital controls and other policies to better regulate global financial flows.[4]

Similarly, the food crisis has encouraged world leaders to question the structure of the global food system. The recent summer 2011 meeting of the G-20[5] focused on measures to tackle the crisis, including a rethinking of ethanol policies (which redirect food to energy production) and regulations to limit speculative activity in commodities markets. France's agricultural minister Bruno Le Maire states that the meeting established a "base for a new global agriculture."[6]

Of course, others argue that the crises provided an opportunity to talk about change, but that substantive reforms have yet to be translated into practice. Henry Saragih, the international coordinator of La Via Campesina ("The Peasant Way"), argues: "The [food] crisis has proven that the neoliberal model has failed and yet the G20 countries are pushing for the same free market solutions and business as usual. We demand systemic change and a new model that puts people first and promotes food sovereignty."[7] Likewise, Ghosh writes about the Western response to the financial crisis: "The stupidity of the current macroeconomic stance in the UK is surprising in itself; but when combined with similar voices in Europe and the US, it is downright astonishing. Three years after the collapse of Lehman Brothers, the global economy is not going through a recovery from financial crisis, but simply entering act two after a brief intermission. On current form this play is a farce that will end in tragedy."[8]

Similar debates, with similarly high expectations for change, have been ongoing in the development field since the 1990s (and much earlier in some cases), intensifying with the onset of the twin crises. By the late 1990s the dominant development policy agenda, called the "Washington Consensus" and recommending liberalization, privatization, and macroeconomic stabilization,[9] had become an object of fierce disagreement within the field. Development critics argued that these free market policies had not generated the dynamic economic growth that was promised, but rather had spawned massive global inequalities, solidified dominance of the global economy by MNCs, contributed to rising global economic fragility and generated growing insecurity for individuals. For example, Shiva writes, "Development was thus reduced to a continuation of the process of colonization. It was an extension of modern Western patriarchy's economic vision based on the exploitation or exclusion of women (of the West and the non-West), on the exploitation and destruction of nature, and on the exploitation and destruction of other cultures."[10]

Today, the debate centers on whether such criticism of the Washington Consensus has resulted in change in the mainstream approach. Marshall, for example, sees the World Bank as making real efforts to address the failures of its past policies and the arguments of critics: "The Bank's response to the important critical voices came rather late, slowly, and often reluctantly, but in many respects the environment of protest and criticism has transformed the institution, opening it up to dialogue, prying open its secret documents, and forcing new communications and listening approaches."[11] By contrast, critics usually admit to some alterations in the orthodox approach, but contend that little of substance has changed. For example, Johnston argues, "whatever the changes in the definition and monitoring of poverty, there is continued belief by neoliberals in the core role of liberalization in poverty reduction."[12] Chang and Grabel similarly argue that "the spin on this new work inaccurately claims that the architects of the Washington Consensus have now 'seen the light', and have genuinely moved to a new way of thinking that transcends their previous policy prescriptions. This, in fact, is not at all the case."[13]

Within the context of this broader debate, in this chapter I address derivatives and the politics of development alternatives. In the first sections, I treat recommendations for derivatives in development as a case study in the development orthodoxy. While derivative instruments do not tell us much about how to alleviate poverty in rural coffee communities, they do shed light on the development establishment and its policy priorities in the "post-Washington Consensus" era. In some respects, derivatives for development suggest a new orientation toward agricultural development within the leading international development organizations, one that recognizes the particularly precarious position of small farmers today. In other respects, however, derivatives represent a continuation of the Washington Consensus, in that they represent a continuing commitment by the development mainstream to high-tech, market-based tools for agricultural development. While derivatives advocacy stems partly from their ideological appeal, as indicated in Chapter 3, I also argue that distinct political advantages are conferred on the institutions that recommend them. Derivatives allow advocates to address prominent critics all the while building new sources of political legitimacy from within the private sector. The political and ideological character of derivatives as poverty alleviation tools helps to explain why derivatives continue to garner mainstream support even with mounting evidence of their inappropriateness in this context.

Perhaps most troubling, this continued affinity for high-tech, market-based solutions is reducing the space available for thinking about imaginative price risk management alternatives that may better serve small producers. Thus, the second part of the chapter highlights several of these alternatives: supply management, intellectual property challenges, Fairtrade, producer unionization, and deglobalization and disengagement. Importantly, each addresses *both* the coffee price risk problem *and* some of the contributors to coffee farmer poverty discussed in Chapter 4 (e.g. oversupply, low and volatile prices, fierce competition, commodity dependence, and global inequalities in wealth and power). This section of the chapter is not an exhaustive accounting of possible alternatives. Rather, I aim to illustrate the many other worlds of coffee that are possible, given the requisite policy space and political will.

Derivatives and Development Politics

Between the late 1970s and mid-1990s, researchers and policymakers in many governments and development institutions became convinced that relatively unobstructed global trade in goods, services, and capital would generate massive returns for the world's poorest people. Combined with national policies to attract foreign capital and promote exports, the privatization of state-owned enterprises, conservative macroeconomic management, and protection of private property rights, a relatively free global market order would energize stagnant sectors of the economy, catalyze job creation, and help usher in a new era of development and poverty alleviation for the South.[14] In the 1990s, this convergence on the proper framework for development was termed the "Washington Consensus," a phrase coined by economist John Williamson, referring to the common opinion on development matters in Washington DC, the capitol of the United States and the location of the headquarters of the World Bank and the International Monetary Fund.

The Washington Consensus in agriculture, which mirrored the contours of the broader agenda, gained traction among policymakers beginning in the early 1980s, as debt crises were bleeding the economies of dozens of Southern states. During the 1970s, many governments incurred heavy foreign debts as oil prices climbed. When commodity prices collapsed in the early 1980s, Southern governments were suddenly faced with the prospect of default—because for many governments, commodity export earnings were the primary source of funds to pay creditors. And default they did, beginning with Mexico in 1982.

The exigencies of the debt crises forced a rethinking of agricultural development policy for two big reasons. First, agriculture was seen to be partly responsible for growing government deficits. Maintaining fixed crop prices for farmers, for example, became more expensive when global commodity prices fell. Subsidies to farmers were also implicated as a contributor to bloated government spending. Second, because many Southern states were seen to be globally competitive only in a handful of commodity products, agricultural exports were viewed in the mainstream as important means of earning the foreign exchange required to repay foreign debts.

The Washington Consensus on Agriculture (WCA)that emerged from this period of crisis and transition was defined by a few key policy prescriptions. It was recommended that Southern states renew their focus on commercial agricultural production for export, and cease their protection and financing of uncompetitive industrial sectors. Within agriculture, the focus was on cutting spending, increasing the efficiency of agricultural production, creating the infrastructure required to facilitate global marketing, and removing policy barriers to global commodity trading. The debtor nations, desperate for loans from the World Bank and the IMF, had little choice but to accept these reforms as conditions for receiving credit (this is called "structural adjustment" via "loan conditionality"). "Structural adjustment . . . was, for one thing, an ideologically driven enterprise to make economies more efficient, in narrow terms, by liberating market forces from state restraints. In the short term, structural adjustment was a program consisting of radical spending cutbacks and trade liberalization designed to allow governments to accumulate the resources and foreign exchange to pay off their massive foreign debt."[15]

Oya argues that the WCA had five policy components in practice: removal of subsidies on inputs for farmers and on consumer food prices; currency devaluation to boost exports; elimination of marketing boards and the like; liberalization of commodity prices; and, the "replacement of subsidized agricultural credit with 'alternative' measures to establish 'sustainable' financial institutions."[16] Typical of neoliberal policy formulations, these recommendations emphasized the greater efficiency of markets relative to government and the importance of the private sector for stimulating growth and competition. Analyzing the matter at the farm level, Kydd and Dorward similarly note that the "Washington Consensus on poor country agriculture" viewed "undercapitalization" and "insufficiently competitive" farms as the primary causes of poverty in rural areas and stagnant Southern agricultural performance.[17] Policy reforms to improve competition (e.g. enabling freer trade and encouraging higher productivity) and facilitate greater private investment in agriculture (e.g. reducing the role of state agencies and lowering taxes on agricultural producers) followed closely from this diagnosis.

Shiva further points out that mainstream agricultural development policy has been characterized, at least since the mid-1960s, by intensive application of sophisticated new technologies to improve productivity, a policy dimension also apparent in the WCA and in contemporary derivatives advocacy. The "Green Revolutions" across Asia that began at this time were predicated on the notion that averting world hunger required massive increases in food production. To this end, new dwarf seed varieties were introduced across Southern states, along with mechanized production techniques, industrial pesticides and fertilizers, and heavy irrigation, with genetically modified seeds added to this list by the 1990s. Combined with land consolidation to reap economies of scale, these new technologies were seen as keys to eliminating hunger and creating prosperous rural communities.[18]

Many of the WCA's recommendations were adopted in the coffee context, discussed in previous chapters. Following the collapse of the ICA in the late 1980s, national governments dismantled their coffee boards, refrained from fixing prices and overtaxing producers, committed themselves to free global coffee trade, reduced or eliminated input and credit subsidies, and cut funding for extension services. In some cases like Vietnam, the mainstream emphasis on expanded commercial agricultural production for export resulted in the creation of coffee export sectors where none had really existed previously. Bacon and colleagues, along with Shiva, note that modern coffee history also reveals the application of sophisticated and expensive technologies to boost productivity. Use of "high yielding seed varieties, agrochemical inputs and significant reduction or outright elimination of shade" are characteristic of technology adopters in coffee (new "sun-tolerant" varieties of coffee allow for more plants, as shade trees can be cut down).[19]

As the WCA was implemented and its effects were more broadly understood, multiple criticisms were leveled against the program. One of the most important criticisms that emerged, at least for our purposes here, is that the WCA overlooked the challenges and constraints these new policies posed for small farmers. Kydd and Dorward argue that the mainstream policy package assumed that smallholder agricultural production was "fundamentally efficient," and did not sufficiently take into account the low prices, high quality standards, fierce competition, and domination by larger firms that smallholders faced when entering the now-free global markets. The WCA thus failed to recognize that smallholder production for the world market is "unlikely to generate the large and dispersed employment gains needed for poverty reduction."[20]

Likewise, Oya argues that WCA fails to comprehend the combined effects of removed government supports and liberalized commodity markets on smallholders. In this environment, farmers are subject to lower and more volatile prices, and are simultaneously deprived of public support in managing these risks (e.g. input subsidies and stabilized prices): "By and large, these effects adversely affected the poorest under-capitalised farmers, who could not afford to buy more expensive inputs . . . while richer farmers and local traders could reap the benefits . . . ."[21] Shiva further points out that the modern-day emphasis on the use of high technology has led small farmers to accumulate enormous debts to adopt these farming methods. With loans frequently collateralized with the farm itself, inability to pay debts often results in seizure of smallholders' lands. In India, peasant farmers are committing suicide en masse to escape these mounting technology-related debts.[22]

Bello, one of the harshest critics of the WCA, argues that this policy package is so biased against smallholders that it really amounts to a thinly disguised effort to rid the Southern countryside of peasants altogether, to make way for corporate agribusiness. Reflecting on the massive dislocation of peasants across the South as a result of the neoliberal agricultural development program, Bello writes: "This was not simply the erosion of national food self-sufficiency or food security but what some students of agricultural trends call 'depeasantization'—the phasing out of a mode of production to make the countryside a more congenial site for intensive capital accumulation. This transformation was a traumatic one for hundreds of millions of people, since peasant production is not simply an economic activity."[23] The foregoing chapters illustrate his point in the coffee context.

Whether or not the development establishment has effectively responded to and incorporated the grievances of critics into its agricultural agenda is a matter of some debate. And, it is in this context that derivatives advocacy provides important insights into the changing contours of the policy orthodoxy. Derivatives advocacy represents a real effort to grapple with the particularly precarious position of smallholders in this context. It implicitly recognizes that the processes of liberalization and globalization have been difficult to manage for some, and that specific policy attention must be paid to those who "lost" under previous versions of the Washington Consensus.

Take, for example, the following statement from UNCTAD:

> Commodity exchanges make it possible for farmers to achieve price predictability and security, despite the volatility, over a crop cycle (and, for storable commodities, for a further six months to one year). This is particularly relevant because, with the withdrawal of government support for developing-country agricultural producers, short-term shocks in the prices of key export products are increasingly felt at the level of the farmer.[24]

In this statement, UNCTAD is considering in part Oya's critique, that is, liberalization decreased public support for farmers and for smallholders this was particularly devastating. That said, the statement stops short of recognizing the role that liberalization and globalization have played in generating price volatility.

Similar thoughtfulness is evident in this statement from several World Bank researchers: "Poverty can be transient and often market-related .... As a result, market-related price and output insurance, delivered directly or indirectly to community households and businesses, may have direct income effects for the insured and economic multiplier effects in the community."[25] As with UNCTAD, the recommendation for derivatives stems directly from the important recognition that liberalized commodity markets generate financial insecurity for those, like peasant farmers, who do not have effective means of managing their volatility.

What is fascinating, however, is *how* the development establishment has internalized this recognition of the special circumstances facing peasant farmers and reformulated its approach to agricultural development in response to critics. Recommendations to employ derivatives in the development context are usually part of a broader package of recommendations and proposals that I call the "market access agenda," a set of proposals that is largely addressed to the unique and difficult position of smallholder farmers operating in a globalized and liberalized economic environment. The market access agenda is a constellation of policies that seek to address recent criticism of the WCA, all the while allowing for continued adherence to the foundational development principles that characterized it. In fact, the market access agenda is identical to the WCA in a number of key respects, though smallholders are now a more central focus. In this manner, the development establishment is able, to some extent, to assuage protest and opposition, all the while consolidating its market-based approach to agricultural development.

The Market Access Agenda

Paralleling the "debating poverty" discussion in the previous chapter, the market access agenda envisions poverty and insecurity among smallholder farmers largely as a consequence of inadequate integration with the world economy. Small farmers just aren't globalized enough and they are suffering as a consequence. UNCTAD writes: "While globalization provides opportunities for economic growth, it also brings increased competition and heightened uncertainty, influencing the extent to which local enterprises can survive and grow. Many small producers are not competitive and are handicapped in doing business and meeting market exigencies."[26]

Indeed, farmers are "poor" because they have no good way of meeting potential buyers of their crop; because rural transportation and crop storage infrastructure is inadequate, encouraging waste and preventing goods from being brought to market; because farmers have no good way of knowing the price their crop commands on global markets; because the quality of the goods they produce do not measure up to global standards; because they are too small and inefficient to effectively compete with lower-cost agribusinesses in a global marketplace; because they do not take advantage of modern technologies that increase productivity, smooth investment, and reduce transaction costs; and because they are not well connected to markets for credit and risk management. The broad problem for small farmers on this account is that they cannot navigate global markets very well, and this deficit results in poverty and insecurity.

The key assumption embedded in the market access agenda is that global markets would pull farmers up out of poverty if only farmers could more successfully and regularly participate in them. Yes, the market context has changed rapidly; yes, volatility is more problematic and competition is more fierce; yes, government is no longer the stabilizing and supportive force it once was. But, for all its faults, this new market context is the best achievable, and farmers will have to adapt. The World Bank argues:

> Far-reaching changes in domestic and global markets are creating big opportunities for farmers and agribusiness entrepreneurs. The demand for high-value primary and processed products is rapidly increasing, driven by rising incomes, faster urbanization, liberalized trade, foreign investment, and advancing technology. These developments are expanding market opportunities, which is important for faster agricultural and nonfarm growth and for greater employment and rural incomes. But the new markets demand quality, timely deliveries, and economies of scale, posing special challenges for smallholders.[27]

The challenge for development institutions, researchers, and policymakers thus has several dimensions. Agricultural development programs must first be dedicated to providing the physical infrastructure required for more effective market integration. The necessary infrastructure has a variety of dimensions, including transportation, information and communications, irrigation, marketing, and finance (credit and risk management). For example, the UNDP recommends "developing a proactive agenda to overcome supply constraints through upgrading of infrastructure like roads, ports, storage facilities."[28] The World Bank highlights marketing infrastructure: "Well-functioning agricultural marketing systems can reduce the cost of food and the uncertainty of supply, improving the food security of poor and nonpoor households. By linking farmers more closely to consumers, these marketing systems transmit signals to farmers on new market opportunities and guide their production to meet changing consumer preferences for quantity, quality, variety, and food safety."[29] UNCTAD emphasizes commodity exchanges in the infrastructure context, arguing that commodity futures exchanges, in addition to helping manage price risk, have other "important impacts on smallholders," including: "transparent market information that reduces information asymmetries and improves farmer cropping and selling activity; upgrade to commodity market infrastructure and practice; and facilitation of farmer financing."[30]

Second, agricultural development programs must also focus their efforts on enabling small farmers themselves, teaching and empowering them to use existing global markets to their advantage. Teaching and empowering can also take a variety of forms, from promotion of commodity exchanges to providing training in the proper use of biotechnology and irrigation systems, support for marketing cooperatives, and quality improvement schemes. For example, UNCTAD discusses a new program that it has recently started to improve small farmer participation in horticultural markets (i.e. fruits, vegetables, herbs, and cut flowers): "UNCTAD has assisted in a partnership between the Swiss supermarket chain Migros and small producers in Ghana. The partnership . . . aims to help them achieve high returns while ensuring traceability and consistent product quality and quantity, to guarantee sustainable methods of production, and to enter into profitable contracts."[31] The World Bank discusses farmer empowerment via marketing cooperatives: "For smallholders, producer organizations are essential to achieve competitiveness . . . . Donors and governments can assist by facilitating the right to organize, training leaders, and empowering weaker members, in particular women and young farmers."[32]

Third, the market access agenda further incorporates recommendations to increase productivity among small farmers, including suggestions for agricultural extension services, limited subsidies for inputs like fertilizers (sometimes called "smart subsidies"), removal of inefficient taxes on the agricultural sector, mechanization and technology application, and more effective risk management. Advocates argue that one big reason global markets are so difficult for smallholders to navigate and profit from is that they do not produce in sufficient quantities to be recognized by exporters and other intermediaries (recall that this is often the case for coffee smallholders), nor do they produce enough to sustain a decent standard of living at current world prices. For example, UNCTAD states, "Improving competitiveness and supply capacities requires targeted national policies complemented by massive international support for enhanced productivity and meeting market requirements."[33] The UNDP similarly recommends "implementing policies to improve productivity, employ appropriate technology in production, develop new skills for cultivation and farm management techniques, promote innovation to boost productivity and create linkages between enterprises, the farming community, universities and research entities."[34]

Fourth and last, there is emphasis on the removal of global barriers to trade and farm productivity, including rich country agricultural subsidies and inefficient ethanol promotion programs in the United States, Europe, and Brazil. Some also suggest that massive amounts of foreign aid are required to renovate Southern agriculture. UNCTAD covers both of these points in a recent report:

> Developing countries may benefit much less from the current dynamism if developed countries use the demand increase as an excuse for taking a

> complacent view of the need for reductions in agricultural tariffs and support to domestic producers, or, worse, if they decide to exploit the market growth for their own exclusive benefit by continuing high levels of support. . . . Aid for trade is a crucial instrument for enabling commodity-dependent developing countries to enjoy the benefits emerging in world markets. Specific areas related to aid for building trade-related infrastructure and improving supply capacity as well as competitiveness are mentioned later in this report.[35]

In some cases, the development establishment recognizes that, even with these efforts, some smallholders will not be able to earn a living from farming. The World Bank thus argues that for some smallholders in "less-favored regions," particularly where environmental degradation is accelerating, diversification into off-farm work or migration to cities will be a more viable option than farming.[36] In other cases, small farmers may not be able to compete if they remain small. The solutions is thus to "get big or get out," to borrow a phrase from former US secretary of Agriculture Earl Butz:. "As agriculture becomes more technology driven and access to consumers is mediated by agroprocessors and supermarkets, economies of scale will pose major challenges for the future competitiveness of smallholders . . . . One way of achieving such productivity gains might be through farm consolidation and mechanization."[37]

Recommendations for derivatives for small farmers cut across all four dimensions of the market access agenda. Derivatives are a means of connecting farmers to global markets, of empowering them to protect themselves from volatility, a means of stimulating production increases, and a mechanism for leveraging policy liberalization. The four points above are also virtually identical to the WCA—witness the emphasis on infrastructure, productivity increases, and liberal policy reform and maintenance—but pay more explicit attention to training and empowerment of smallholders such that they can survive, compete, and prosper in the global marketplace.

At heart, the market access agenda contains a genuine concern for the plight of smallholders that sits awkwardly and paradoxically alongside a deeper commitment to maintaining the contemporary globalized and liberalized world agricultural system. As Engles argues, the post-Washington Consensus period at the World Bank has involved a "greater concern for the social costs of adjustment and poverty in general," but that the concern is merely instrumental, aimed at the "expansion and revision of the Washington Consensus." She writes, "Overall, there is limited evidence that the Bank has moved beyond its traditional concern with economic growth within a market capitalist framework."[38] The market access agenda does not propose revolutionary nor systemic change, but rather small reforms around the margins of the system such that peasants and other peripheral actors might share a bit more in global prosperity than they do currently.

The Washington Consensus Revisited

Despite its newfound concern for smallholder farmers, the development establishment remains grounded by many of its old assumptions and biases. The market access agenda, including derivatives advocacy, reflects a strongly held belief in the beneficent and progressive power of free markets in agriculture, and the prosperity-inducing effects of technological innovation. In an important sense, derivatives for development recommendations are amalgams of recent development criticism and long-standing orthodox ideological biases—that is, smallholders require more attention from policymakers, free-markets are the best institutions for agricultural development, and sophisticated technology application is critical for farm success. In this manner, derivatives satisfy, if only partially and theoretically, the complaints of critics without requiring substantive revision of major orthodox development tenets.

Further, and as Woods emphasizes in her discussion of the World Bank and the IMF, global economic and development institutions are additionally constrained in their policy recommendations by a politics of survival and the perceived, related need to retain power and relevance on the global stage. Woods writes, "Often Fund and Bank prescriptions are based neither on clear evidence nor on pure expert analysis or predictions. Instead they reflect bureaucrats trying to square political pressures and institutional constraints."[39] Derivatives, by quelling protest and solidifying private sector alliances, thus also serve an important strategic, political function for the development establishment.

There are two ideological biases, frequently associated with the Washington Consensus in agriculture, that are exemplified by the derivatives approach to agricultural price risk management. First, the case of derivatives in development exhibits what Joseph Stiglitz calls "market fundamentalism." This concept here refers to the dogmatic adherence to market-based approaches to development, to the exclusion of alternative policies. In the derivatives context, at least three interrelated dimensions of market fundamentalism are apparent: policy action on the basis of assumptions and models that bear little resemblance to reality; the belief that problems with free markets can be solved with free markets; and resistance to nonmarket alternatives.

On the matter of bad theory, Stiglitz writes in reference to the World Bank and the IMF: "The international financial institutions have pushed a particular ideology—market fundamentalism—that is both bad economics and bad politics; it is based on premises concerning how markets work that do not hold even for developed countries, much less for developing countries."[40] This tendency is highly visible in the derivatives context, where theoretical assumptions about how and for whom derivatives markets work have led to a large effort to promote the institutions at the expense of potentially more viable options and without adequate consideration of contradictory empirical evidence and unintended consequences (see Chapter 3 for discussion of the large gap between theory and practice, and Chapter 4 for unintended consequences).

In contrast to the World Bank, where market fundamentalism has long been identified by critics, UNCTAD's consistent support for commodity exchanges and modern financial instruments for smallholders is surprising. This organization is often viewed as a more moderate voice in mainstream development debates, countering the market fundamentalism of World Bank and IMF and carving out a space for alternative approaches. Mojarov and Arda note that UNCTAD, in the commodity context, favors an "approach stressing the balanced roles of governments and the markets."[41] In fact, the first secretary-general of UNCTAD, Raul Prebisch, was an important heterodox theorist of commodity dependence (with not insignificant Marxist leanings, in my opinion), who frequently noted that structural inequalities in the global economy contributed to the deteriorating economic position of countries in the South. It is outside the scope of this discussion to offer a detailed analysis of UNCTAD and its changing ideological leanings. Rather, I intend only to point out that UNCTAD's recent advocacy of derivative instruments appears out of character and casts some doubt on the "balance" of its current approach to commodities. While the World Bank's market fundamentalism has been an object of criticism for some time (see Stiglitz above), UNCTAD appears to only recently be moving in this direction, at least as far as derivatives and development are concerned.

Market fundamentalism in the derivatives and development context further exhibits odd and insular understandings of cause, effect, and appropriate policy solutions. Along these lines, I have been confounded by the fact that UNCTAD and the World Bank are advocating commodity derivatives exchanges for development at the same time that they indict financial speculation in commodity derivatives markets. In a widely celebrated report released in 2011 and coauthored by researchers from UNCTAD, the FAO, and the World Bank among other organizations, the development establishment condemns financial speculation in the context of the food crisis. Yet, the report completely fails to consider this admonition in relation to efforts to promote derivatives and commodity exchanges across the South.

To the contrary, in the space of one paragraph the development establishment argues that financial speculation in derivatives markets has contributed to recent price volatility *and* that derivatives markets offer a workable solution to the problem:

> While analysts argue about whether financial speculation has been a major factor, most agree that increased participation by non-commercial actors such as index funds, swap dealers and money managers in financial markets probably acted to amplify short term price swings and could have contributed to the formation of price bubbles in some situations . . . . It is clear however that well functioning derivatives markets for agricultural commodities, could play a significant role in reducing or smoothing price fluctuations—indeed, this is one of the primary functions of commodity futures markets.[42]

How can derivatives markets be both the problem *and* the solution?[43] One of the great paradoxes of derivatives advocacy, visible in the writings of both UNCTAD and the World Bank, is that it simultaneously represents a response to criticism of the market-based approach to agricultural development as well as an attempt to extend the reach of the free market in the agricultural context. Indeed, derivatives advocates are, all at once and without even a hint of irony, admitting that liberalized and globalized commodity markets are not without flaw (e.g. they allow volatility to be passed through directly to smallholders), but that such flaws can be compensated for by applying a different set of globalized and liberalized markets (derivatives). The idea that market problems can be met with market solutions is another important dimension of the orthodoxy's market fundamentalism on display in the derivatives context. UNCTAD and the World Bank take this fundamentalism even further—to the point of self-contradiction—in the 2011 report cited above, arguing that the *same* markets (derivatives) are both a cause of and the solution to agricultural price volatility.

Moreover, that derivatives advocacy has actually picked up speed in the face of growing criticism and evidence that suggests the multiple shortcomings of this strategy suggest a problematic resistance to thinking about substantive alternatives, specifically alternatives that fall outside of the neoliberal, free market umbrella. Speaking to this dimension of market fundamentalism, Margaret Thatcher's famous invocation—"there is no alternative"—has been so derided in the critical development literature that it has been given its own acronym, TINA. In the case under consideration here, where the market access agenda does offer some alternatives to derivatives markets, these tend to be constrained by the same promarket bias apparent in the derivatives context.

For example, some researchers recommending derivatives have also suggested that warehouse receipt systems may serve a critical credit and risk management function for farmers. Varangis, Larson, and Anderson, writing for the World Bank, argue that warehouse systems may help to manage price risk in contexts where derivatives are inappropriate or unavailable.[44] UNCTAD also recommends warehouse receipt financing to farmers' associations in the global South, along with a number of other financial instruments for risk management including derivatives, forward contracting, and repos.[45] With the option of storing crops in warehouses, farmers can wait to market their crop until global prices recover from the glut of coffee on the world market during the harvest season. In this manner, farmers could get higher prices than would be possible without storage. In the interim, that is, while waiting to sell, the warehouse receipt can be used as collateral to procure more loans.

While an in-depth analysis of warehouse receipt systems is not possible here, it is sufficient to note the real similarities this "alternative" has to derivatives-based risk management solutions. The price risk management alternatives that are offered in the mainstream discourse are, like derivatives, largely based upon market provision of services (fee-based services provided by private, for-profit firms), designed to be complementary to a liberalized and globalized agricultural system, and make little effort to address any of the underlying and deeply interconnected causes of poverty among coffee farmers (e.g. oversupply, long-term price decreases, price volatility, fierce competition, commodity dependence, loss of government support for smallholder agriculture, and global inequalities in wealth and power). Market fundamentalism in the agricultural development orthodoxy thus promotes mental monocultures, limits policy imaginations, and forecloses consideration of substantive alternatives.

Derivatives advocacy in development further displays "techno-fundamentalism," or an abiding faith in the restorative and progressive power of technology to solve human problems. As indicated in the previous chapters, derivatives markets are exceptionally sophisticated financial technologies. Those who craft derivatives contracts are sometimes referred to as "nuclear financial engineers," working in the field of "particle finance." In this context, derivatives recommendations join a long list of technologies—financial, biotechnological, information and communications, transport, processing, and marketing—that have come to be considered critical to agricultural success.

Overoptimism about the power of technology is endemic in the general derivatives literature, as well as in the work of derivatives advocates in the development context. From a more general perspective, Robert Shiller, for example, envisions a new kind of society based upon technology-induced cultural change and risk management innovations in finance: "Ultimately, *The New Financial Order* is about applying risk management technology to the major problems of our lives. That is, it depicts an electronically integrated risk management culture designed to work in tandem with the already existing economic institutions of capitalism to promote wealth" (interesting here as well is how Shiller depicts derivatives as complementary to existing institutions, underscoring arguments from the previous chapter).[46] Like Shiller, UNCTAD expresses similarly utopian sentiments in the specific case of derivatives and development: "Technological progress can serve the poor as well as the rich. The same forces that are now upsetting the landscape of established futures exchanges are also providing the basis for a new, more inclusive system of market-based risk management, which can help address the age-old problem of farmers' vulnerability to price risk."[47]

I do not intend here to indict technology in general, or to present myself as a modern-day Luddite. What I do want to suggest, however, is that techno-fundamentalism among derivatives advocates has at least two dangerous side-effects in the context of coffee and poverty. To start, "quick fixes" for agriculture based upon sophisticated new technologies prevent adequate consideration of underlying, systemic causes of poverty among coffee farmers. With derivatives comes the risk of assuming that poverty among peasant coffee farmers, related to problems of price volatility, can be "solved" relatively painlessly without changing the underlying structure of the global coffee chain. This assumption is embedded in the work of derivatives advocates where price volatility is deemed "manageable" without challenging the underlying liberalized and globalized production structure (refer to Chapter 4 for the discussion on the "symbiosis" between the coffee derivatives chain and the underlying coffee chain).

The case of concentrated animal feeding operations (CAFOs) for cows in the United States provides a useful analogy to the case of derivatives for coffee farmers under examination here. CAFOs are integrated operations for raising livestock in which a very large population of animals are raised and fattened on relatively small plots of land. The cattle raised in CAFOs are not grazed on grass; instead they are fed corn and are kept in close quarters with one another, reducing the land requirements and thus the costs of livestock production. When cows live in such close proximity to one another, eating food to which they are unaccustomed, disease incubates and spreads rapidly. In the United States, government agencies have recommended and CAFO operators have undertaken to regularly treat the cattle with antibiotics to reduce the likelihood of disease and mass infection. The techno-fix provided by antibiotics allows for the continuation of CAFO operations, rather than pushing us to question a system for producing food that systematically degrades the land

(CAFOs, and corn production, are horribly toxic for the land and groundwater that lie underneath), the cows (who have a miserable existence), and the people who eat them (who grow sick and obese from eating meat raised on corn in festering conditions). Joel Salatin, food activist and owner of Polyface Farm in Virginia, notes:

> I'm always struck by how successful we have been at hitting the bull's-eye of the wrong target. I mean we have learned—for example, in cattle we have learned how to plant, fertilize and harvest corn using global positioning satellite technology, and nobody sits back and asks, "But should we be feeding cows corn?" We've become a culture of technicians. We're all into the how of it and nobody's stepping back and saying "But why?"[48]

Continuing on, though related to the first point, techno-fundamentalism also results in a lack of consideration of unintended consequences. Paul Virilio, echoing Salatin above, has generally commented how today "new technologies are going hand in hand with an uncritical 'technicity'."[49] Science fiction writer Isaac Asimov meant precisely this when he wrote, "The saddest part of life right now is that science gathers knowledge faster than society gathers wisdom."[50]

For derivatives and coffee farmers, faith in the progressive power of technology, as with faith in markets, leads to an overlooking or diminishing of evidence that suggests that these markets and technologies may not work in the way we expect. It also results in failure to adequately consider unintended consequences, for example, rising inequality along the coffee chain and increased volatility in coffee cash markets. The same might be said for the market access agenda more generally, which, for example, recommends all kinds of technologies to increase production without considering the impact of this supply expansion in aggregate (e.g. more oversupply, lower long-term prices, fiercer competition).

Putting ideology aside for a moment, there is good reason to believe that a politics of survival further informs derivatives advocacy. Global institutions, like most institutions, want to survive, persist in furthering their agenda, and retain power and relevance in their area of work. In the development context, this results in an effort on the part of development institutions to advocate policies that deflect popular criticism and protest, and cultivate new sources of political legitimacy.

Derivatives serve an important function relative to critical voices in the agricultural development debate. Derivatives recommendations represent consideration of and response to criticisms regarding the unintended consequences of globalization (price volatility, in this case) and the specific neglect of smallholder producers in the Washington Consensus on

Agriculture. By working to include small farmers in derivatives markets, the development establishment can address *both* these market exigencies and the previous detrimental neglect of peasant producers all at once, thereby satisfying the demands of development critics. In this context, Craig and Porter have referred to recent changes in the development orthodoxy in terms of the "rise of inclusive liberalism."[51] With the neoliberal consensus coming under attack in the 1990s from many quarters, the development orthodoxy has, these authors argue, shifted its political strategy to accommodate criticism and reconsolidate its ideological dominance moving forward:

> It involves elaborating a liberal consensus to reach well beyond mere market liberalization, to include concerns about security, stability, risk, safety, inclusion and participation. All of these are de-politicized, consensual rationales, absolutely suited to a global liberal order without serious ideological rival. Here, the ideological and political task is to imagine and create ways to offer the most excluded of the poor some stake in the wider liberal order, while at the same time protecting it from legitimate contest. Great efforts are made to be seen to "include" those classic liberal subjects, the vulnerable: the excluded, the poor, the marginal, the child. Whereas a previous neo-liberalism would have left these to sink or swim in the frank market, "inclusive" liberalism won't let them get away so easily.[52]

Derivatives advocacy, especially recent efforts to establish intermediaries and other kinds of passed-on price insurance, exemplifies this turn to "inclusive liberalism," a political effort to relegitimize the orthodox vision of agricultural development while maintaining the original neoliberal core.

Derivatives for development also helps to solidify already close relationships between international development institutions and powerful private interests, generating new sources of legitimacy and support for the development establishment from the private sector. While the World Bank usually works closely with private financial institutions—the World Bank really is a bank and works closely with private financial firms particularly on matters of client debt rescheduling—partnerships and collaborations in the derivatives context provide opportunities to forge new business relationships and cooperative ventures. As mentioned in Chapter 2, the World Bank has recently begun working with JP Morgan to provide derivatives products to its clients. There are plans to extend this program in the future to include other large derivatives providers. Chapter 3 discussed various intermediation efforts undertaken by the World Bank, often in conjunction with private financial services providers.

UNCTAD too appears to be positioning itself closely to some big financial players in the derivatives context. The following quote is taken from a recent report from UNCTAD, coauthored by the Swiss Futures and Options Association, and based upon the proceedings of the Emerging Markets Forum at the 2006 International Bürgenstock Conference, a prominent international gathering of global derivatives industry experts. I quote the report at length as it exposes the uncomfortably close, "friendly" relationship between UNCTAD and the derivatives industry, despite UNCTAD's assertions of its "impartiality" on the matter of expanding commodity exchanges in the South:

> As an international organization with considerable accumulated knowledge of commodity sector development, UNCTAD is ideally placed to overcome the trust gap that often still exists between the public and private sectors in developing countries and which hinders investments in trade-related institutions. An organization like UNCTAD brings a measure of impartiality to the discussion on the use of modern risk management and financing tools, and thus helps potential users of these tools to feel more comfortable about such use. Its role is really that of an "honest broker," informing those active in the commodity sector of the new possibilities open to them, assisting in the evaluation of the benefits of new tools and the implications of their use... UNCTAD will continue actively supporting the development of commodity exchanges in interested countries, with a particular focus on the introduction of new instruments that can boost agricultural growth and reduce rural poverty.... There are many further opportunities out there which are yet to be realized and much poverty that could be alleviated if only decision-makers know how to utilize modern financial tools for managing commodity production and trade, particularly the commodity exchange. With the continued support of our stakeholders in government and friends in the industry, we will stand for a brighter future in this domain.

Along similar lines, there is some evidence of crossover in employment between the development establishment and the derivatives industry. As of the date of this writing in March 2012, the managing director of the Indian Multi-Commodity Exchange (MCX) is a former employee of the World Bank and UNCTAD. He also sits on the Board of Directors of Bourse Africa, the new commodity exchange headquartered in Botswana and promoted by the Financial Technologies Group that works out of India.[53] The CEO of the new Ethiopian Commodity Exchange also worked formerly as a senior economist for the World Bank and for the UN, and also previously directed the International Food Policy Research Institute, a prominent development think tank located in Washington DC.[54] This crossover might be considered evidence of the orientation of new Southern exchanges to the development needs of local actors, but at the same time it casts doubt on the impartiality of derivatives recommendations and illustrates how derivatives advocacy has pushed international development organizations into closer relations with powerful private financial firms.

Taken together, these ideological prejudices and political strategies restrict and limit consideration of policy alternatives and lead to policy recommendations that are divorced from the underlying realities of agricultural production. In the specific case of derivatives and coffee, it would seem that these factors contribute to a general tendency among advocates to overlook the growing body of empirical evidence that points to serious problems with derivatives-based programs for coffee smallholders, to ignore the probable and devastating unintended consequences that derive from integrating derivatives into development and encouraging their expansion, and to dismiss workable alternatives.

Indeed, there are many innovative and imaginative solutions to the price risk problem that combine price risk management with other mechanisms that address some of the underlying causes of coffee farmer poverty. Of course, no single one of these solutions is appropriate in every context; nor will any one solution magically heal the global coffee economy's ailments. Rather, policymakers will likely have to consider a large variety of alternative solutions, and how these might be integrated with one another, setting the stage for a coffee economy that is just and remunerative for all.

The Alternatives

The inadequacy of derivatives-based solutions in the coffee context strongly suggests that policymakers and researchers consider the alternatives. I do not mean to suggest that derivatives are not useful to certain actors at certain times. Rather, the evidence suggests that derivatives are not very effective tools for smallholders, who are the overwhelming majority of coffee farmers around the world.

As it happens, there are a variety of alternatives that policymakers may want to consider in addition to, or instead of, derivatives and the other market-oriented, fee-based alternatives suggested by the market access agenda. In the remainder of this section, I spotlight five price risk management arrangements that may better work for coffee smallholders. Some of these arrangements also carry significant benefits for governments who depend on coffee sales for export and tax revenues. Also important is that each of these alternatives, in addition to mitigating or preventing coffee price risk, also addresses some of the underlying causes of coffee farmer poverty such as oversupply, inequalities in wealth and power in coffee production and distribution, long-term declines in coffee prices, and fierce competition among producers. This section in no way exhausts the possibilities, nor does it offer a comprehensive analysis of the alternatives, but is simply designed to present innovative and imaginative options that seem to deserve more attention from the development community than they currently receive.

Supply Management

Despite opposition from the mainstream, supply management for coffee—involving cooperative efforts to restrict global coffee supplies—has produced results in the past and has garnered interest from coffee-producing states periodically since the fall of the ICA in 1989. As noted in chapters 3 and 4, researchers have found that the ICA, with its system of international coffee quotas and domestic marketing boards, did work to raise and stabilize prices. The FAO notes that international collaboration to restrict supplies via such commodity agreements worked well for coffee, even if the arrangement failed in other commodity contexts (e.g. sugar, rubber, cocoa, tin).[55] In addition, the ICA regime worked to stabilize and raise government export and tax revenues, particularly for the most coffee-dependent states, generating significant macroeconomic benefits alongside those for farmers.

In the context of the discussion of monopolization in Chapter 4, supply management creates new monopolies upstream along the coffee chain to counterbalance the power of monopolistic firms further downstream. In this manner, farmers may be able to get higher and more stable prices for their crops in both the short- and long-term. Specifically, governments insert themselves into the coffee chain between producers and the world market. To the extent that governments represent the interests of their farmers, the countermonopoly established by the public can make price negotiation and market access less difficult for smallholders. Recall that scholars found that the ICA did serve to balance, even if only partially, the power of corporate consumers from the North.

It is also important for policymakers to note that supply management is largely incompatible with derivatives-based risk management schemes. This strategy involves government determination of prices, and derivatives traders would likely shy away from trading in such an environment. It may also be the case that the derivatives industry, in the future, comes to be a powerful opponent of supply management, as new exchanges are established, profits from speculative derivatives trading soar, and firms come to rely on derivatives-based risk management strategies.

While some have pointed to the inefficiencies associated with supply management systems, systems in which prices are raised above their "natural" equilibrium price and in which public officials are given incentives for rent-seeking,[56] others suggest that the primary obstacle to pursuing supply management currently is not economic, but political. The FAO, for example, argues that new commodity agreements face two major sets of problems: technical and political. On the technical side, producing countries might need assistance in designing and initially financing a supply management arrangement (e.g. initial buffer stocks might need financing, among other aspects of the scheme). On the political side, "designing workable supply management mechanisms and maintaining the continuing commitment of the parties to the discipline of an agreement are problematic, and free-rider problems persist with those suppliers outside the agreement."[57] Free-riding, which occurs when nonmembers to an agreement take advantage of the high prices established by members, or when members cheat on their commitments, undermined efforts to manage supplies in 2001 by the Association of Coffee Producing Countries (ACPC). As prices fell during the 1998–2002 coffee crisis, 19 producing countries agreed to retain 20 percent of their supplies in a bid to raise coffee prices above US$0.95 per pound. The FAO reports that "only Brazil, Colombia, Costa Rica, and, temporarily, Vietnam cooperated," with other countries retaining minimal or no supplies at all. For this reason, the FAO notes that a "high degree of commitment must exist" among a relatively large proportion of coffee-producing states for an agreement of this sort to be viable.[58]

The political will of consuming countries is also lacking in this context. As mentioned previously, the commitment of the United States to the ICA was critical to the success of the agreement because the United States is the world's largest coffee consumer and its participation encouraged other coffee-consuming states to join the agreement. Without the participation of consumers, there is a higher risk of free-riding, that is, cheating, as producers can ship however much coffee they choose to consumers without sanction. Lack of support from the global North leads the FAO to argue that: "The manipulation of commodity prices based on the management of supply appears to be regarded with some degree of skepticism, at least by the consuming countries, partly because previous attempts have proved to be ineffective and unsustainable, and partly because many countries, the developed consuming nations in particular, are no longer prepared to support them."[59]

Further, there is also political opposition to a new agreement from some of the large Northern multinationals that govern the coffee chain. A 2001 report from Oxfam relates the opinions of the world's four largest coffee roasters on reinstating a supply management regime. Kraft, Sara Lee, and Procter & Gamble each expressed their strong opposition to "price interference."[60] Interestingly, Nestlé was found to be in favor of supply management due to the fact that a large proportion of the company's coffee business is in instant coffee. Instant coffee production is very capital intensive and green coffee beans make up only a small proportion of overall costs. For this reason, price stability is cited as more important by the roaster than low prices. In fact, Nestlé is sometimes at a disadvantage when prices fall because competitors can slash prices more dramatically.[61]

Currently, there is a renewed interest in supply management as a consequence of the global food crisis. With prices rising so rapidly, public officials in North and South face enormous political pressure to reduce prices and mitigate future price increases. Some researchers have seized on the urgency of the situation, recommending decisive action to cooperatively manage global food supplies. In a presentation at a 2010 UNDP conference on the food crisis, Nissanke argues, "The failure of the earlier ICAs [international commodity agreements] should not be an excuse for non-action now."[62] In the context of food crops, and recognizing the role that commodity speculators have played in generating recent volatility, Nissanke argues for the international establishment of both real and virtual buffer stocks of grains, such that global price volatility in both cash and futures markets might be curbed via selective accumulation and release of these stockpiles.[63] Ghosh agrees that management of food price volatility "requires international arrangements and co-operative interventions, such as strategic grain reserves, commodity boards and other measures to stabilise world trade prices." In a slightly different vein, Ussher argues for the creation of an international commodity fund that would oversee global commodity supplies in the context of developing and maintaining a global commodity reserve currency. This proposal, based on the earlier work of Nicholas Kaldor, would merge commodity price stabilization via supply management with mechanisms for stimulating full employment and macroeconomic stabilization (i.e. balance of payments).[64] Whether or not such recommendations are extended to the range of commodities, to include nonfood crops like coffee, remains to be seen (Ussher's proposal already includes coffee).

Intellectual Property Challenges

For over a decade, the international community has bickered about intellectual property rights (IPRs) and their global enforcement. Traditionally, it has been the rich countries who have lobbied for trade agreements in which poorer countries are required to monitor and enforce IPRs granted in the rich countries. Recent negotiations at the WTO about "trade-related intellectual property rights" (TRIPs) have stalled due to the North—South cleavage on this issue. Often framed with reference to antiretroviral therapies (ARVs) used by people suffering from HIV/AIDS (human immunodeficiency virus/acquired immunodeficiency syndrome), Southern negotiators have argued that preserving the IPRs of Northern pharmaceutical corporations comes at the horrific cost of denying generic ARVs to the growing Southern population that is seropositive or lives with AIDS. Even in more trivial contexts, the IPR issue has resulted in heated international exchanges, for example, when the Motion Picture Association of America recently tried to get the Government of China to better enforce copyright protections among purveyors of bootlegged movies.

Recent moves by the government of Ethiopia somewhat turns the matter on its head. Taking a page from the playbooks of the rich countries, the Government of Ethiopia recently filed for trademark protection in the US Patent Office in an attempt to squeeze more money from the multinational coffee retailer Starbucks on behalf of Ethiopian coffee farmers. This case illustrates another potential means by which policymakers may secure higher and more stable prices for coffee farmers, while simultaneously counterbalancing the market power of multinationals downstream. As most introductory microeconomic textbooks note, intellectual property rights, such as trademarks, patents, and copyrights, have long been used to secure monopoly power and are a powerful way for producers to extract higher prices from consumers.

Prior to 2005, Starbucks, one of the largest US coffee retailers, had been marketing several "special origin" coffees from Ethiopia—Sidamo, Harar, and Yirgacheffe. *Fortune* reports that Ethiopian coffee farmers received a mere US$1 per pound for Shirkina Sun-Dried Sidamo coffee, a product that fetched US$26 per pound in Starbucks retail outlets.[65] Other special origin Ethiopian beans were also subject to enormous mark-ups, with farmers receiving very little from the retailer.

In 2005, the Government of Ethiopia's Intellectual Property Office filed for three trademarks, one for each coffee origin, with the US Patent Office in a bid to get Starbucks to pay farmers more for their coffee. "It was an attempt to use tools usually reserved for corporations in developed economies to wrest profit from their distributors. By seizing control of these brands, the Ethiopian government planned to force those who sell its coffee into licensing agreements, eventually obtaining a larger share of the sales."[66] In a testament to the political power of the largest coffee players, the trademarking initiative was foiled when a lobbying group, the National Coffee Association of USA, brought significant pressure to bear on US patent authorities.[67]

Despite only limited success with the trademarking initiative, the public scandal that followed (protests were led by Oxfam) was successful in raising prices for Ethiopian growers. Starbucks, facing the public outcry, voluntarily signed a licensing agreement that involves paying higher prices for these special origin coffees, prices that are stable over the duration of the agreement.

Arslan and Reicher find that the increases in prices following the agreement between Starbucks and the Ethiopian Government were positive and statistically significant, estimated at about 7–15 percent.[68]

The Government of Jamaica has also successfully employed IPRs to protect the prices received by growers and counterbalance the power of traders, roasters, and retailers downstream. The Coffee Industry Board of Jamaica (CIB) is responsible for overseeing and enforcing the use of its two trademarked special origin coffees: Jamaica Blue Mountain® and Jamaica High Mountain Supreme®. The CIB is responsible for licensing hullers, roasters, and domestic dealers, with only properly licensed firms permitted to process and market these coffees abroad. The board also generally ensures "the integrity of the brand" and undertakes advertising and promotional work to support the specialty coffee industry.[69]

While not yet pursuing trademarks, the Coffee Board of Kenya in 2010 embarked on a program to brand Kenyan coffees. Taking another page from the playbook of Northern multinationals and the successes of producers in Colombia (more below), the board aimed at creating an identifiable logo and image that represents and symbolizes Kenyan coffees in the minds of consumers that in turn will help augment prices for farmers over the long term. The branding initiative in Kenya was funded by the European Union at a cost of 500 million Kenyan shillings.[70]

Trademarking and branding coffees in this way supports price risk management and other coffee development goals. By public scandal or by legal protections, IPRs can be utilized by policymakers and governments to secure higher and more stable prices for farmers by facilitating licensing agreements with traders, roasters, and retailers. Higher coffee prices for farmers mean greater tax and export revenues for governments as well. As with supply management, such strategies additionally confer more leverage and negotiating power on producers and producing governments, counterbalancing to some degree the influence of monopolists downstream. There are a variety of high-quality, special origin coffees that are not presently trademarked for which IPR strategies might be viable. For example, high-quality coffees from Sumatra in Indonesia, from the Kenyan highlands, as well as some of those from Mexico may qualify for trademarking in the future.

That said, IPR-based strategies are likely not viable for many coffee producers and coffee-producing governments. Gaining leverage from trademarking requires that coffees be of an especially high quality and in relatively high demand in Northern markets. While such strategies may work for already famous and popular coffees, like the very fine varieties from Ethiopia and Jamaica referenced above, they are less tenable for producers of lower-quality beans, which are generally purchased and roasted in large batches without regard to their origin. For example, Robusta coffees and Brazilian Arabicas, both of generally lower quality by global standards, would not likely benefit from IPR strategies. Branding, which does not necessarily require high quality nor that producers satisfy a variety of trademarking rules (dependent on the jurisdiction where a trademark is sought), may be a viable option for a broader range of coffees.

Producer Unionization

The market access agenda does reference, to some extent, the importance of cooperative producer organization for finance and marketing purposes. However, there is a potentially much larger role that could be played by producer unions that undertake a wide range of activities, both economic *and* political, on behalf of member farmers. While the cooperatives recommended in the market access agenda are limited in their role and function, the Colombian coffee sector provides an interesting example of the potential for producer organizations to serve a variety of roles and to counterbalance the power of multinational consumers downstream.

The National Federation of Coffee Growers of Colombia (FNC), founded in the 1920s, is a nonprofit organization that represents over 500,000 coffee-producing families across the country and aims to "represent them both nationally, and internationally defend their rights and seek ways to improve their quality of life."[71] The organization is run democratically, with municipal, regional, and national representatives to the National Congress of Coffee Growers elected periodically by members. The National Coffee Committee, representing the Congress and comprised of members of the FNC Board of Directors, meets regularly with officials from the Colombian government to draft domestic coffee policy and "directs the representation of Colombian coffee grower's interests in the international arena."[72]

The crucial political role that could be played by producer organizations, exemplified in the Colombian context, is not an aspect of cooperative organization sufficiently emphasized in the mainstream development literature. The FNC does not merely negotiate with exporters and international traders, as with most marketing cooperatives. Nor does it merely facilitate access to credit markets, as with finance cooperatives. The FNC performs these tasks, and many others besides, but also provides a vehicle for political voice and participation by growers who might otherwise be too poor and too small to be taken seriously by government and the international community.

In addition to political representation domestically and internationally, the FNC provides a number of other services for its members. At the farm level, the FNC assists growers in being competitive, meeting international quality standards, and getting remunerative prices for their crop. The FNC operates a research center and an extension services program that provide growers with technical assistance maintaining and planting trees, and with international certification and meeting quality standards. It also assists farmers in adding value to their crop by introducing limited coffee-processing technologies (e.g. to wash the beans before export, allowing for higher prices). The FNC also facilitates access to credit markets and cheap fertilizers.

In addition, the FNC now offers fixed prices to growers that protect them from international price volatility.[73] Giovanucci describes the price risk management system that prevailed prior to the 1998–2002 coffee crisis: "The NFCG [FNC] holds, as a primary responsibility the transference of a fair market price to coffee growers and guaranteeing the purchase of all coffees offered so long as they comply with the pre-determined quality standards.... Farmers typically receive around 70–75% of the FOB [free on board] price, when selling their coffee through the coop system ... *This is one of the higher rates in the world*."[74] The Colombian system relied on a "stabilization fund" that facilitated saving in boom years such that funds were available to fix prices to farmers during times of falling prices. Giovanucci does note, however, that after 2001–02, the FNC had a difficult time sustaining high fixed prices due to funding problems associated with the coffee crisis (maintaining a fixed price is expensive when global prices are falling). That said, the FNC resumed offering fixed prices to farmers, with the financial assistance of the Colombian Government, in 2008 as global coffee prices fell.[75] (Recall that this is partly due to the slowdown in demand associated with the recession in the North, and partly due to the liquidation of long positions by index speculators.) Bearing on previous discussions, Giovanucci cautions that the price protections provided by the FNC, along with many other services, may be reinforcing coffee dependence and thus farmer vulnerability.[76]

Also related to price risk management, the FNC oversees the promotion and maintenance of the Juan Valdez® trademark and brand. The trademark is cooperatively owned by 20,000 shareholder-growers across Colombia and is one of the most well-recognized coffee brands globally.

The FNCs efforts on "connectivity" aim to link geographically separated smallholders to modern information and communications technologies via "connectivity centers," 68 of which were slated to come online in 2011. Farmers are also provided with identification cards that allow them quick and easy access to FNC services.

At the community level, the FNC undertakes technical training on coffee growing and coffee management, as well as spearheading a host of community development projects. The FNC notes that "in 8 decades these initiatives have reached over 3 million people." The organization has built 12,000 aqueducts, 19,000 classrooms for 188,000 students, 15,000 km of roads serving over

5 million Colombians, and more than 500 hospitals and health centers that serve over 3 million people.[77]

Environmentally, the FNC is active in training farmers in soil and land conservation. The organization has overseen the creation of 450 hectares of "biodiversity corridors" across coffee-growing regions, in addition to planting trees across 65,000 hectares of land and facilitating environmentally friendly certification for 27,000 hectares of land planted with coffee.[78] Cenicafé, the FNC's scientific research center, has also pioneered a technique for washing coffee beans that has reduced water consumption from 40 liters to one liter per unit of washed Arabica beans.

It is hard to say, particularly given the brevity of this discussion, whether or not the Colombian model of producer unionization is viable in other country settings. While the FNC has the advantage of over 80 years of operation, strong support from the Colombian government, and working in a region that supports cultivation of some of the finest coffees in the world—advantages that may not be available in other contexts—the Colombian model nevertheless illustrates the multidimensional benefits obtainable via organization and collective action among smallholders, suggesting that further research and investigation is warranted.

Fairtrade

Markets for ethically traded, organic, bird-friendly (i.e. shade-grown), special origin, and other specialty coffees have generated increasing interest over the past decade or so, particularly given the relatively more secure position of farmers producing for these markets during the coffee crisis. The fact that prices tend to be higher and often more stable in specialty markets (prices are fixed in the case of Fairtrade) recommends the markets as means of protecting the incomes of coffee farmers from the vagaries of the global coffee market.

Fairtrade is an independent, private, nonprofit certification and labeling initiative that incorporates principles of economic, social, and environmental justice. As such, scholars have noted that Fairtrade networks are "counter-hegemonic" and represent "globalization from below."[79] The Fairtrade Labeling Organizations International (FLO) notes that Fairtrade allows farmers "to escape from poverty and provide themselves and their families with a decent standard of living."[80] Among the movement's many goals is to ensure that farmers receive a "fair" or "remunerative" price for their crop, one that covers the "costs of sustainable production." Raynolds, Murray, and Taylor describe the movement as follows: "The Fairtrade movement is an effort to link socially and environmentally conscious consumers in the North with producers engaged in socially progressive and environmentally sound farming in the South."[81] Bacon usefully distinguishes between organic and shade-grown coffees on the one hand and Fairtrade coffees on the other. The former specialty coffees represent efforts to certify the ***production*** process, while the latter represent efforts to certify the *trade* process.[82]

Fairtrade organizations link farmers directly with roasters and other consumers, who pay a fixed price per pound of coffee. The reduction in the number middlemen along the path from field to cup is one way in which Fairtrade coffee networks are able to maintain higher prices for farmers. As of March 2012, the Fairtrade price is US$1.40/pound for washed Arabica beans and US$1.01/pound for washed Robusta beans.[83] If world market prices exceed the Fairtrade price, farmers receive the higher world price. In addition, producers receive a US$0.10/pound premium dedicated to social and community investment, which ultimately helps producers gain access to better financing, community-owned and operated transportation and communications systems, technical assistance, and health and education services.

Currently, the FLO has 20 member labeling organizations in 21 countries that certify the following commodities: coffee, tea, rice, bananas, mangoes, cocoa, cotton, sugar, honey, fruit juice, nuts, fresh fruit, quinoa, herbs, spices, and wine.[84] Almost 1.5 million farmers and workers, represented by over 600 producer organizations in 51 countries, currently reap the benefits of Fairtrade.[85] In the coffee context, however, Fairtrade sales are only a small proportion of the total. In 2005, Fairtrade sales were less than 1 percent of total global coffee production, by volume. Baffes and colleagues note that "differentiated" coffee sales, that is, trade outside of "traditional channels" including fairly traded, organic, and other "niche" coffees, accounted for roughly 6–8 percent of global consumption. They also report that, of the 240,000 60 kg bags of Fairtrade coffee consumed in 2001, over 40 percent was consumed in Germany and the Netherlands.[86]

Figure 5.1 illustrates the trend in Fairtrade Robusta coffee prices since 1989 relative to the price established on LIFFE's Robusta futures market. Please note that Fairtrade prices rise when the London price increases, but do not fall below the minimum price floor established by the FLO.

Fairtrade coffee networks are a recent and relatively successful example of a coffee chain in which roasters, international traders, and exporters along the coffee chain have been replaced by a nonprofit organization that governs the coffee trade with an eye toward fair and stable prices for coffee growers. In an important sense, the Fairtrade system is one in which the for-profit monopolists that govern the traditional coffee chain are replaced by a non-for-profit monopolist in the context of an alternative chain. The Fairtrade coffee commodity chain, like the traditional chain, is characterized by marked

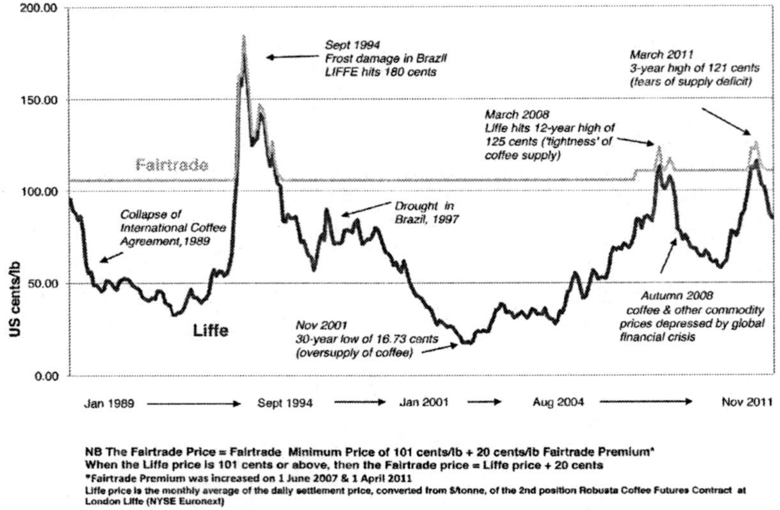

Figure 5.1 Fairtrade Robusta prices relative to future Robusta prices, 1989–2011
Source: Fairtrade Foundation/Fairtrade International, "Robusta Coffee Price Chart," http://www.fairtrade.org.uk/includes/documents/cm_docs/2010/r/robusta_pricechart_89_10_aug10.pdf, accessed December 8, 2011.

levels of concentration insofar as all Fairtrade coffee must first pass through one of several certifying organizations before it reaches the final consumer market.

The Fairtrade system eliminates entirely the need to rely on the coffee derivative chain as it incorporates price risk management into the underlying chain structure. Certification is the process by which coffees are verified by the Fairtrade Labeling Organization (FLO) or one of its affiliates, ensuring that coffees are produced under fair and sustainable conditions and that growers receive the guaranteed minimum price established by the FLO. Relative to derivatives-based price risk management strategies that involve procuring risk management products from financial monopolies, Fairtrade involves reliance on a potentially more beneficent monopolist to act as a marketing channel to Fairtrade consumers and to provide risk management services.

Thus far, Fairtrade has met with real success in maintaining stabilized and relatively high coffee prices for participating growers. In some cases, small farmers excluded from the traditional coffee chain have been able to sell through the Fairtrade chain, realizing more stable and remunerative prices. For example, in Mexico, Calo and Wise find that: "Fair Trade premiums... have proven highly remunerative for those able to sell their coffee in Fair Trade markets, and certification costs are negligible. With prices fixed at levels meant to exceed production costs, Fair Trade premiums have been a lifeline for those able to gain access to this market."[87] Bacon, who pictures Fairtrade as an antidote to problems caused by market concentration along the traditional coffee chain, makes similar findings regarding the stabilizing impact of Fairtrade certification on the livelihoods of small coffee farmers in Nicaragua.[88]

However, some have found that Fairtrade coffee chains are also exclusive to some degree, much like the traditional coffee and coffee derivatives chains. Several researchers report that certification requires not only paperwork but also that coffee be available in sufficient quantities and qualities.[89] For this reason, small farmers that are organized into cooperatives have had more success participating in Fairtrade coffee networks than have unorganized smallholders. That Mexican coffee farmers have a long tradition and history of cooperative organization partly explains their recent successes.

It is also important to note that Fairtrade is not and cannot be a comprehensive solution to the problems that smallholder coffee farmers face. Put simply, it is unlikely that all coffee farmers can be Fairtrade farmers. At some point, as more coffee farmers enter the Fairtrade market, it will become difficult to maintain the higher Fairtrade price unless demand increases significantly. That said, there are potentially a variety of steps that policymakers could take to make Fairtrade markets more accessible for smallholders. Specifically, policymakers' support for cooperative organization, provision of extension services to assist in meeting certification requirements, and promotion of Fairtrade products could all assist in expanding opportunities for small farmers.

Disengagement and Diversification

The last type of strategy, disengagement and diversification, involves creating opportunities for and encouraging small coffee producers to participate in more decentralized and deglobalized commodity chains that are less subject to monopolistic control, price volatility, and fierce competition. As many researchers have pointed out, globalized systems of commodity production frequently lend themselves to monopolization. As production becomes more geographically fragmented, large and sophisticated multinational firms are in a better position than others to organize, monitor, control, and profit from production processes that span large geographic distances. Economic geographer Peter Dicken notes that in a globalized economy, transnational corporations have distinct advantages in that they can "coordinate and control various processes and transactions within transnational production networks," "take advantages of geographical differences in the distribution of factors of production," and "switch and reswitch resources and operations between locations."[90] Further, globalized and liberalized commodity markets are generally characterized by high levels of market volatility. The relationship between monopolization, volatility, and globalization potentially recommends participation in local alternative chains as a means of protecting coffee farmers from global competition, price volatility, and exclusion and manipulation by global coffee monopolies.

Along these lines, Bello comments extensively on the work of Via Campesina, a global political and social organization dedicated to improving the lives of the global peasantry and reforming the global agricultural system. Along with political resistance and protest geared toward delegitimizing the current neoliberal agricultural regime, Via Campesina articulates an alternative vision of the global food system called "food sovereignty." Focusing on production of food items for local consumption, the food sovereignty vision incorporates ideas of land justice, democratic participation, the subjection of food production to social needs rather than profit logics, "valorizing peasant knowledge," and a balance between agriculture and industry.[91] Focus on the Global South, a nonprofit think tank and policy research organization, associates Via Campesina's vision with the process of "deglobalization." Deglobalization involves "making production for the domestic market, rather than production for export, the center of gravity for agriculture" and "using trade policy to protect local agriculture from destruction."[92]

In the coffee context, disengaging from monopoly by encouraging coffee smallholders to engage in food production for local consumption has several advantages. Those peasants who "switch" to local food production may enjoy more stable prices, less exclusive markets for their products, and fewer dealings with monopolists. Further, smallholders would have food to eat if and when volatility and exclusion became problematic in local markets and result in falling cash incomes (many small coffee producers today go hungry when relative prices change, for example, when coffee prices fall relative to food prices). Further, moving farmers out of coffee reduces supplies on the coffee market, potentially reducing competitive and price pressures along the coffee chain itself. Ponte notes that the International Coffee Organization has recently been considering "quality" initiatives that would remove inferior coffees from the global market.[93] It is possible that these quality initiatives could be productively complemented with efforts to promote local food production.

Disengagement and deglobalization may also generate positive spillovers in the context of the ongoing food crisis. Greater emphasis on local food production can work to reduce the negative impact of high global prices on the urban poor, who no longer have to rely on global food systems for nourishment. Locally produced food carries the further benefit of not saddling governments with rising import bills when global food prices rise, as they have recently. Ghosh notes that generally "Countries in which a very large proportion of the basic food requirement is met through domestic supply (China, India) are therefore less likely to experience the volatility *if* they have in place adequate institutional arrangements to ensure domestic production and distribution."[94] Stimulating diversification toward local food production thus not only benefits coffee farmers, who are more removed from the price dynamics and power plays that characterize the global market, but also benefits local food markets and the urban poor.

While, in theory, derivatives-based risk management schemes could be employed alongside diversification/deglobalization schemes—with different kinds of producers participating in different schemes—the spirit of the two models are not at all commensurable. The vision of the global agricultural system promoted by Bello, Vía Campesina, and Focus on the Global South, among others, pictures systems of local food production for local consumption that are almost completely separated from global markets. The notion of "sovereignty" in agricultural production militates against agricultural risk management systems in which poor smallholders must depend on for-profit financial MNCs for their safety and security. Shiva, another prominent advocate of deglobalization and diversity in agricultural production, recognizes that some crops (like coffee perhaps) are necessarily global in nature and may not fit neatly into such a model, given that they are produced in one region of the world and consumed largely in another. She argues that Fairtrade is the proper global counterpart to localized food production systems, because each have in mind the health of the Earth and the livelihoods of smallholders, priorities much less visible in the derivatives context.[95]

Conclusion

Derivatives for development represent an important departure from the previous agricultural orthodoxy, the Washington Consensus on Agriculture. Rather than overlooking the plight of smallholders confronting policy liberalization and market globalization as in the past, derivatives advocates have turned their gaze squarely to small farmers and are attempting to craft policies and programs that specifically target this community.

Yet, despite this new orientation, derivatives recommendations, and the market access agenda of which they are a part, retain many of the old biases and prejudices that characterized the WCA. In the face of mounting evidence of the shortcomings and dangers of derivatives in the agricultural development context, derivatives advocates nevertheless hold fast to market-based policies and programs based on high technologies that meet their political needs and validate their ideological leanings. Indeed, while the benefits of derivatives for smallholders are far from clear, it does appear that derivatives advocacy is highly politically advantageous for advocates. Derivatives markets allow for continued adherence to the agricultural status quo, all the while quelling criticism and generating new sources of political legitimacy from powerful private interests.

One of the biggest costs of this kind of "inclusive liberalism"—liberalism that consolidates its global dominance by superficially reaching out to marginalized communities and peoples—is the closure of the policy space available for thinking about alternatives. As the dominant agricultural vision comes to appear "softer," more "inclusive," and "caring," its political legitimacy is enhanced and viable alternatives based on different priorities and visions are pushed to the margins of policy discourse.

This is all the more dangerous given that imaginative, interesting, and viable alternatives do exist in the coffee context. Supply management, intellectual property challenges, Fairtrade, producer unionization, and deglobalization, representing only a few of many innovative alternatives, give us a glimpse of the other worlds of coffee that are possible. It is critical that policymakers look beyond the veneer of inclusion offered by derivatives-based solutions and seriously consider other programs and policies that may more consistently work to assist small coffee farmers.

CHAPTER 6

Conclusions

No society can surely be flourishing and happy, of which the far greater part of the members are poor and miserable. It is but equity, besides, that they who feed, cloath and lodge the whole body of the people, should have such a share of the produce of their own labor as to be themselves tolerably well fed, cloathed and lodged.[1]

Like so many small farmers today, small coffee farmers face serious challenges to their well-being and survival. Some of these challenges, price risk among them, have intensified with the globalization, liberalization, commercialization, and financialization of the world's food systems over the past several decades. Periodic, catastrophic price crises, along with short-term volatility and long-term declines in coffee prices, compromise farmers' access to food, water, shelter, fuel, medicine, education, and investment opportunity, eroding the freedom of farmers and their families to live decent, happy, and healthy lives.

In some respects, recommendations that derivatives be used as antipoverty tools in this context are bewildering. Ceding the well-being of poor farm families to often inefficient and always volatile financial markets defies popular understanding of terms like "security" and "risk management." Deploying complex and expensive financial instruments in contexts where individuals and families have poor access to information and training and often cannot afford to purchase basic necessities to some extent involves turning a blind eye to the exigencies of small farm life in the developing world. Placing small coffee farmers, who already face enormous pressures from powerful roasters and traders, into another context where they also must navigate the rules and standards established by powerful Northern multinationals seems potentially dangerous. In the contexts of the global food crisis and the Great Recession, deployment of derivatives as development tools is also questionable, given the role that these instruments played (and continue to play) in facilitating market volatility and financial insecurity.

Despite the good intentions of researchers and policymakers, the evidence generally suggests that derivatives are inappropriate tools for comprehensively and systematically addressing coffee farmer price risk. While coffee price risk has significant long-term dimensions, derivatives offer only short-term solutions. While effective hedging requires efficient markets, futures and options markets are plagued by predictive deficiencies and speculative excesses. While small farmers likely require risk management tools that are cheap (or free), easily scaled down to take account of their small lot sizes, and operable without extensive and expensive training, derivatives exchanges offer products tailored to the needs of the largest, wealthiest, and most technically savvy traders.

This mismatch, between the nature of the problem and the character of the tool, is compounded by the superficial treatment of commodity price risk that derivative instruments offer. As with many problems in the global food system, coffee price dynamics and the vulnerability of small farmers to them are rooted in broad and complex historical processes underpinned by a radically unequal global distribution of wealth and power. Market liberalization and globalization, reduced government expenditure and assistance to agriculture, dominance of agribusiness, commodity dependence, fierce global competition, and market oversupply are, at least in part, consequences of gross maldistributions of resources and influence across North and South, empire and colony, core and periphery, monopolists and competitive producers, and agribusiness and the peasantry. Derivatives do nothing to address these inequalities and the array of hardships that stem from them, nor do proponents of derivatives for development acknowledge the key role played by such dynamics in the context of farm-level poverty.

To the contrary, derivatives work through various mechanisms to enhance and aggravate these maldistributions. Uneven access to risk management tools in a volatile market setting is one conduit. That derivatives provide new business opportunities for some actors along the coffee chain, those that already command the lion's share of profits and power, and not for others like small farmers provides a further mechanism for widening inequalities. Another derives from the tendency for derivatives market volatility to spill over into cash markets, resulting in a scenario where the profits of derivatives traders, brokers, exchanges, and clearinghouses come at the cost of volatile food and crop prices for the rural and urban poor.

Yet, when viewed from a different angle, it is decidedly unsurprising that derivatives have come to and remain at the forefront of debates about insecurity and risk management in the development context. The foregoing chapters illustrated that derivatives display a variety of other highly desirable characteristics independent of their usefulness for small farmers and applicability in solving problems of poverty and insecurity in rural communities. Derivatives are market-based solutions to the producer price risk problem that generally conform to the broader neoliberal orientation that characterizes the development mainstream. The instruments reinforce and support the mainstream emphasis on liberalization, globalization, and commercial crop production for export in the agricultural context, all the while allowing for a more caring and "inclusive" orientation toward the global peasantry. Derivatives appeal to the belief that technological innovation holds the key to development, a sentiment that is particularly strongly held with regard to agriculture, where Green Revolutions and cutting-edge technologies have historically been praised as the keys to agricultural success.

The expansion of derivatives markets across the global South and their integration into development agendas also promote the interests of powerful private financial firms and extends the reach of formal financial markets, consistent with the broader global process of financialization. The apparent marriage of financial interests with development interests, in the context of derivatives for small farmers, further creates opportunities for new political alliances and helps the international development establishment cultivate new sources of political legitimacy.

Indeed, derivatives are not merely experimental tools for rural poverty alleviation. They are also political and ideological instruments deployed by international development institutions in the interests of policy consistency, political legitimacy, and the retention of long-held beliefs in the benefits of free markets and advanced technologies for agricultural development. The political and ideological character of derivatives in the development context have at least two consequences that give reason for real concern. First, the political and ideological usefulness of derivatives for the development establishment has led empirical evidence that counters the enthusiasm of advocates—for example, evidence regarding market inefficiency, market access, the thus-far unenviable track record of many intermediaries, and unintended consequences—to be downplayed or ignored. Thus, derivatives continue to be recommended in the face of growing evidence of their inadequacy and inappropriateness as development tools.

Second, and related to the first point, the political and ideological character of derivatives has resulted in a reluctance, and in some cases an inability, to consider alternatives that fall outside the neoliberal umbrella. Alternatives that require government intervention (such as supply management), alternatives that require localization and disengagement from the global market (such as de-globalization strategies), and alternatives that address inequalities in wealth and power by counterbalancing coffee monopolies (like producer unionization and intellectual property challenges) are all variously discounted or overlooked.

In other words, when stripped of their political utility and ideological appeal, derivatives are revealed as instruments poorly configured to meet the urgent needs of small coffee farmers confronting volatile markets. What is more, the political and ideological attraction to derivatives among advocates works as a fig-leaf of sorts to conceal in mainstream analyses the dangers to small farmers posed by global expansion of derivatives markets and their integration into development agendas. What other possible worlds of coffee are obscured by this veil?

Several empirical conclusions drawn throughout the book bear repeating here, given their potential impact on policymaking. First, and speaking to one of the great ironies of the modern-day growth and expansion of derivatives markets, is that those who are touted as the primary beneficiaries of this trend—smallholder farmers and other small local actors—appear upon closer analysis among those least likely to systematically gain. In fact, the only clear winners from integrating derivatives into development that I have been able to discern from the foregoing analysis is the derivatives industry itself, those actors along the coffee chain sufficiently wealthy, powerful, large, and technically savvy to venture into the markets, and the mainstream development institutions that are recommending the instruments.

It is true that under the right conditions, farmers and other small local players may be able to effectively use derivatives on an intermittent basis, or, more permanently with the right kind of intermediary. It is even more likely that governments of commodity-dependent countries can use the instruments to their advantage, potentially trading futures and options to manage short-term fluctuations in export and tax revenues and issuing commodity-linked bonds to finance various expenditures.

Yet, the benefits even to Southern governments of expanding and deepening derivatives markets are not clear-cut and are certainly not guaranteed. The inefficiencies and short-termism that plague agricultural commodity derivatives markets are problematic for governments looking to hedge price risk, just as they are for individual farmers. The potential for speculative transactions in derivatives markets to generate volatility in cash markets is also an issue that warrants concern from government officials. Particularly troubling in this context is the likelihood that local commodity exchanges will have to allow significant speculative activity, probably foreign speculators in addition to local ones, to generate sufficient market liquidity to sustain the exchange.

Second, establishing and maintaining derivatives markets is an expensive and difficult undertaking. Despite constant assertions that derivatives represent a "non-interventionist" approach to price risk management and that they require relatively little public spending, in reality Southern governments are, and will continue to, spend scarce resources on regulation and monitoring, promotion and sponsorship of new exchanges, and licensing, among other ongoing financial obligations. And, given the trend toward merger and partnership between already-established and new exchanges, as well as the tendency for the markets to be heavily populated by Northern speculators where regulations allow, it is likely that scarce public funds from the South will leak out toward the North, as Northern firms utilize Southern markets for personal gain.

In addition to these expenses, hooking small farmers up to derivatives markets via intermediaries appears to require government support of some kind. The most successful intermediary discussed in Chapter 3, at least in terms of project duration, is the ASERCA program, a facility funded and administered by the Government of Mexico. This is hardly the nongovernmental approach advertised by derivatives advocates. As also mentioned in that chapter, there is a growing recognition that private intermediaries (such as local banks or exporters who pass on price insurance to farmers) will require some kind of incentive to perform this service. This implies that subsidization, tax concessions, or other costly inducements will be required of Southern governments.

Along these lines, there is also reason to believe that retooling derivatives markets such that they better match the price risk problem producers face will require government intervention. Ronald McKinnon, one of the earliest advocates of substituting derivatives markets for publicly operated buffer stock programs, argues that this proposal is only workable where there are "distant" futures markets. Absent the independent formation of private markets that extend sufficiently far forward, he suggests that government will have to act as a market-maker, taking up long positions to match short positions by farmers. However, this would not be a costless undertaking.

Third, derivative-based solutions to price risk management problems do not adequately address the underlying factors that drive farming communities to poverty. In fact, derivatives may actually work at cross-purposes with development goals. This is the case, for example, as derivatives deepen inequalities along the coffee commodity chain, to the detriment of smallholders. This is also the case, as another example, where the protection afforded by derivatives encourages continued specialization and dependence on coffee production for export. In addition to reinforcing commodity dependence, this may also contribute to long-term declines in coffee prices. Evaluating coffee price risk solutions requires a broader framework and understanding of poverty than that which is currently embedded in the recommendations of derivatives proponents, lest derivatives undermine other important development goals and poverty-alleviation efforts.

Last, viable alternatives to derivatives do exist, despite their being downplayed in the mainstream. Critically, the alternatives spotlighted in Chapter 5 not only address price risk but also variously address underlying contributors to farmer poverty, vulnerability, and disempowerment (such as market oversupply, commodity dependence, market power imbalances, and poor political representation). Policymakers may also want to consider the compatibility of derivatives with these alternative strategies. The evidence presented throughout suggests that derivatives are not a stand-alone strategy for price risk management, and, at the very least, will need to be complemented by other programs and policies. It would be unfortunate if, by accepting the derivatives solution, officials closed off the opportunity to pursue other viable alternatives. For example, as derivatives markets become more embedded, it may be more difficult, politically and economically, to pursue supply management strategies.

In the context of supply management, policymakers may be able to seize on the political momentum generated by the food price crisis in order to forge a new consensus and alliances among Southern governments and between North and South. Intellectual property challenges may also come with the benefit of having some existing political momentum. IPRs have for over a decade been advocated by Northern states, core firms, and mainstream international development organizations. Employing these same tools to assist poor coffee farmers may thus come with a preexisting benediction from existing centers of global power. While arguably the most radical of the alternatives, localization and disengagement strategies may also benefit from the political momentum generated by the ongoing food crisis. The global community is rapidly recognizing that import dependence and the disappearance of subsistence agriculture have undermined food security and antipoverty efforts in many developing countries. Movements toward sustainable food production for domestic consumption may thus have a broader and more receptive audience than at past times. Further, the success of certain countries, like Mexico, with ethical trading networks (Fairtrade), suggests the need for further consideration of such strategies and policy measures to assist producers who would like to participate in the markets. This is also the case with producer unionization, with Colombia providing a successful example of the broad array of functions that a producer union can perform for small farmers.

Looking forward, the foregoing analysis yielded a variety of findings that may illuminate future research and thinking about the politics of insecurity, financialization, globalization, inequality, commodity chains, derivatives, and development. I highlight some of these findings below.

With Polanyi (and with Marx to some extent), many on the Left have argued that a "global politics of insecurity," issuing from the process of globalization and capitalist expansion, is a force that is undermining the neoliberal policy orthodoxy and creating opportunities to forge a new kind of global economy. Individuals, families and communities will only take so much insult and injury to their economic welfare and to social stability—political movements to counter the destabilizing influence of free and volatile markets will arise and push for reform or overturn the existing order. For Polanyi, societies will make moves toward "social self-protection" in the face of massive social destruction by capitalist markets, implementing policies and programs to limit the reign of (and thus damage from) free markets and compensate for their failures and oversights. Polanyi saw this process at work in the manner in which governments and communities responded to the 1930s Great Depression, with the erection of barriers to free trade and capital movements and the creation of new social programs to temper market excess.[2] Marx envisioned a more revolutionary process of change, but also one that was ultimately responsive to the incredible insecurity wrought by capitalist expansion. Capitalism, as it expands, "digs its own grave" by undermining the well-being of those (the proletariat) upon which the system depends. At some critical juncture, the insecurity of proletariat results in revolutionary overthrow of the capitalist system.[3]

For a more modern example of this line of thought, take, for example, the following statement from Gray:

> The central paradox of our time can be stated thus: economic globalization does not strengthen the current regime of global *laissez-faire*. It works to undermine it.... The swift waxing and waning of industries and livelihoods, the sudden shifts of production and capital, the casino of currency speculation—these conditions trigger political counter-movements that challenge the very ground rules of the global free market.[4]

Along these lines, and as discussed in Chapter 5, many have argued that the global food and financial crises are generating the political momentum and policy space required to put in place a new kind of economic and financial policies. Similar arguments have been made regarding the development crisis spawned by the Agricultural Washington Consensus.

The case of derivatives for development suggests that the global politics of insecurity is not necessarily a force for substantive change, in contrast to assertions like those above. Rather than a counterhegemonic force, the politics of insecurity have been to some extent co-opted by the orthodoxy and turned in the interests of *sustaining* the capitalist, neoliberal order in Southern agriculture. The case examined in the foregoing chapters illustrates that the World Bank and UNCTAD, among other segments of the development mainstream, are cognizant of and responsive to the insecurities wrought by globalization of agricultural commodity markets. Yet, the solutions offered to the problem wholly conform with neoliberal ideas about the importance of global markets, the desirability of liberal economic regimes and state nonintervention in the economy, and the key role for advanced technology (here, financial technologies) in propelling progress. In this manner, a global politics of insecurity is transformed from a force for change into a force for stasis. Indeed, the politics of insecurity have provided a context for the creation and consolidation of "inclusive liberalism."

The process of financialization dovetails in interesting ways with consolidation of the inclusive liberal framework in Southern agriculture. The case of derivatives for development illustrates that financialization in the South has been aided by development agencies employing the rhetoric of inclusive liberalism. Specifically, derivatives markets are growing, expanding, and deepening in part because they are conceived and promoted as innovative solutions to the market-generated insecurities confronting peasant farmers. It does not necessarily matter that empirically derivatives markets do not perform this role very well. Ertuk and colleagues quote Wallerstein on this point: "Capitalist civilization has not only been a successful civilization. It has above all been a seductive one. It seduces even its victims and opponents."[5]

Similar to my findings for derivatives for coffee farmers, these authors find in the US and UK cases that the promises of financialization for ordinary people have largely been broken, with large segments of the middle classes in both countries precluded from taking advantage of expanded financial product offerings for a variety of reasons. Ertuk and colleagues ultimately conclude that "democratizing finance" is not really about providing ordinary individuals and families with new products to improve their well-being. Rather, the rhetoric of democratic finance is a means of fostering political support for the substitution of private markets for public risk management arrangements. The authors write: "If we think cynically about the practical effects of the promise of democratized finance, it is not really about how many more at some future date will be provided for through individual saving and investment; rather, it is about changing the agenda so that individual provision becomes more attractive as a substitute to [the] state . . . ."[6] By these lights, what matters is that "democratizing finance" provides political legitimacy for risk privatization, whether or not this process confers real welfare benefits on individuals and families.

Even as democratizing derivatives falls short of its promises to farmers, the market-expanding process it legitimates carries with it real dangers—namely, aggravating global maldistributions of wealth and power, and facilitating greater market volatility and individual insecurity. In this context, the commodity chain framework has proven quite useful as a heuristic, exploratory, and diagnostic tool. In Chapter 4, I employed commodity chains to map the interactions between the "real" and financial economies, between the main (coffee) commodity chain and one ancillary chain (the derivatives chain) that services it. Among the more provocative implications of the analysis, at least for future commodity chain research, is that, in the case of derivatives, it increasingly appears that the "ancillary" chain is leading and the coffee chain is actually subordinate to it in important ways. That future prices increasingly direct cash market behavior is clear evidence to this effect. Too often, logistical, financial, risk management, and other "support" services are considered marginal or contingent, rather than driving global production processes and relationships.

The commodity chain framework also proved to be a useful tool for exploring problems of inequality in the global economy and diagnosing derivatives for development recommendations from this perspective. Not merely heuristic tools, commodity chains can in this way be proactively deployed as evaluative tools in the context of economic and development policy. Specifically, for coffee and derivatives, a commodity chain framework assisted me in thinking about the likely unintended consequences of particular policy recommendations.

The framework further enabled me to think about alternatives to derivatives that would address some of the underlying causes of coffee farmer poverty. If poverty in this context is (at least partially) linked to concentrations of wealth and power along the commodity chain, one way of thinking about antipoverty policies is by conceiving means to alter the structure of the chain—for example, by challenging, substituting for, and disengaging from monopolistic nodes. In contrast to the commodity chain literature on "industrial upgrading," the discussion of price risk management alternatives (Chapter 5) suggests that development policy might also be directed toward altering the structure of the chain itself. Industrial upgrading represents attempts to improve the welfare of actors in marginal nodes of the chain by encouraging them to "upgrade" or move to a different node on the chain where competition is less and profits higher.[7] Implicit in such recommendations is the notion that the chain's structure is given, and that poor participants in it can only better their lot by changing their position within it. Similarly, recommendations are also sometimes given for "attracting" a monopolist to a particular locale, which is thought to generate positive spillovers for local communities who can now work more closely with powerful and profitable firms.[8]

Yet, in the coffee context, the five alternatives highlighted in Chapter 5 each represent an alternative to industrial upgrading that seeks to alter the relative distribution of power and profit along the chain. Intellectual property challenges and producer unions "challenge" the power of monopolistic traders and roasters by counterbalancing their market power with the creation of other monopolies upstream at the producer node. Supply management and Fairtrade represent methods of "substituting for monopoly," as public and nonprofit monopolies, respectively, are substituted for private, for-profit ones. "Disengaging" from monopoly, as with strategies for localization and deglobalization, seeks to remove small farmers from the orbit of the big monopolists, instead encouraging participation in chains where power and profit are less unevenly distributed. These all constitute viable alternatives to industrial upgrading strategies, and suggest potentially new ways of deploying commodity chains in the development policy context.

Notes

Chapter 1

1. R. H. Tawney, *Land and Labor in China* (New York: ME Sharpe, 1966), 77.
2. The World Bank's 2008 *Agriculture for Development: World Development Report* (Washington, DC: World Bank, 2008) estimates that 1.5 billion people from the developing world are smallholder farmers. With a world population of about 6.775 billion in September 2011, and not counting the shrinking small farm population in the United States, Europe, and Japan, this means that more than one in every five people on Earth is a small farmer.
3. Lindsay Stringer, Chasca Twyman, and Leah Gibbs, "Learning from the South," *The Geographic Journal*, 174:3 (2008), 238.
4. Oxfam, "Dumping without Borders" (Oxfam Briefing Paper, August 2003), 5.
5. Oxfam, "Dumping," 8.
6. Aparna Pallavi, "Empty Fields Stare at Farm Widows," *India Together* (August 23, 2007), accessed on November 3, 2011, http://www.indiatogether.org/2007/aug/agr-barefield.htm
7. Michael Pollan, *The Omnivore's Dilemma* (New York: Penguin, 2006).
8. Pollan, *Omnivore's Dilemma*, 53.
9. William Greider, "The Last Farm Crisis," *The Nation* (November 20, 2000), 1.
10. Charis Gresser and Sophia Tickell, *Mugged: Poverty in Your Coffee Cup* (London: Oxfam, 2002), 6.
11. Gresser and Tickell, *Mugged*, 11.
12. See, e.g., John Vidal and Claire Provost, "US Universities in Africa Land-Grab," *The Guardian*, June 8, 2011; Bretton Woods Project, "World Bank Policies 'Enabling' African Land Grab," September 14, 2011; CRBM, "The Vultures of Land Grabbing," 2010, accessed on November 29, 2011, http://farmlandgrab.org/wp-content/uploads/2010/11/VULTURES-completo.pdf.
13. Food price data from the FAO's "food price index," accessed on September 29, 2011, www.fao.org.
14. See Raj Patel's *Stuffed and Starved: The Hidden Battle for the World Food System* (Brooklyn, NY: Melville House, 2008) for a great introduction to the world food system and the challenges it poses for policy.

15. Sara Murray, "Most Food Stamp Recipients Have No Earned Income," *The Wall Street Journal*, September 26, 2011.
16. BIS, "Statistical Annex," *BIS Quarterly Review* (June 2011).
17. PERLS are "principal exchange rate linked securities"; KIKOs are "knock-in knock-out" contracts; and TARNs are "targeted redemption notes." See Frank Partnoy, *FIASCO* (New York: Penguin, 1999); and, Randall Dodd, "Playing with Fire," *Finance and Development*, 46:2 (June 2009).
18. FIA, "Annual Volume Survey: 2010 Record Volume" (March 2011), www.futuresindustry.org.
19. Nelson Schwartz and Julie Creswell, "Who Created This Monster?," *The New York Times*, March 23, 2008.
20. Beat Balzli, "How Goldman Sachs Helped Greece Mask Its True Debt," *Der Spiegel*, February 8, 2010.
21. Robert Shiller, *The New Financial Order* (Princeton, NJ: Princeton University Press, 2003), 1.
22. Indeed, this has already happened. Derivatives on the Case-Shiller housing price indices (20 major residential market indices are available) have been trading on the Chicago Mercantile Exchange for the past several years.
23. UNCTAD, *Commodity Policies for Development* (Geneva: UNCTAD, 2005), 8.
24. ITF, *Lessons Learned* (ITF, 2006), http://www.itf-commrisk.org/itf.asp?page=13, accessed on November 17, 2006; the ITF is no longer in operation.
25. Jacob Hacker, "Privatizing Risk Without Privatizing the Welfare State: The Hidden Politics of Social Welfare Retrenchment in the United States," *American Political Science Review*, 98:2 (2004); "Dismantling the Health Care State? Political Institutions, Public Policies and the Comparative Politics of Health Reform," *British Journal of Political Science*, 34:4 (2004); *The Great Risk Shift* (Oxford: Oxford University Press, 2006); "The Privatization of Risk and the Growing Economic Insecurity of Americans," Social Science Research Council, http://privatizationofrisk.ssrc.org/Hacker/index.html (2006).
26. Karl Polanyi, *The Great Transformation* (Boston: Beacon, 2001), 259.
27. Dick Bryan and Michael Rafferty, *Capitalism with Derivatives* (New York: Palgrave, 2006), 212.
28. John Gray, "From the Great Transformation to the Global Free Market," in *The Globalization Reader*, 3rd ed., eds. Lechner and Boli (Malden, MA: Blackwell, 2008), 25.
29. Gerald Epstein (ed.), *Financialization and the World Economy* (Cheltenham, UK: Edward Elgar, 2005), 3.
30. This term is taken from Walden Bello, *The Food Wars* (London: Verso, 2009).

Chapter 2

1. Michael Savoy in Lamon Rutten, "Going Rural with Smart Finance," *Hindu Business Line*, March 21, 2007.

2. This name is somewhat misleading. Future prices frequently serve as "benchmark" prices that sellers around the world reference in pricing their goods. This implies an opposite meaning to the one embedded in the definition of derivatives. Rather than future prices being derivative, it is cash prices that are frequently the derivative. The relation between spot and future prices is a matter of significant debate and disagreement among economists and financial experts.
3. Some take issue with this distinction. For example, Bryan and Rafferty in *Capitalism with Derivatives* argue that such a distinction is untenable largely because so many derivatives trades contain elements of both hedging and speculation: "Unfortunately, in actual markets, the behavioral differences between the two types of market participants are much harder to delineate. Studies have not only found a range of reasons for (or types of) both hedging and speculation, but, at any point in time, market participants may be engaged in both speculative-type and hedging-type activities . . . " (p. 202).
4. Adam Tickell, "Unstable Futures," in *Global Capitalism versus Democracy*, eds. Panitch and Leys (London: Merlin, 1999), 249.
5. Dick Bryan and Michael Rafferty, *Capitalism with Derivatives* (New York: Palgrave, 2006), 43.
6. See, for example, Randall Dodd, "The Virtues of Prudential Regulation," in *Capital Markets Liberalization and Macroeconomics Overview Book*, eds. Ocampo and Stiglitz (New York: Oxford University Press, 2005), available online at www.financialpolicy.org; Michael Darby, "Over-The-Counter Derivatives and Systemic Risk to the Global Financial System," in *NBER Working Paper Series* (Cambridge, MA: National Bureau of Economic Research, 1994).
7. If Southwest hedged long with futures, the airline would pay the derivatives market when oil prices fall, precluding both losses and gains on the price of oil. If Southwest hedged with options, and oil prices fell, the airline would likely not exercise the option, but would be out the initial premium paid to enter the contract. In this way, hedging serves to *stabilize* incomes, revenues, and/or asset values.
8. Dave Carter, Dan Rogers, and Betty Simkins, "Fuel Hedging in the Airline Industry: The Case of Southwest Airlines," *Case Research Journal* (2004, online article), 3.
9. David Koenig, "Airlines that Hedged against Fuel Costs Reap Benefits," *The Washington Post*, October 21, 2005.
10. Susan Newman, "Financialization and Changes in Social Relations Along Commodity Chains: The Case of Coffee," *Review of Radical Political Economics* 41:4 (2009), 547.
11. Bryan and Rafferty, *Capitalism with Derivatives*, 2.
12. A useful and entertaining primer on pit trading in commodity futures can be found in the movie *Trading Places*, starring Eddie Murphy and Dan Akroyd.
13. Bryan and Rafferty, *Capitalism with Derivatives*, 47.
14. Frank Partnoy, *FIASCO* (New York: Penguin, 1999).

15. Pauline Tiffen and Guido Fernandez, *Report on the BMI-FEDA Hedging Program, El Salvador*, Commodity Risk Management Group at the World Bank (Washington, DC: The World Bank, October 2005); CRMG, "Price Risk Management Work Summary," Commodity Risk Management Group at the World Bank (Washington, DC: The World Bank, May 2005).
16. Thomas Liaw, and Ronald Moy, *The Irwin Guide to Stocks, Bonds, Futures and Options: A Comprehensive Guide to Wall Street's Markets* (New York: McGraw-Hill, 2001), 281.
17. Ibid.
18. Joanne Morrison, "ICE Adds Brazilian Flavor to Coffee Futures Market," *FIA Magazine*, March/April 2011.
19. Jon Gregory, *Counterparty Credit Risk* (West Sussex: John Wiley & Sons, 2010), 7.
20. BIS, "Statistical Annex," *BIS Quarterly Review* (June 2011).
21. CIA World Factbook, "World: Economy," accessed on December 5, 2011, www.cia.gov.
22. FIA, "Annual Volume Survey: 2010 Record Volume" (March 2011), www.futuresindustry.org.
23. ISDA, "Definition: Notional Principal," accessed on December 5, 2011, http://www.isda.org/educat/faqs.html#7.
24. BIS, "Statistical Annex" (June 2011).
25. Adam Gross, "The New Order of Global Derivatives Trading," PowerPoint presentation at FAO International Conference on Commodity Exchanges and their Role in Market Development and Transparency, May 15, 2007, available via UNCTAD website, www.unctad.org.
26. FIA, "2010 Record Volume," *Future Industry* (March 2011) and FIA, "Annual Volume Survey: 2008 A Wild Ride," *Future Industry* (March/April 2009), www.futuresindustry.org.
27. FIA, "2010 Record Volume."
28. BIS, "Statistical Annex" (June 2011).
29. Walden Bello, *The Food Wars* (London: Verso, 2009), Introduction.
30. *Wall Street Journal*, "US Plans Tougher Rules on Commodities," June 4, 2008.
31. Galen Burghardt, "Volume Surges Again," *Futures Industry* (March/April 2008).
32. FIA, "2010 Record Volume."
33. Ibid.
34. Gross, "The New Order of Global Derivatives Trading."
35. Chen Jia, "Focus Turns to Futures Trading as Commodities Surge," *China Daily*, February 10, 2011.
36. See George DeMartino, *Global Economy, Global Justice* (New York: Routledge, 2000); Eric Helleiner, *States and the Reemergence of Global Finance* (Ithaca, NY: Cornell University Press, 1994); Ngaire Woods, *The Globalizers* (Ithaca, NY: Cornell, 2006); Peter Dicken, *Global Shift*, 5th ed. (New York: Guilford, 2007).
37. Leo Melamed, *For Crying Out Loud* (New York: Wiley and Sons, 2009), xiii.
38. BIS, "Statistical Annex" (June 2011); FIA, "2010 Record Volume."

39. Jorge Cardenas, "The World Coffee Crisis," *World Coffee Conference* (London: ICO, 2001), 2.
40. UNCTAD, *Commodity Policies for Development* (Geneva: UNCTAD, 2005), 8.
41. Jerry Markham, *The History of Commodity Futures Trading and Its Regulation* (New York: Prager, 1987), 12.
42. Ibid., 24.
43. Ibid., 110.
44. Ibid., 104.
45. Justin Fox, "Commodity Futures Modernization Act," *Time* (December 31, 2008).
46. Asani Sarkar, "Indian Derivatives Markets," The New York Federal Reserve, http://www.newyorkfed.org/research/economists/sarkar/derivatives_in_india.pdf, accessed on November 3, 2011.
47. Chen Jia, "Fortelling the Future for Profit," *China Daily*, December 1, 2011.
48. Randall Dodd and Stephanie Griffith-Jones, *Report on Chile's Derivatives Markets: Stabilizing or Speculative Impact* (ECLAC, 2006), http://policydialogue.org/files/events/DoddGriffith-Jones_Chiles_derivatives_markets.pdf, accessed on November 3, 2011.
49. Jennifer Clapp and Eric Helleiner, "Troubled Futures," *Review of International Political Economy*, 2010.
50. Nicholas Economides, "The Impact of the Internet on Financial Markets," *Journal of Financial Transformation* 1:1 (2001), 10.
51. Perry Mehrling, *Fischer Black and the Revolutionary Idea of Finance* (Hoboken: John Wiley & Sons, 2005), 9.
52. Alfred Steinherr, *Derivatives: The Wild Beast of Finance* (West Sussex: John Wiley & Sons, 2000), 24.
53. Melamed, *For Crying Out Loud*, xv.
54. Richard Teweles and Frank Jones, *The Futures Game* (New York: McGraw-Hill, 1999), 154.
55. Hélyette Geman, *Commodities and Commodity Derivatives* (West Sussex: John Wiley & Sons, 2005), 163.
56. Melamed, *For Crying Out Loud*, xv.
57. Olatundun Janet Adelegan, "The Derivatives Market in Sub Saharan Africa," *IMF Working Paper* (Washington, DC: IMF, 2009), 18.
58. For information on the Bank's promotional work in the derivatives context see, for example: Stijn Claessens and Ronald Duncan (eds.), *Managing Commodity Price Risk in Developing Countries* (Baltimore, MA: Johns Hopkins University Press for the World Bank, 1993); ITF, *Mexico: Price Risk Management, Phase 2 Report* (Washington, DC: World Bank/ITF, 2002); Donald Larson and Jonathan Coleman, *The Effects of Option-Hedging on the Costs of Domestic Price Stabilization Schemes* (Washington, DC: The World Bank, 1991); Donald Larson, Panos Varangis, and Nanae Yabuki, *Commodity Risk Management and Development* (Washington, DC: The World Bank, 1998); Donald Larson, Jock Anderson, and Panos Varagis, "Policies on Managing Risk in Agricultural Markets," *The*

World Bank Research Observer 19:2 (2004); Panos Varangis, Donald Larson, and Jock Anderson, *Agricultural Markets and Risks: Management of the Latter, Not the Former* (Washington, DC: The World Bank, 2002); Panos Varangis and Donald Larson, *Dealing with Commodity Price Uncertainty* (Washington, DC: The World Bank, 1996); World Bank, *Dealing with Commodity Price Volatility in Developing Countries: A Proposal for a Market-Based Approach* (Washington, DC: The World Bank, 1999); World Bank, *Managing Agricultural Production Risk* (Washington, DC: World Bank, Agricultural and Rural Development Department, 2005), 32727-GLB; World Bank, *Rural Finance Innovations: Topics and Case Studies* (Washington, DC: The World Bank, 2005).

59. see: http://treasury.worldbank.org/bdm/htm/hedging_products.html.
60. For more information on UNCTAD's derivatives promotion see UNCTAD, *Commodity Policies for Development*; UNCTAD, *The World's Commodity Exchanges*, proceedings of the 27th Bürgenstock Conference (Bürgenstock: UNCTAD, 2006); UNCTAD, *Examination of the Effectiveness and Usefulness for Commodity Dependent Countries of New Tools in Commodity Markets: Risk Management and Collateralized Finance* (Geneva: United Nations, 1998); UNCTAD, *Report of the Expert Meeting to Examine the Effectiveness and Usefulness for Commodity-Dependent Countries of New Tools in Commodity Markets: Risk Management and Collateralized Finance* (Geneva: United Nations, 1998); UNCTAD, *Farmers and Farmers' Associations in Developing Countries and Their Use of Modern Financial Instruments* (United Nations, 2002); UNCTAD, *Enabling Small Commodity Producers and Processors in Developing Countries to Reach Global Markets* (Geneva: United Nations, 2006); UNCTAD, *The Development Role of Commodity Exchanges* (Geneva: United Nations, 2007). See also the International Trade and Commodities Division's website on "helping small commodity producers reach global markets," http://www.unctad.org/Templates/Page.asp?intItemID=4020&lang=1, accessed on December 5, 2011.
61. See, e.g.: UNDP, *Commodity Development Strategies in the Integrated Framework* (Geneva: UNDP, 2009); FAO, *Commodity Exchanges and Derivatives Markets: Evolution, Experience and Outlook in the Cereal Sector* (Rome: FAO, 2007); FAO, *Managing Supplies to Raise International Agricultural Commodity Prices* (Rome: FAO Committee on Commodity Problems, 2007).
62. See: http://www.dce.com.cn/portal/cate?cid=1114585896100.
63. See: www.mcx.com.
64. USDA Economic Research Service, "Farm Risk Management: Risk Management Strategies," http://www.ers.usda.gov/Briefing/RiskManagement/Strategies.htm, accessed on July 7, 2011.
65. See, e.g., USAID, *Commodity Futures Exchange: An Assessment and Conceptual Framework for Establishing a Commodity Futures Exchange in Egypt* (Washington, DC: USAID, 2007).
66. ITF, *Mexico: Phase 2 Report*, 2002.
67. See: www.gbot.mu.
68. See: www.mcx.com/aboutus/aboutus.htm.

69. World Bank, "World Bank Group Announces New Instrument to Help Food Producers and Consumers in Developing Nations Deal with Volatile Prices," press release on June 21, 2011.
70. There is a large and growing literature on "vulnerability" and "livelihood insecurity." See, e.g., Steven Devereux, "Livelihood Insecurity and Social Protection: A Re-Emerging Issue in Rural Development," *Development Policy Review* 19:4 (2001); Christopher Bacon, "Confronting the Coffee Crisis: Can Fair Trade, Organic, and Specialty Coffees Reduce Small-Scale Farmer Vulnerability in Northern Nicaragua?" *World Development* 33: 3 (2005); Jonathan Morduch, "Between the State and the Market: Can Informal Insurance Patch the Safety Net?" *The World Bank Research Observer* 14:2 (1999).
71. Ulrich Hess and Andrea Stoppa, "Design and Use of Weather Derivatives in Agricultural Policies," *WTO Conference Paper*, Capri, Italy, June 2003.
72. Simon Miller, "Weather Builds on Derivatives Sales in 2011," in *Financial Risk Today*, www.financialrisktoday.com, May 23, 2011.
73. Joanne Morrison, "ICE Adds Brazilian Flavor . . . ."
74. Panos Varangis, Jerry Skees, and Barry Barnett, "Weather Indexes for Developing Countries," in *Climate Risk and the Weather Market*, ed. Robert Dischel (London: Risk Books, 2002), p. 1 of article.
75. Calum Turvey, "Weather Derivatives for Specific Event Risk in Agriculture," in *Review of Agricultural Economics* 23:2 (2001); World Bank, *Managing Agricultural Risk* (Washington, D.C.: World Bank, 2005).
76. World Bank, *Managing Agricultural Risk*, 14.
77. Ulrich Hess, Kaspar Richter and Andrea Stoppa, "Weather Risk Management for Agri-business and Agriculture in Developing Countries," in *Climate Risk and the Weather Market*, ed. Robert Dischel (London: Risk Books, 2002) p. 1 of article.
78. Weather Risk Management Association, "Great Weather Risk Management Transactions," http://www.wrma.org/risk_transactions.html, accessed on July 7, 2011.
79. World Bank, *Managing Agricultural Risk*, 35.
80. Ibid., 51.
81. IFC, "Global Index Insurance Facility," http://www.ifc.org/ifcext/gfm.nsf/Content/Insurance-GIIF, accessed on July 7, 2011.
82. Syngenta Foundation for Sustainable Agriculture, "Risk Management," http://www.syngentafoundation.org/index.cfm?pageID=43, accessed on July 7, 2011.
83. Micro Ensure, "Weather Index Crop Insurance," http://www.microensure.com/products-weather.asp, accessed on July 7, 2011.
84. Oli Brown, Alec Crawford, and Jason Gibson, *Boom or Bust: How Commodity Price Volatility Impedes Poverty Reduction, and What to Do about It* (Winnepeg: International Institute for Sustainable Development, 2008), 1.
85. Paul Cashin, John McDermott, and Alasdair Scott, *Booms and Slumps in World Commodity Prices* (Washington, DC: The International Monetary Fund, 1999), 4.
86. Ibid., 13–18.

87. FAO, "Price Volatility in Agricultural Markets," in *Economic and Social Perspectives* (Policy Brief 12), December 2010.
88. FAO, *Commodity Exchanges and Derivatives Markets*, 1.
89. UNCTAD, *The World's Commodity Exchanges*, iv.
90. Jubilee Debt Campaign, *A New Debt Crisis?* (London: Jubilee Debt Campaign, March 2009).
91. Sovereign defaults have lots of nasty consequences that commodity-linked bonds arguably help avoid. Governments in default often have to resort to austerity (witness Greece's current debt problems), cutting popular social programs and environmental preservation initiatives, among other expenditure reductions. Susan George's book *The Debt Boomerang* (London: Pluto, 1992) is a great resource on these points.
92. World Bank, *Rural Finance Innovations*, 15; Eduardo L. Leao de Sousa and Fernando L. Pimentel, *Study on the Cedula de Produto Rural (CPR)—Farm Product Bond in Brazil* (Washington, DC: The World Bank, 2005), 11.
93. Earl Stennis, Musa Pinar and Albert Allen, "The Futures Market and Price Discovery in the Textile Industry," *American Journal of Agricultural Economics* 65:2 (1983), 308.
94. In David DeRosa (ed.), *Currency Derivatives* (New York: Wiley & Sons, 1998), 143.
95. Theodore Schultz, "The Theory and Measurement of Price Expectations," *The American Economic Review* 39:3 (1949), 1.
96. Jeannette Herrmann in Claessens and Duncan (eds.), *Managing Commodity Price Risk*, 428.

Chapter 3

1. Kabra, Kamal, Comments on the Forward Market Regulation Act, Standing Committee on Food, Consumer Affairs and Public Distribution (Ministry of Consumer Affairs, Food and Public Distribution, Department of Consumer Affairs, Government of India, 14th Lok Sabha, 17th Report, December 2006), 16–17, emphasis added.
2. Timothy Geithner, "Implications of Growth in Credit Derivatives for Financial Stability," Speech at NYU's Stern School of Business Third Credit Risk Conference, May 16, 2006.
3. Eleni Gabre-Madhin, "An Eye on the Future: Can the Ethiopia Commodity Exchange Succeed without Futures?," www.ecx.com.et, May 2007.
4. Standing Committee on Food, Consumer Affairs and Public Distribution (2006–07), "Forward Contracts (Regulation) Amendment Bill, 2006," Ministry of Consumer Affairs, Food and Public Distribution, Department of Consumer Affairs, Government of India, 14th Lok Sabha, 17th Report, December 2006.
5. David Harvey, *A Brief History of Neoliberalism* (Oxford: Oxford University Press, 2005), 2.

6. Dani Rodrik, "Goodbye Washington Consensus, Hello Washington Confusion?," *Journal of Economic Literature* 44:4 (December 2006).
7. Kenneth Arrow, "Uncertainty and the Welfare Economics of Medical Care," *American Economic Review* 53:5 (1963), 947.
8. David Moss, *When All Else Fails* (Cambridge, MA: Harvard University Press, 2002), 3. Moss is quoting Kenneth Arrow in part of this excerpt.
9. World Bank, *Social Protection Sector Strategy: From Safety Net to Springboard* (Washington, D.C.: World Bank, 2001), 16.
10. Robert Shiller, "Radical Financial Innovation," Cowles Foundation Discussion Paper #1461, Cowles Foundation for Research in Economics, Yale University (April 2004), 7.
11. Milton Friedman, "The Reduction of Fluctuations in the Incomes of Primary Producers," *The Economic Journal* 64:256 (December 1954), 698.
12. Ronald McKinnon, "Futures Markets, Buffer Stocks and Income Stability for Primary Producers," *Journal of Political Economy* 75:6 (1967), 860.
13. See, e.g.: Mary Bohman, Lovell Jarvis and Richard Barichello, "Rent Seeking and International Commodity Agreements: The Case of Coffee," *Economic Development and Cultural Change* 44:2 (1996); Takamasa Akiyama et al., *Commodity Market Reforms: Lessons of Two Decades* (Washington, D.C.: World Bank, 2001).
14. Jeanette Herrmann, "Integration of the International Rice Market," in *Managing Commodity Price Risk in Developing Countries*, eds. Stijn Claessens and Ronald Duncan (Baltimore, MD: Johns Hopkins Press/World Bank, 1993), 427.
15. Anne Peck, "The Economic Role of Traditional Commodity Futures Markets," in *Futures Markets: Their Economic Role* (Washington, D.C.: American Enterprise Institute, 1985), 56–7.
16. Friedman, "The Reduction of Fluctuations in the Incomes of Primary Producers," 703.
17. David Newbery and Joseph Stiglitz, *The Theory of Commodity Price Stabilization* (Oxford: Oxford University Press, 1981), 177.
18. Stijn Claessens and Ronald Duncan (eds.), *Managing Commodity Price Risk in Developing Countries* (Baltimore, MA: Johns Hopkins University Press for the World Bank, 1993), 17.
19. Robert J. Meyers, "Incomplete Markets and Commodity-Linked Finance in Developing Countries," *World Bank Research Observer* 7:1 (1992), 79–80.
20. UNCTAD, *Farmers and Farmers' Associations in Developing Countries and Their Use of Modern Financial Instruments* (Geneva: UNCTAD, 2002), 6.
21. Herrmann, "Integration of the International Rice Market"; Newbery and Stiglitz, *The Theory of Commodity Price Stabilization*; McKinnon, "Futures Markets, Buffer Stocks . . . ."
22. Herrmann, "Integration of the International Rice Market," 428.
23. McKinnon, "Futures Markets, Buffer Stocks . . . ."

24. Anne Peck, "Hedging and Income Stability: Concepts, Implications and an Example," *American Journal of Agricultural Economics* 57:3 (August 1975), 410.
25. Jorge Cardenas, "The World Coffee Crisis," *World Coffee Conference* (London: ICO, 2001), 2.
26. Bryan Lewin, Daniele Giovanucci and Panos Varangis, *The Coffee Market: New Paradigms in Global Supply and Demand* (Washington, D.C.: World Bank, 2004), 21.
27. Robert Bates, *Open Economy Politics: The Political Economy of the World Coffee Trade* (Princeton, NJ: Princeton University Press, 1997), 18.
28. Cardenas, "The World Coffee Crisis," 1.
29. Celine Charveriat, *Bitter Coffee* (London: Oxfam 2001), 5.
30. John Baffes, Bryan Lewin, and Panos Varangis, "*Coffee: Market Settings and Policies*" (Washington, D.C.: World Bank, 2005), accessed on January 13, 2007, http://siteresources.worldbank.org/INTGAT/Resources/GATChapter16.pdf, 297.
31. Lewin, Giovanucci and Varangis, *The Coffee Market.*
32. Charveriat, *Bitter Coffee*, 5.
33. FAO, *Commodity Market Review, 2003–2004* (Rome: Food and Agriculture Organization, Commodities and Trade Division, 2003), 6.
34. Lewin, Giovanucci and Varangis, *The Coffee Market*, 19.
35. Lamon Rutten and Rita Youssef, "Market-based Price Risk Management" (Winnipeg: IISD, 2007), 8.
36. Paul Cashin, John McDermott and Alasdair Scott, *Booms and Slumps in World Commodity Prices* (Washington, D.C.: The International Monetary Fund, 1999), 4.
37. Ibid.
38. Christopher Gilbert, "Trends and Volatility in Agricultural Commodity Prices," in *Agricultural Markets and Trade*, eds. Alexander Sarris and David Hallam (Cheltenham, UK: Edward Elgar, 2006), 31.
39. See, e.g., Joseph Love, "Raul Prebisch and the Origins of the Doctrine of Unequal Exchange," *Latin American Research Review* 15:3 (1980), 45–72.
40. Robert Schaeffer, *Understanding Globalization* (Lanham, MD: Rowman and Littlefield, 2005), 157–9.
41. Gilbert, "Trends and Volatility . . . ."
42. Stefano Ponte, "The 'Latte Revolution'? Regulation, Markets and Consumption in the Global Coffee Chain," *World Development* 30:7 (2002), 1101.
43. Data from the ICO. www.ico.org.
44. Baffes, Lewin and Varangis, *Coffee*, 297.
45. Geoff Sayer, *Coffee Futures: The Impact of Falling World Prices on Livelihoods in Uganda* (London: Oxfam, 2002), 11. Although still very dependent on coffee export earnings, Uganda's dependence has declined significantly since the 1970s-80s when coffee exports accounted for some 80–90 percent of total export earnings.
46. FAO, *Commodity Market Review*, 7.

47. Lewin, Giovanucci and Varangis, *The Coffee Market*, xi.
48. Charis Gresser and Sophia Tickell, *Mugged: Poverty in Your Coffee Cup* (London: Oxfam, 2002), 7.
49. Antony Wild, *Coffee: A Dark History* (London: Fourth Estate, 2004), 1.
50. Charveriat, *Bitter Coffee*, 2.
51. ILO, *Economic Security for a Better World* (Geneva: International Labor Organization, 2004), 11.
52. Rutten and Youssef, "Market-based Price Risk Management," 16.
53. Robert Holzmann and Steen Jorgenson, "Social Risk Management," Social Protection Discussion Paper Series #0006 (Washington, D.C.: World Bank, 2000) 7.
54. UNCTAD, *Farmers and Farmers' Associations in Developing Countries . . .*, 3.
55. Sayer, *Coffee Futures*, 10.
56. Kelly Watson and Moira Laura Achinelli, "Context and Contingency: The Coffee Crisis for Conventional Small-Scale Coffee Farmers in Brazil," *The Geographic Journal* 174:3 (2008), 227–9.
57. Gresser and Tickell, *Mugged.*
58. ITF, *Mexico: Price Risk Management, Phase 2 Report* (Washington, D.C.: World Bank/ITF, 2002), 6.
59. Hallie Eakin, Catherine Tucker, and Edwin Castellanos, "Responding to the Coffee Crisis: A Pilot Study of Farmers' Adaptations to the Coffee Crisis," *The Geographic Journal* 172:2 (2006), 164 and 168–9.
60. Néstor Osorio, "The Global Coffee Crisis: A Threat to Sustainable Development" (August 2002), Submission to the World Summit on Sustainable Development, Johannesburg, 2002, available via www.ico.org.
61. Deborah Sick, "Coping with the Crisis: Costa Rican Households and the International Coffee Market," *Ethnology* 36:3 (1997).
62. Eakin, Tucker and Castellanos, "Responding to the Coffee Crisis"; Christopher Bacon, "Confronting the Coffee Crisis: Can Fair Trade, Organic, and Specialty Coffees Reduce Small-Scale Farmer Vulnerability in Northern Nicaragua?" *World Development* 33:3 (2005); World Bank, *Shocks and Social Protection: Lessons from the Central American Coffee Crisis* (Washington, D.C.: The World Bank, 2005).
63. Charveriat, *Bitter Coffee.*
64. Gresser and Tickell, *Mugged.*
65. Lewin, Giovanucci and Varangis, *The Coffee Market.*
66. Schaeffer, *Understanding Globalization*, 157.
67. Jamie Lee, "Sicom Taps Indian Market with Cross-listing Accord," *The Business Times Singapore*, May 27, 2009.
68. Sushil Mohan and James Love, "Coffee Futures: Role in Reducing Coffee Producers' Price Risk," *Journal of International Development* 16:7 (2004), 984.
69. Ibid., 1000.
70. Ibid.
71. Ibid.

72. Ibid.
73. Ibid.
74. R. Salvadi Easwaran and P. Ramasundaram, "Whether Commodity Futures Market in Agriculture is Efficient in Price Discovery?—An Econometric Analysis," *Agricultural Economics Research Review* 21 (2008), 343–4.
75. Jens-Peter Loy, "Relative Forecasting and Hedging Efficiency of Agricultural Futures Markets in the European Union: Evidence for Slaughter Hog Contracts," Paper prepared for presentation at the Xth EAAE Congress 'Exploring Diversity in the European Agri -Food System,' Zaragoza (Spain), August 28–31, 2002, 5.
76. Todd Groome, Nicholas Blancher, Francois P. Haas, and John Kiff, *The Limits of Market-Based Risk Transfer and Implications for Managing Systemic Risks* (Washington, D.C.: IMF), 17.
77. Richard Teweles and Frank Jones, *The Futures Game* (New York: McGraw-Hill, 1999), 41.
78. Randall Fortenberry and Hector Zapata, "Developed Speculation and Underdeveloped Markets," University of Wisconsin-Madison, Department of Agricultural Economics Staff Paper, 2004, 15–16.
79. Joanne Morrison, "ICE Adds Brazilian Flavor to Coffee Futures Market," *FIA Magazine*, March/April 2011.
80. Marcy Nicholson, "UPDATE 3-ICE committee recommends Brazilian coffee-trade," *Reuters*, October 14, 2010.
81. Randall Dodd, "From Fat Years to Lean Years: What if Joseph Had Used Derivatives?," Financial Policy Forum Working Paper, 2007.
82. McKinnon, "Futures Markets, Buffer Stocks . . . ," 857.
83. Sergio Lence, "Do Futures Benefit Farmers?," *American Journal of Agricultural Economics* 91:1 (2009).
84. Sergio Lence and Marvin Hayenga, "The Pitfalls of Multi-Year Rollover Hedges," *American Journal of Agricultural Economics* 83:1 (2001), 107–19.
85. UNCTAD, *The Development Role of Commodity Exchanges* (Geneva: United Nations, 2007).
86. Dodd, "From Fat Years to Lean Years," 25–6.
87. CRMG, "Price Risk Management Work Summary," Commodity Risk Management Group at the World Bank (Washington, D.C.: The World Bank, May 2005), 21.
88. Morrison, "ICE Adds Brazilian Flavor to Coffee Futures Market," emphasis added.
89. In reality, margins are usually maintained by a "clearing member" of the exchange. The clearinghouse then ensures the solvency of the clearing members. But it is the clearinghouse that establishes margin levels. See Chapter 4.
90. Ronald Anderson and Jean-Pierre Danthine, "The Time Pattern of Hedging and the Volatility of Future Prices," *The Review of Economic Studies* 50:2 (1983), 249.
91. Rutten and Youssef, "Market-based Price Risk Management," 22.

92. Nataliia Gerasymenko and Oleksandr Zhemoyda, "New Challenges for Risk Management in AgriFood Industry," (Paper prepared for presentation at the 113th EAAE Seminar "A resilient European food industry and food chain in a challenging world," Chania, Crete, Greece, September 3–6, 2009), 3.
93. Rutten and Youssef, "Market-based Price Risk Management," 21.
94. Sushil Mohan, "Market-Based Price Risk Management for Coffee Producers," *Development Policy Review* 25:3 (2007), 347.
95. Peter Gibbon, *The Commodity Question: New Thinking on Old Problems* (United Nations Development Program, 2005), 16.
96. Sheridan Roberts, *The Global Information Society: A Statistical View* (Santiago: United Nations, 2008).
97. UNCTAD, *Enabling Small Commodity Producers and Processors in Developing Countries to Reach Global Markets* (Geneva: United Nations, 2006), 4–5.
98. Jason Potts, *Building a Sustainable Coffee Sector Using Market-Based Approaches: The Role of Multi-Stakeholder Cooperation* (UNCTAD/IISD, 2003), 3, emphasis added.
99. Marcel Fafchamps and Ruth Vargas Hill, *Coffee Hedging in the Market: Exporter, Trader and Producer Data from Uganda* (Washington, D.C.: World Bank, 2006).
100. Mohan, "Market-based Price Risk Management for Coffee Producers," 348–9.
101. UNCTAD, *Enabling Small Commodity Producers*, 15.
102. Ulrich Kleih, Gideon Onumah and Ruth Butterworth, "Training Manual on Market Information System, Uganda—Coffee" (Common Fund for Commodities and Uganda Coffee Development Authority, 2006), 1.
103. Adam Tickell, "Unstable Futures," in *Global Capitalism versus Democracy*, eds. Panitich and Leys (London: UK: Merlin, 1999).
104. Stephen Figlewski, "Derivative Risks, Old and New," NYU Stern School of Business Working Paper No. FIN-98–033 (December 1998).
105. ITF, *Lessons Learned.*
106. CRMG, "Price Risk Management Work Summary," 3.
107. ITF, *Mexico: Phase 2 Report*, 4.
108. Yevgeny Kuznetsov and Carl Dahlman, *Mexico's Transition to a Knowledge-Based Economy: Challenges and Opportunities* (Washington, D.C.: The World Bank, 2008), 79.
109. CRMG, "Price Risk Management Work Summary," 11–12.
110. UNDP, *Uganda Human Development Report, 2007* (Geneva: United Nations Development Program, 2007), 54–6.
111. Watson and Achinelli, "Context and Contingency," 230.
112. ITF, *Mexico: Phase 2 Report*, 21.
113. Ibid., 21.
114. Ibid., 36.
115. CRMG, "Lessons Learned—Price Risk Management" (Washington, D.C.: The World Bank, 2005), 1.
116. ITF, *Mexico: Phase 2 Report*, 27–8.

117. www.infoaserca.gob.mx/coberturas/participantes2005.pdf and www.infoaserca.gob.mx/coberturas/participantes2004.pdf, accessed on August 1, 2007 and August 2, 2007.
118. From FAOSTAT.
119. From ITF, *Mexico: Phase 2 Report.* Average farm size is 2.69 hectares.
120. Ibid.
121. World Bank, *Brazil: Access to Financial Services* (Washington, D.C.: The World Bank, Brazil Country Management Group 2004), 206.
122. Baffes, Lewin and Varangis, *Coffee*, 306.
123. Eduardo L. Leao de Sousa and Fernando L. Pimentel, *Study on the Cedula de Produto Rural (CPR)—Farm Product Bond in Brazil* (Washington, D.C.: The World Bank, 2005), 5.
124. World Bank, *Brazil: Access to Financial Services*, 206.
125. Non-transferrable so a secondary market will not emerge.
126. Dodd, "From Fat Years to Lean Years," 26.
127. Ibid.
128. Leao de Sousa and Pimentel, *Study on the Brazilian CPR*, 5.
129. World Bank, *Rural Finance Innovations: Topics and Case Studies* (Washington, D.C.: The World Bank, 2005), 14.
130. Commodity linked bonds are increasingly being advocated to developing country governments for this very reason.
131. World Bank, *Rural Finance Innovations*, 15.
132. Leao de Sousa and Pimentel, *Study on the Brazilian CPR*, 11.
133. World Bank, *Rural Finance Innovations*, 15.
134. Leao de Sousa and Pimentel, *Study on the Brazilian CPR*, 11.
135. Stephanie Daniels and Seth Petchers, *The Coffee Crisis Continues* (London: Oxfam America, 2005), 30.
136. World Bank, *Rural Finance Innovations*, 15
137. Ibid.; Rodrik, "Goodbye Washington Consensus, Hello Washington Confusion?"
138. CRMG, "Lessons Learned—Price Risk Management."
139. Ibid., 2.
140. in Gibbon, *The Commodity Question*, 17.
141. CRMG, "Price Risk Management Work Summary," 11–12
142. UNCTAD, *Farmers and Farmers' Associations.*
143. CRMG, "Price Risk Management Work Summary," 25.

Chapter 4

1. Karl Marx and Friedrich Engels, *The Communist Manifesto* (New York: Penguin, 1998), 57.
2. The Law of Unintended Consequences is that there always are some.
3. Randall Dodd, "Subprime: Tentacles of a Crisis," in *Finance and Development* 44:4 (December 2007).

4. See, e.g., Dodd, "Subprime"; Robert Wade, "The First World Debt Crisis of 2007–2010 in Global Perspective," *Challenge*, July-August 2008.
5. Monsanto, "Roundup Ready System," http://www.monsanto.com/weedmanagement/Pages/roundup-ready-system.aspx, accessed on October 6, 2011.
6. William Neumann and Andrew Pollack, "U.S. Farmers Cope with Roundup-resistant Weeds," *The New York Times*, May 3, 2010.
7. World Bank, *Agriculture for Development: World Development Report, 2008* (Washington, D.C.: The World Bank, 2008).
8. UNCTAD, *Farmers and Farmers' Associations in Developing Countries and Their Use of Modern Financial Instruments* (United Nations, 2002).
9. Lamon Rutten and Rita Youssef, *Market-based Price Risk Management* (Winnipeg: IISD, 2007).
10. UNCTAD, *Commodity Policies for Development* (Geneva: UNCTAD, 2005).
11. UNDP, *Commodity Development Strategies in the Integrated Framework* (Geneva: UNDP, 2009).
12. UNCTAD, "Report of the Expert Meeting on Enabling Small Commodity Producers and Processors in Developing Countries to Reach Global Markets" (UNCTAD: Geneva, January 2007), 2.
13. Ibid., 5.
14. Ibid., 3.
15. See, e.g., Ngaire Woods, *The Globalizers* (Ithaca, NY: Cornell, 2006); Walden Bello, *The Food Wars* (London: Verso, 2009); Arturo Escobar, *Encountering Development* (Princeton, NJ: Princeton University Press, 1995); Michael Edwards, "The Irrelevance of Development Studies," *Third World Quarterly* 11:1 (1989).
16. Terence Hopkins and Immanuel Wallerstein, "Commodity Chains: Construction and Research," *Commodity Chains and Global Capitalism*, eds. Gereffi and Korzeniewicz (Westport, CT: Praeger, 1994).
17. Immanuel Wallerstein, "The Modern World-System as a Capitalist World-Economy," *The Globalization Reader*, eds. Lechner and Boli (Malden, MA: Blackwell, 2008), 59.
18. Wallerstein, "The Modern World-System . . . ," 59.
19. In this tradition "monopoly" refers to concentrated market structures in which one firm dominates, as well as those in which only a few firms dominate. This latter structure is referred to in neoclassical economics as "oligopoly."
20. Charis Gresser and Sophia Tickell, *Mugged: Poverty in Your Coffee Cup* (London: Oxfam, 2002).
21. Immanuel Wallerstein, *The Politics of the World-Economy* (Cambridge: Cambridge University Press, 1984), 15.
22. Antony Wild, *Coffee: A Dark History* (London: Fourth Estate, 2004), 1.
23. Steven Topik, "Historicizing Commodity Chains," in *Frontiers of Commodity Chain Research*, ed. Jennifer Bair (Stanford University Press, 2009), 43.
24. Harry Magdoff, *Imperialism: From the Colonial Age to the Present* (New York: Monthly Review, 1978), 97.

25. L. S. Stavrianos, *Global Rift* (New York: William Morrow and Company, 1981), 95.
26. Wild, *Coffee*, 173.
27. Topik, "Historicizing Commodity Chains," 44–5.
28. Ibid., 46.
29. Stavrianos, *Global Rift*, 300.
30. Ibid., 300.
31. Ibid., 300–1.
32. Yoshida Masao, *Agricultural Marketing Intervention in East Africa* (Tokyo: Institute of Developing Economies, 1984), 19.
33. Magdoff, *Imperialism*, 119. See also, Vladimir Lenin, *Imperialism: The Last Stage of Capitalism* (New York: International, 2002).
34. John A. Hobson, "The Economic Taproot of Imperialism," *Imperialism* (www.marxists.org, 1902).
35. Topik, "Historicizing Commodity Chains," 48.
36. Kelly Watson and Moira Laura Achinelli, "Context and Contingency: The Coffee Crisis for Conventional Small-Scale Coffee Farmers in Brazil," *The Geographic Journal* 174:3 (2008), 228.
37. Robert Rice, "The Land Use Patterns and the History of Coffee in Eastern Chiapas, Mexico," *Agriculture and Human Values* 14 (1997), 127–43.
38. Stavrianos, *Global Rift*, 670.
39. Mike Davis, "Late Victorian Holocausts," *The Development Reader*, eds. Chari and Corbridge (New York: Routledge, 2008), 21.
40. Bello, *Food Wars*, 27.
41. Wild, *Coffee*, 15.
42. During WWII, the US signed onto the Inter-American Coffee Agreement (IACA), which collapsed after the war.
43. Wild, *Coffee*; Ponte, "The 'Latte Revolution'?."
44. Wild, *Coffee*, 199.
45. John Talbot, "The Struggle for Control of a Commodity Chain," *Latin American Research Review* 32:2 (1997), 121.
46. Robert Bates, *Open Economy Politics: The Political Economy of the World Coffee Trade* (Princeton, NJ: Princeton University Press, 1997), 18.
47. See Susan George, *The Debt Boomerang* (London: Pluto, 1992); Bello, *Food Wars*; Woods, *The Globalizers*.
48. Topik, "Historicizing Commodity Chains," 57.
49. Ibid., 56.
50. See, e.g. Woods, *The Globalizers*; Bello, *Food Wars*.
51. Ponte, "The 'Latte Revolution'?," 1105.
52. Gresser and Tickell, *Mugged*, 21.
53. Wild, *Coffee*, 226.
54. Susan Newman, "Financialization and Changes in Social Relations Along Commodity Chains: The Case of Coffee," *Review of Radical Political Economics* 41:4 (2009), 554.

55. Ponte, "The 'Latte Revolution'?," 1108.
56. Topik, "Historicizing Commodity Chains," 58.
57. Ponte, "The 'Latte Revolution'?"
58. Gresser and Tickell, *Mugged*; Topik, "Historicizing Commodity Chains"; John Talbot, *Grounds for Agreement* (Lanham, MD: Rowman and Littlefield, 2004).
59. Bates, *Open Economy Politics*.
60. Ponte, "The 'Latte Revolution'?," 1106.
61. Gresser and Tickell, *Mugged*, 20.
62. Benoit Daviron and Stefano Ponte, *The Coffee Paradox* (London: Zed Books, 2005), 95.
63. Ponte, "The 'Latte Revolution'?"
64. NKG, "Facts and Figures" and "Group Companies," http://www.nkg.net/aboutus/factsandfigures and http://www.nkg.net/groupcompanies, accessed December 7, 2011.
65. Carlos Guadarrama-Zagasti, "A Grower Typology Approach to Assessing the Environmental Impact of Coffee Farming in Veracruz Mexico," *Confronting the Coffee Crisis*, eds. Bacon et al. (Cambridge, MA: MIT Press, 2008), 134–5.
66. Wild, *Coffee*, 212.
67. ITF, "Lessons Learned."
68. UNCTAD, *World's Commodity Exchanges*, proceedings of the 27th Bürgenstock Conference (Bürgenstock: UNCTAD, 2006), iv.
69. Goggin in UNCTAD, *World's Commodity Exchanges*, 41.
70. Eileen Rabach and Eun Mee Kim, "Where Is the Chain in Commodity Chains? The Service Sector Nexus," *Commodity Chains and Global Capitalism*, eds. Gereffi and Korzeniewicz (Westport, CT: Praeger, 1994), 131.
71. Some of the exchanges, for example, the BM&F, also offer "spread" contracts designed mostly for index speculators rolling their positions.
72. Richard Teweles and Frank Jones, *The Futures Game* (New York: McGraw-Hill, 1999), 30–1.
73. Nicholas Economides, "Network Economics with Application to Finance," *Financial Markets, Institutions & Instruments*, 2:5 (1993), 1.
74. Economides, "Network Economics," 4, italics in original.
75. Economides, "Network Economics"; Ian Domowitz and Benn Steil, "Automation, Trading Costs and the Structure of the Securities Trading Industry," *Brookings-Wharton Papers on Financial Services* (1999).
76. Simon in UNCTAD, *The World's Commodity Exchanges*, 11.
77. UNCTAD, *Progress in the Development of African Commodity Exchanges* (Addis Ababa: UNCTAD/African Union, 2005), 20.
78. Ibid., 19–20.
79. James Doran, "The Mating Game," *Futures Industry* (Outlook, 2008).
80. David Loader, *Clearing and Settlement of Derivatives* (Amsterdam: Elsevier, 2005), 35.
81. Ibid., 36.
82. Leo Melamed, *For Crying Out Loud* (New York: Wiley and Sons, 2009), xiv.

83. Wallace Turbeville, *Derivatives Clearinghouses in an Era of Financial Reform* (Washington, D.C.: Roosevelt Institute, 2010), 6.
84. Ibid.
85. Turbeville, in *Derivatives Clearinghouses* notes that in the past the clearinghouses were actually created by their members, though today many are publicly traded entities. This suggests that, depending on the case in question, it may be the members controlling the clearinghouses and not the clearinghouses determining the membership.
86. Melamed, *For Crying Out Loud*, xv.
87. quoted in Louise Story, "A Secretive Banking Elite Rules Trading in Derivatives," *The New York Times*, December 11, 2010.
88. Ibid.
89. LCH Clearnet, "Current Membership," http://www.lchclearnet.com/membership/ltd/current_membership.asp, accessed August 16, 2011
90. Euronext, "Membership Directory," http://www.euronext.com/forourclient/mbs/market/list.jsp?lan=EN&cha=1663&MEP=8631, accessed August 16, 2011
91. BM&F, "Brokerage Houses and Other Participants," http://www.bmfbovespa.com.br/shared/iframe.aspx?altura=1100&idioma=en-us&url=www2.bmf.com.br/pages/portal/bmfbovespa/associados2/associadosPesquisa2.asp, accessed August 16, 2011
92. TRX Futures, "About Us," http://www.trxfutures.com/aboutus, accessed September 20, 2011.
93. Newman, "Financialization and Changes . . . ."
94. Euronext, "Robusta Coffee," http://www.euronext.com/editorial/wide/editorial-3050-EN.html, accessed August 16, 2011.
95. Newman, "Financialization and Changes . . . ," 548.
96. Michael Masters and Adam White, "Accidental Hunt Brothers" (July 2008), http://www.loe.org/images/content/080919/Act1.pdf, accessed November 17, 2011, 9.
97. Masters and White, "Accidental Hunt Brothers," ii.
98. Tim Wise, "Food Price Volatility" (January 27, 2011), http://triplecrisis.com/food-price-volatility, accessed on September 27, 2011. Italics in original.
99. Master and White, "Accidental Hunt Brothers," ii.
100. Ponte, "The 'Latte Revolution'?," 1107.
101. Benjamin Davis, "The Adjustment Strategies of Mexican Ejidatarios in the Face of Neoliberal Reform," *CEPAL Review* 72: (December 2000), 103.
102. Newman, "Financialization and Changes," 548.
103. Gross in UNCTAD, *World's Commodity Exchanges*, 8.
104. Peter Blogg and Surendra Kotecha, "NYSE Liffe Robusta Coffee Futures," Presentation for the ICO by representatives of NYSE Liffe, March 16, 2009.
105. See, e.g., Jonathan Wheatley, "Brazil Exchanges in Global Party Mood," *Financial Times*, February 28, 2008.

106. BM&F, "About Us," http://www.bmfbovespa.com.br/en-us/bmfbovespa/about-us/history/history.aspx?Idioma=en-us, accessed September 27, 2011.
107. Commodities Bureau, "NYSE Euronext Completes MCX Stake Deal," http://www.financialexpress.com/news/nyse-euronext-completes-mcx-stake-deal/330034/3, accessed on September 27, 2011.
108. UNCTAD, *World's Commodity Exchanges.*
109. Rabach and Kim, "Where Is the Chain . . . ," 125.
110. Farmer associations in the United States have already presented this grievance to the CFTC; see, e.g., Bob Stallman, "Statement of the American Farm Bureau Federation" to the CFTC, April 22, 2008, accessed December 7, 2011, http://www.cftc.gov/ucm/groups/public/@newsroom/documents/file/event042208_stallman.pdf.
111. Masters and White, "Accidental Hunt Brothers," 20.
112. Ibid.
113. Ibid., 10.
114. Jayati Ghosh, "The Unnatural Coupling: Food and Global Finance," IDEAs Working Paper Series, Paper # 08/2009 (2009), 3.
115. Ibid., 5.
116. Ibid., 19.
117. Executive Director of ICO, "October 2008 Coffee Market Report," http://dev.ico.org/documents/cmr1008e.pdf, accessed October 6, 2011, 1.
118. Masters and White, "Accidental Hunt Brothers."
119. Dick Bryan and Michael Rafferty, *Capitalism with Derivatives* (New York: Palgrave, 2006), 63.
120. Robert Pindyck, "The Dynamics of Commodity Spot and Futures Markets: A Primer," *The Energy Journal* 22:3 (2001), 1–29.
121. This is the case, for example, with Ethiopian coffee farmers interviewed in the documentary film *Black Gold.*
122. Newman, "Financialization and Changes . . . ."

Chapter 5

1. Vandana Shiva, in "In the Footsteps of Gandhi: An Interview with Vandana Shiva" by Scott London, http://www.scottlondon.com/interviews/shiva.html, accessed October 14, 2011.
2. Edmund Andrews, "Greenspan Concedes Error on Regulation," *The New York Times*, November 23, 2008.
3. Paul Krugman, "How Did Economists Get It So Wrong?," *The New York Times*, October 2, 2009.
4. Ilene Grabel, "Not Your Grandfather's IMF," *Cambridge Journal of Economics* 35:5 (2011).
5. Group of 20; represents the world's largest economies.
6. Javier Blas, "G20 Attacked on Food Crisis Plan," *The Financial Times*, June 23, 2011.

7. Via Campesina, "G20 excludes poor countries," press release, http://www.viacampesina.org/en/index.php?option=com_content&view=article&id=969:g20-exludes-poor-countries-and-pushes-business-as-usual-small-farmers-demand-system-change&catid=15:news-from-the-regions&Itemid=29, accessed October 7, 2011.
8. Jayati Ghosh, "Spooked into Austerity," http://triplecrisis.com/tag/financial-crisis/page/2/, accessed October 7, 2011.
9. Dani Rodrik, "Goodbye Washington Consensus, Hello Washington Confusion?," *Journal of Economic Literature* 44:4 (December 2006).
10. Vandana Shiva, "Development as a New Project of Western Patriarchy," in *Reweaving the World*, eds. Diamond and Orenstein (San Francisco, CA: Sierra Club, 1990), 189–90. For less radical critiques, see, e.g.: Serra, Spiegel and Stiglitz, eds., *The Washington Consensus Reconsidered* (New York: Oxford, 2008).
11. Katherine Marshall, *The World Bank* (New York: Routledge, 2008), 151.
12. Deborah Johnston, "Poverty and Distribution: Back on the Neoliberal Agenda?," in *Neoliberalism: A Critical Reader*, eds. Saad-Fihlo and Johnston (London: Pluto Press, 2005), 138.
13. Ha-Joon Chang and Ilene Grabel, *Reclaiming Development* (London: Verso, 2004), 2.
14. For a good overview of the Washington Consensus see, e.g., John Williamson, "Did the Washington Consensus Fail?," speech before the Peterson Institute for International Economics (Washington, DC: November 6, 2002).
15. Walden Bello, *The Food Wars* (London: Verso, 2009), 30.
16. Carlos Oya, "Sticks and Carrots for Farmers in Developing Countries," in *Neoliberalism: A Critical Reader*, eds. Saad Fihlo and Johnston (London: Pluto, 2005), 129.
17. Johnathan Kydd and Andrew Dorward, "The Washington Consensus on Poor CountryAgriculture," *Development Policy Revew* 19:4 (2001), 467–78.
18. Vandana Shiva, "The Economics of Peace," Speech at the Economics of Peace Conference in Sonoma, CA, October 2009, http://vimeo.com/7429355, accessed October 20, 2011; Vandana Shiva, *The Violence of the Green Revolution* (London: Zed Books, 1992).
19. María Elena Martinez-Torres, "The Benefits and Sustainability of Organic Farming by Peasant Coffee Farmers in Chiapas Mexico," in *Confronting the Coffee Crisis*, eds. Christopher M. Bacon, V. Ernesto Méndez, Stephen R. Gleissman, David Goodman, and Jonathan A. Fox (Cambridge, MA: MIT Press, 2008), 103.
20. Ibid., 471.
21. Oya, "Sticks and Carrots," 131.
22. Shiva, "Economics of Peace."
23. Bello, *Food Wars*, 35.
24. UNCTAD, *Commodity Policies for Development* (Geneva: UNCTAD, 2005), 8.
25. Donald Larson, Jock Anderson, and Panos Varagis, "Policies on Managing Risk in Agricultural Markets," *The World Bank Research Observer* 19:2 (2004), 210.

26. UNCTAD, *Commodity Policies for Development*, 5.
27. World Bank, *Agriculture for Development: World Development Report* (Washington, DC: World Bank, 2008), 118.
28. UNDP, *Commodity Development Strategies in the Integrated Framework* (UNDP, 2009), 44.
29. World Bank, *Agriculture for Development*, 118.
30. UNCTAD, *Expert Meeting on the Trade and Development Implications of Financial Services and Commodity Exchanges (Part I), Item 3: Trade and Development Implications of Commodity Exchanges* (Geneva: UNCTAD, September 2007), 5.
31. UNCTAD, *Commodity Policies for Development*, 5.
32. World Bank, *Agriculture for Development*, 14.
33. UNCTAD, *Commodity Policies for Development*, 4.
34. UNDP, *Commodity Development Strategies*, 44.
35. UNCTAD, *Commodity Policies for Development*, 4.
36. World Bank, *Agriculture for Development*, 192.
37. Ibid., 92.
38. Susan Engels, *The World Bank and the Post-Washington Consensus in Vietnam and Indonesia* (London: Routledge, 2010), 72, 75.
39. Ngaire Woods, *The Globalizers* (Ithaca, NY: Cornell, 2006), 4.
40. Joseph Stiglitz, "Globalism's Discontents," *American Prospect* 13:1 (January 14, 2002), 1.
41. Alexei Mojarov and Mehmet Arda, "Commodities," in *Beyond Conventional Wisdom in Development Policy: An intellectual history of UNCTAD, 1964–2004*, eds. Shigehisa Kasahara and Charles Gore (New York: United Nations, 2004), 124.
42. UNCTAD, FAO, World Bank, OECD, IFAD, IMF, IFPRI, WFP, UNDP, and UN-HLTF, "Price Volatility in Food and Agricultural Markets" (June 2011), 12; see also pp. 21–3, http://www.oecd.org/document/20/0,3746,en_2649_37401_48152724_1_1_1_37401,00.html.
43. Some experts, including UNCTAD and friends in the report cited directly above this note, have argued that OTC commodity derivatives are the real problem (e.g. the commodity swaps discussed in the previous chapter), while exchange-traded futures and options present no such difficulties. This is an unsustainable assumption, given that swap dealers trade heavily on the organized exchanges to lay off the risk they incur by dealing the OTC instruments in the first place. Already, there are speculative position limits in place on the exchanges, but these failed to curb recent volatility as exemptions were made for swaps trading. Others have argued that there are important regulatory efforts afoot, to place limits on the future positions of swap speculators, that would take bad speculation out of the markets, rendering them more functional (e.g. Clapp and Helleiner, "Troubled Futures"). But, not only have the position limits established in the Dodd-Frank Bill not gone into effect (this Bill is the primary emphasis in Clapp and Helleiner's article), there is serious opposition to these provisions from the financial sector. Additionally, *Forbes* reported in October 2011 ("CFTC Position Limits Rule Divides Agency, Angers

Market Participants," November 19, 2011) that the CFTC has yet to define the term "swap," which will not only delay the rule's implementation, but will also potentially dilute the regulation's impact depending on how the term is defined. Similar regulations, being considered in the EU, have also yet be approved by legislators (see the recent press release from the European Commission, "New rules for more efficient, resilient and transparent financial markets in Europe," http://europa.eu/rapid/pressReleasesAction.do?reference=IP/11/1219&format=HTML&aged=0&language=en&guiLanguage=en, accessed October 20, 2011).

44. Larson, Anderson, and Varangis, "Policies on Managing Risk in Agricultural Markets."
45. UNCTAD, *Farmers and Farmers' Associations*, 18. "Repos" are repurchase agreements; farmers temporarily sell their crop to a bank in exchange for quick cash, and agree to repurchase it in the future at a fixed price.
46. Robert Shiller, *The New Financial Order* (Princeton, NJ: Princeton University Press, 2003), x.
47. UNCTAD, *The Global Trading Village* (Bürgenstock: UNCTAD, 2000), preface.
48. Joel Salatin, quoted in the movie *Food, Inc.*, quote pulled from the International Movie Database at http://www.imdb.com/title/tt1286537/quotes, accessed October 20, 2011.
49. Carlos Oliviera, "The Silence of the Lambs: Paul Virilio in Conversation," http://www.alchemists.com/visual_alchemy/manifesto/virilio1.html, accessed October 7, 2011.
50. Isaac Asimov and Jason Shulman, *Isaac Asimov's Book of Science and Nature Quotations* (New York: Grove Press, 1990).
51. David Craig and Doug Porter, "The Third Way and the Third World: Poverty Reduction and Social Inclusion Strategies in the Rise of 'Inclusive' Liberalism," *Review of International Political Economy* 12:2 (2005), 226–63.
52. Ibid., 392.
53. Bourse Africa, list of directors on the board, http://www.bourseafrica.com/Directors-boards-members.html, accessed October 21, 2011.
54. TED, speaker biography, http://www.ted.com/speakers/eleni_gabre_madhin.html, accessed on October 21, 2011.
55. FAO, *Managing Supplies to Raise International Agricultural Commodity Prices* (Rome: FAO Committee on Commodity Problems, 2007), 3.
56. Rent-seeking in this case refers to time and money spent trying to gain access to the world coffee market via domestic public officials. In many cases, access under the ICA was regulated by marketing boards who distributed a select number of export licenses to certain firms. Only these firms were permitted to export coffee legally. As you might imagine, would-be exporters had an incentive to lobby and do favors for public officials to procure a license. Rent-seeking behaviors, thought to be inefficient because they represent wasted time and money, are common side-effects of bureaucratically managed economic systems.
57. FAO, *Managing Agricultural Supplies*, 4.

58. Ibid., 4.
59. Ibid., 5.
60. Stephanie Daniels and Seth Petchers, *The Coffee Crisis Continues* (Boston, MA: Oxfam America, 2005), 59.
61. Ibid., 43, 59.
62. Machiko Nissanke, *A Case for Innovative Commodity Stabilization Measures* (Geneva: Global Commodities Forum, March 2010), 11.
63. Ibid., 12.
64. Leanne Ussher, "International Price Stability, Full Employment and Global Balances: The Case for a Commodity Reserve Currency," draft of paper from Economics Department at Queens College, City University of New York, March 2008, http://www.qc-econ-bba.org/RePEc/pdf/0001.pdf, accessed November 29, 2011.
65. Stephen Farris, "Starbucks versus Ethiopia," *Fortune*, February 26, 2007.
66. Ibid.
67. Oxfam, "Starbucks opposes Ethiopia's plan to trademark specialty coffee names that could bring farmers an estimated $88 million annually," press release, November 25, 2006.
68. Aslihan Arslan and Christopher Reicher, "The Effects of the Coffee Trademarking Initiative and Starbucks Publicity on Export Prices of Ethiopian Coffee," Kiel Institute for the World Economy Working Paper #1606 (March 2010), 13.
69. CIB, http://www.ciboj.org/cib/, accessed October 11, 2011.
70. US$175,000 at the prevailing 1:2883 exchange rate on October 11, 2011. "Coffee Board of Kenya's New Brand," http://www.youtube.com/watch?v=fMNk3gOhZvg&feature=player_detailpage accessed October 11, 2011.
71. FNC, "About Us," http://www.federaciondecafeteros.org/particulares/en/quienes_somos, accessed October 28, 2011.
72. FNC, "The Branches of the FNC," http://www.federaciondecafeteros.org/particulares/en/que_hacemos/representacion_gremial/organos_gremiales_de_la_federacion_de_cafeteros/, accessed October 28, 2011.
73. FNC, "Home page," www.federaciondecafeteros.org, accessed October 28, 2011.
74. Daniele Giovanucci, *Colombia: Coffee Sector Study* (Washington, DC: The World Bank, 2002), 6.
75. USDA Foreign Agricultural Service, *GAIN Report: Colombia Coffee, Semi-Annual 2008* (Washington, DC: USDA, 2008), 3, emphasis added.
76. Giovanucci, *Colombia*, 10.
77. FNC, "Sustainability that Matters," http://www.federaciondecafeteros.org/particulares/en/sostenibilidad_en_accion, accessed October 28, 2011.
78. Ibid.
79. Laura Raynolds, Douglas Murray, and Peter Taylor, "The Future of Fair Trade Coffee: Dilemmas Facing Latin America's Small-Scale Producers," *Development in Practice* 16:2 (2006), 80.

80. FLO, "Impact," http://www.fairtrade.net/impact.html, accessed March 31, 2008.
81. Raynolds, Murray and Tailor, "The Future of Fair Trade Coffee," 80.
82. Martinez-Torres, "The Benefits and Sustainability," 500.
83. FLO, "Coffee," http://www.fairtrade.net/coffee.0.html, accessed October 11, 2011.
84. FLO "About Fairtrade," http://www.fairtrade.net/about_fairtrade.html, accessed May 26, 2008.
85. FLO, "Facts and Figures," http://www.fairtrade.net/figures.html, accessed May 26, 2008.
86. John Baffes, Bryan Lewin, and Panos Varangis, *Coffee: Market Settings and Policies* (Washington, DC: World Bank, 2005), accessed on January 13, 2007, http://siteresources.worldbank.org/INTGAT/Resources/GATChapter16.pdf, 207.
87. Muriel Calo and Timothy Wise, *Revaluing Peasant Coffee Production: Organic and Fair Trade Markets in Mexico* (Medford, MA: Tufts University Global Development and Environment Institute, 2005), 1.
88. Martinez-Torres, "The Benefits and Sustainability."
89. Ibid.; Raynolds, Murray, and Taylor, "The Future of Fair Trade Coffee."
90. Peter Dicken, *Global Shift*, 5th ed. (New York: Guilford, 2007), 106–7.
91. Bello, *Food Wars*, 135–7.
92. Ibid., 145.
93. Ponte, "The 'Latte Revolution'?"
94. Jayati Ghosh, "The Unnatural Coupling: Food and Global Finance" (2009),, 17.
95. Shiva, "Economics of Peace,".

Chapter 6

1. Adam Smith, *The Wealth of Nations* (New York: Modern Library, 2000), 90.
2. Karl Polanyi, *The Great Transformation* (Boston: Beacon, 2001).
3. See, e.g., Karl Marx and Friedrich Engels, *The Communist Manifesto* (New York: Penguin, 1998); Karl Marx, "The German Ideology," *The Marx-Engels Reader*, ed. Robert Tucker, 2nd ed. (New York: WW Norton, 1978).
4. John Gray, *False Dawn: The Delusions of Global Capitalism* (New York: WW Norton, 1998), 7.
5. Ismail Erturk, Julie Froud, Sukhdev Johal, Adam Leaver, and Karel Williams, "The Democratization of Finance? Promises, Outcomes and Conditions," *Review of International Political Economy* 14:4 (October 2007), 553.
6. Ibid., 572.
7. E.g. Gary Gereffi makes the argument that the East Asian Tiger economies achieved high and sustained levels of economic growth over time by "upgrading" their position in the textile commodity chain; see "International Trade and Industrial Upgrading in the Apparel Commodity Chain," *Journal of International Economics* 48: (1999). Sefano Ponte similarly argues that small coffee farmers can improve their position in the global coffee economy by "upgrading" to specialty

coffee production for the global market and away from mass produced coffees, though he recognizes that estates are likely better positioned to do this than small producers; see Stefano Ponte, "The 'Latte Revolution'? Regulation, Markets and Consumption in the Global Coffee Chain," *World Development* 30:7 (2002).

8. See, e.g., Jeffery S. Rothstein, "Economic Development Policymaking Down the Global Commodity Chain: Attracting an Auto Industry to Silao, Mexico," *Social Forces* 84:1 (September 2005), 49–69.

References

Adelegan, Janet Olatundun. "The Derivatives Market in Sub Saharan Africa." *IMF Working Paper* (Washington, D.C.: IMF, 2009).

Akiyama, Takamasa et al. *Commodity Market Reforms: Lessons of Two Decades* (Washington, D.C.: World Bank, 2001).

Anderson, Ronald and Danthine, Jean-Pierre. "The Time Pattern of Hedging and the Volatility of Future Prices." *The Review of Economic Studies* 50:2 (1983), 249–66.

Andrews, Edmund. "Greenspan Concedes Error on Regulation." *The New York Times* (October 23, 2008).

Arrow, Kenneth. "Uncertainty and the Welfare Economics of Medical Care." *American Economic Review* 53:5 (1963), 941–73.

Arslan, Aslihan and Reicher, Christopher. "The Effects of the Coffee Trademarking Initiative and Starbucks Publicity on Export Prices of Ethiopian Coffee." *Kiel Institute for the World Economy Working Paper #1606* (March 2010).

Asimov, Isaac and Shulman, Jason. *Isaac Asimov's Book of Science and Nature Quotations* (New York: Grove Press, 1990).

Bacon, Christopher. "Confronting the Coffee Crisis: Can Fair Trade, Organic, and Specialty Coffees Reduce Small-Scale Farmer Vulnerability in Northern Nicaragua?." *World Development* 33:3 (2005), 497–511.

Baffes, John. *Restructuring Uganda's Coffee Industry: Why Going Back to the Basics Matters* (Washington, D.C.: The World Bank, 2006).

Baffes, John, Lewin, Bryan and Varangis, Panos. *Coffee: Market Settings and Policies* (Washington, D.C.: World Bank, 2005).

Balzli, Beat. "How Goldman Sachs Helped Greece Mask Its True Debt." *Der Spiegel* (February 8, 2010).

Bates, Robert. *Open Economy Politics: The Political Economy of the World Coffee Trade* (Princeton NJ: Princeton University Press, 1997).

Bello, Walden. *The Food Wars* (London: Verso, 2009).

BIS. "Statistical Annex." *BIS Quarterly Review*. June 2011.

Blas, Javier. "G20 Attacked on Food Crisis Plan." *The Financial Times* (June 23, 2011).

Blogg, Peter and Kotecha, Surendra. "NYSE Liffe Robusta Coffee Futures." Presentation for the ICO by representatives of NYSE Liffe, March 16, 2009.

Bohman, Mary, Jarvis, Lovell and Barichello, Richard. "Rent Seeking and International Commodity Agreements: The Case of Coffee." *Economic Development and Cultural Change* 44:2 (1996), 379–404.

Bretton Woods Project. "World Bank Policies 'Enabling' African land grab." September 14, 2011.

Brown, Oli, Crawford, Alec and Gibson, Jason. *Boom or Bust: How Commodity Price Volatility Impedes Poverty Reduction, and What to Do about It* (Winnepeg: International Institute for Sustainable Development, 2008).

Bryan, Dick and Rafferty, Michael. *Capitalism with Derivatives* (New York: Palgrave, 2006).

Burghardt, Galen. "Volume Surges Again." *Futures Industry* (March/April 2008).

Bussolo, Maurizio et al. *The Impact of Commodity Price Changes on Rural Households: The Case of Coffee in Uganda* (Washington, D.C.: The World Bank, 2006).

Calo, Muriel and Wise, Timothy. *Revaluing Peasant Coffee Production: Organic and Fair Trade Markets in Mexico* (Medford, MA: Global Development and Environment Institute, 2005).

Cardenas, Jorge. "The World Coffee Crisis," in *World Coffee Conference* (London: ICO, 2001), http://www.ico.org/event_pdfs/cardenas.pdf

Carter, Dave, Rogers, Dan and Simkins, Betty. "Fuel Hedging in the Airline Industry: The Case of Southwest Airlines." Case Research Journal (online article), 2004.

Cashin, Paul, McDermott, John and Scott, Alasdair. *Booms and Slumps in World Commodity Prices.* (Washington, DC: The International Monetary Fund, 1999).

Chang, Ha-Joon and Grabel, Ilene. *Reclaiming Development* (London: Verso, 2004).

Charveriat, Celine. *Bitter Coffee* (London: Oxfam, 2001).

Claessens, Stijn and Duncan, Ronald, eds. *Managing Commodity Price Risk in Developing Countries* (Baltimore, MA: Johns Hopkins University Press for the World Bank, 1993).

Clapp, Jennifer and Helleiner, Eric. "Troubled Futures." *Review of International Political Economy* (2010), iFirst, 1–27.

Craig, David and Porter, Doug. "The Third Way and the Third World: Poverty Reduction and Social Inclusion Strategies in the Rise of 'Inclusive' Liberalism." *Review of International Political Economy* 12:2 (2005), 226–63.

CRBM. "The Vultures of Land Grabbing." 2010. http://farmlandgrab.org/wp-content/uploads/2010/11/VULTURES-completo.pdf, accessed November 29, 2011.

CRMG. *Lessons Learned—Price Risk Management* (Washington, D.C.: The World Bank, 2005).

CRMG. *Price Risk Management Work Summary* (Washington, D.C.: The World Bank/CRMG, May 2005).

Daniels, Stephanie and Petchers, Seth. *The Coffee Crisis Continues* (Boston, MA: Oxfam America, 2005).

Darby, Michael. "Over-The-Counter Derivatives and Systemic Risk to the Global Financial System." *NBER Working Paper Series* (Cambridge, MA: National Bureau of Economic Research, 1994).

Daviron, Benoit and Ponte, Stefano. *The Coffee Paradox* (London: Zed Books, 2005).

Davis, Benjamin. "The Adjustment Strategies of Mexican Ejidatarios in the Face of Neoliberal Reform." *CEPAL Review* 72: (2000), pp. 99–118.

Davis, Mike. "Late Victorian Holocausts," in *The Development Reader*, Sharad Chari and Stuart Corbridge, eds. (New York: Routledge, 2008), pp. 14–30.

DeMartino, George. *Global Economy, Global Justice* (New York: Routledge, 2000).

DeRosa, David, ed. *Currency Derivatives* (New York: Wiley & Sons, 1998).

Devereux, Steven. "Livelihood Insecurity and Social Protection: A Re-Emerging Issue in Rural Development." *Development Policy Review* 19:4 (2001), 507–19.

Dicken, Peter. *Global Shift*, 5th edition. (New York: Guilford, 2007).

Dischel, Robert, ed. *Climate Risk and the Weather Market* (London: Risk Books, 2002).

Dodd, Randall. "From Fat Years to Lean Years: What if Joseph Had Used Derivatives?," *Financial Policy Forum Working Paper*, 2007.

Dodd, Randall. "Playing with Fire." *Finance and Development.* June 2009.

Dodd, Randall. "Subprime: Tentacles of a Crisis," in *Finance and Development*, December 2007.

Dodd, Randall. "The Virtues of Prudential Regulation." Washington DC: Financial Policy Forum Report, January 2004.

Dodd, Randall and Griffith-Jones, Stephanie. "Report on Chile's Derivatives Markets: Stabilizing or Speculative Impact." ECLAC, 2006.

Domowitz, Ian and Steil, Benn. "Automation, Trading Costs and the Structure of the Securities Trading Industry." *Brookings-Wharton Papers on Financial Services* (1999).

Doran, James. "The Mating Game." *Futures Industry* (Outlook 2008).

Eakin, Hallie, Tucker, Catherine and Castellanos, Edwin. "Responding to the Coffee Crisis: A Pilot Study of Farmers' Adaptations to the Coffee Crisis." *The Geographical Journal* 172:2 (2006), 156–71.

Easwaran, R. Salvadi and Ramasundaram, P. "Whether Commodity Futures Market in Agriculture is Efficient in Price Discovery?—An Econometric Analysis." *Agricultural Economics Research Review* 21 (2008), 337–44.

Economides, Nicholas. "The Impact of the Internet on Financial Markets." *Journal of Financial Transformation* 1 (2001), 8–13.

Economides, Nicholas. "Network Economics with Application to Finance." *Financial Markets, Institutions & Instruments* 2:5 (1993), 89–97.

Edwards, Michael. "The Irrelevance of Development Studies." *Third World Quarterly* 11:1 (1989), 116–35.

Engels, Susan. *The World Bank and the Post-Washington Consensus in Vietnam and Indonesia* (London: Routledge, 2010).

Epstein, Gerald, ed. *Financialization and the World Economy* (Cheltenham, UK: Edward Elgar, 2005).

Erturk, Ismail, Froud, Julie, Johal, Sukhdev, Leaver, Adam and Williams, Karel. "The Democratization of Finance? Promises, Outcomes and Conditions." *Review of International Political Economy* 14:4 (2007), 553–75.

Escobar, Arturo. *Encountering Development* (Princeton NJ: Princeton University Press, 1995).

Executive Director of ICO. "October 2008 Coffee Market Report." http://dev.ico.org/documents/cmr1008e.pdf, accessed October 6, 2011.

Fafchamps, Marcel and Hill, Ruth Vargas. *Coffee Hedging in the Market: Exporter, Trader and Producer Data From Uganda* (Washington, D.C.: World Bank, 2006).

FAO. *Commodity Exchanges and Derivatives Markets: Evolution, Experience and Outlook in the Cereal Sector* (Rome: FAO, 2007).

FAO. *Commodity Market Review, 2003–2004* (Rome: Food and Agriculture Organization, Commodities and Trade Division, 2003).

FAO. *Managing Supplies to Raise International Agricultural Commodity Prices* (Rome: FAO Committee on Commodity Problems, 2007).

FAO. "Price Volatility in Agricultural Markets." *Economic and Social Perspectives.* Policy Brief 12 (Dec 2010).

Farris, Stephen, "Starbucks versus Ethiopia," *Fortune*, February 26, 2007.

FIA. "Annual Volume Survey: 2010 Record Volume." *Future Industry* (March 2011).

FIA. "Annual Volume Survey: 2008 A Wild Ride." *Future Industry* (March/April 2009).

Figlewski, Stephen. "Derivative Risks, Old and New." *NYU/Stern Working Paper No. FIN-98–033* (December 1998).

Fortenberry, Randall and Zapata, Hector. "Developed Speculation and Underdeveloped Markets." University of Wisconsin-Madison, Department of Agricultural Economics Staff Paper (2004).

Fox, Justin. "Commodity Futures Modernization Act," *Time* (December 31, 2008).

Friedman, Milton. "The Reduction of Fluctuations in the Incomes of Primary Producers." *The Economic Journal* 64:256 (1954), 704–729.

Gabre-Madhin, Eleni. "An Eye on the Future: Can the Ethiopia Commodity Exchange Succeed Without Futures?." www.ecx.com.et, May 2007.

Geithner, Timothy. "Implications of Growth in Credit Derivatives for Financial Stability." Speech at NYU's Stern School of Business Third Credit Risk Conference, May 16, 2006.

George, Susan. *The Debt Boomerang* (London: Pluto, 1992).

Gerasymenko, Nataliia and Zhemoyda, Oleksandr. "New Challenges for Risk Management in AgriFood Industry." Paper prepared for presentation at the 113th EAAE Seminar, Chania, Crete, Greece, September 3–6, 2009.

Gereffi, Gary. "International Trade and Industrial Upgrading in the Apparel Commodity Chain." *Journal of International Economics* 48: (1999), 37–70.

Ghosh, Jayati. "Spooked into Austerity." http://triplecrisis.com/tag/financial-crisis/page/2/, accessed October 7, 2011.

Ghosh, Jayati. "The Unnatural Coupling: Food and Global Finance" (2009).

Gibbon, Peter. *The Commodity Question: New Thinking on Old Problems* (UNDP, 2005).

Gilbert, Christopher. "Trends and Volatility in Agricultural Commodity Prices," in *Agricultural Markets and Trade*, Alexander Sarris and David Hallam, eds. (Cheltenham, UK: Edward Elgar, 2006).

Giovanucci, Daniele. *Colombia: Coffee Sector Study* (Washington, D.C.: The World Bank, 2002).

Giovannucci, Daniele, Lewin, Bryan and Swinkels, Rob. *The Socialist Republic of Vietnam: Coffee Sector Report* (Washington, D.C.: World Bank, 2004).

Grabel, Ilene. "Not Your Grandfather's IMF." *Cambridge Journal of Economics* 35:5 (2011), 805–30.

Gray, John. *False Dawn: The Delusions of Global Capitalism* (New York: WW Norton, 1998).

Gray, John. "From the Great Transformation to the Global Free Market," in *The Globalization Reader*, Lechner and Boli, eds., 3rd edition (Malden, MA: Blackwell, 2008), pp. 25–31.

Gregory, Jon. *Counterparty Credit Risk* (West Sussex: John Wiley & Sons, 2010).

Greider, William. "The Last Farm Crisis." *The Nation* (November 2000).

Gresser, Charis and Tickell, Sophia. *Mugged: Poverty in Your Coffee Cup* (London: Oxfam, 2002).

Groome, Todd, Blancher, Nicholas, Haas, Francois P. and Kiff, John. *The Limits of Market-Based Risk Transfer and Implications for Managing Systemic Risks* (Washington, D.C.: IMF, 2006).

Gross, Adam. "The new order of global derivatives trading," PowerPoint presentation at FAO International Conference on Commodity Exchanges and their Role in Market Development and Transparency, 15 May 2007.

Guadarrama-Zagasti, Carlos. "A Grower Typology Approach to Assessing the Environmental Impact of Coffee Farming in Veracruz Mexico," in *Confronting the Coffee Crisis*, Bacon et al., eds. (Cambridge, MA: MIT Press, 2008), pp. 127–154.

Hacker, Jacob. "Dismantling the Health Care State? Political Institutions, Public Policies and the Comparative Politics of Health Reform." *British Journal of Political Science* 34:4 (2004).

Hacker, Jacob. "Privatizing Risk Without Privatizing the Welfare State: The Hidden Politics of Social Welfare Retrenchment in the United States." *American Political Science Review* 98:2 (2004), 243–60.

Hacker, Jacob. *The Great Risk Shift* (Oxford: Oxford University Press, 2006).

Hacker, Jacob. "The Privatization of Risk and the Growing Economic Insecurity of Americans." Social Science Research Council, 2006. http://privatizationofrisk.ssrc.org/Hacker/index.html.

Harvey, David. *A Brief History of Neoliberalism* (Oxford: Oxford University Press, 2005).

Helleiner, Eric. *States and the Reemergence of Global Finance* (Ithaca: Cornell University Press, 1994).

Hess, Ulrich and Stoppa, Andrea. "Design and Use of Weather Derivatives in Agricultural Policies." *WTO Conference Paper*, Capri, Italy, June 2003.

Hobson, John A. *Imperialism.* www.marxists.org, 1902.

Holzmann, Robert and Jorgenson, Steen. *Social Risk Management* (Washington, D.C.: World Bank, 2000).

Hopkins, Terence and Wallerstein, Immanuel. "Commodity Chains: Construction and Research," in *Commodity Chains and Global Capitalism*, Gereffi and Korzeniewicz, eds. (Westport, CT: Praeger, 1994), pp. 17–19.

ILO. *Economic Security for a Better World* (Geneva: International Labor Organization, 2004).

ITF. *Mexico: Price Risk Management, Phase 2 Report* (Washington, D.C.: World Bank/ITF, 2002).

Jia, Chen. "Focus Turns to Futures Trading as Commodities Surge." *China Daily* (February 10, 2011).

Jia, Chen. "Fortelling the Future for Profit." *China Daily* (December 1, 2011).

Johnston, Deborah. Poverty and Distribution: Back on the Neoliberal Agenda?, in *Neoliberalism: A Critical Reader*, Saad-Fihlo and Johnston, eds. (London: Pluto Press, 2005), pp. 135–41.

Jubilee Debt Campaign. *A New Debt Crisis?* (London: Jubilee Debt Campaign, March, 2009).

Kabra, Kamal. Comments on the Forward Market Regulation Act. Standing Committee on Food, Consumer Affairs and Public Distribution. Ministry of Consumer Affairs, Food and Public Distribution, Department of Consumer Affairs, Government of India, 14th Lok Sabha, 17th Report, December 2006.

Kleih, Ulrich, Onumah, Gideon and Butterworth, Ruth. "Training Manual on Market Information System, Uganda—Coffee." Common Fund for Commodities and Uganda Coffee Development Authority, 2006.

Koenig, David. "Airlines That Hedged Against Fuel Costs Reap Benefits." *The Washington Post* (October 21, 2005).

Krugman, Paul. "How Did Economists Get It So Wrong?" *The New York Times* (September 2, 2009).

Kuznetsov, Yevgeny and Dahlman, Carl. *Mexico's Transition to a Knowledge-Based Economy: Challenges and Opportunities* (Washington, D.C.: The World Bank, 2008).

Kydd, Johnathan and Dorward, Andrew. "The Washington Consensus on Poor CountryAgriculture." *Development Policy Review* (2001).

Larson, Donald, Anderson, Jock and Varagis, Panos. "Policies on Managing Risk in Agricultural Markets." *The World Bank Research Observer* 19:2 (2004), 199–230.

Larson, Donald and Coleman, Jonathan. *The Effects of Option-Hedging on the Costs of Domestic Price Stabilization Schemes* (Washington, D.C.: The World Bank, 1991).

Larson, Donald, Varangis, Panos and Yabuki, Nanae. *Commodity Risk Management and Development* (Washington, D.C.: The World Bank, 1998).

Leao de Sousa, Eduardo L. and Pimentel, Fernando L. *Study on the Cedula De Produto Rural (CPR)—Farm Product Bond in Brazil* (Washington, D.C.: The World Bank, 2005).

Lee, Jamie. "Sicom Taps Indian Market with Cross-listing Accord." *The Business Times Singapore* (May 27, 2009).

Lence, Sergio. "Do Futures Benefit Farmers?." *American Journal of Agricultural Economics* 91 (2009), 154–67.

Lence, Sergio and Hayenga, Marvin. "The Pitfalls of Multi-Year Rollover Hedges." *American Journal of Agricultural Economics* 83 (2001), 107–19.

Lenin, Vladimir. *Imperialism: The Last Stage of Capitalism* (New York: International, 2002).

Lewin, Bryan, Giovanucci, Daniele and Varangis, Panos. *The Coffee Market: New Paradigms in Global Supply and Demand* (Washington, D.C.: World Bank, 2004).

Liaw, Thomas and Moy, Ronald. *The Irwin Guide to Stocks, Bonds, Futures and Options: A Comprehensive Guide to Wall Street's Markets* (New York: McGraw-Hill, 2001).

Loader, David. *Clearing and Settlement of Derivatives* (Amsterdam: Elsevier, 2005).

Love, Joseph. "Raul Prebisch and the Origins of the Doctrine of Unequal Exchange." *Latin American Research Review* 15:3 (1980), 45–72.

Loy, Jens-Peter. "Relative Forecasting and Hedging Efficiency of Agricultural Futures Markets in the European Union: Evidence for Slaughter Hog Contracts," Paper prepared for presentation at the Xth EAAE Congress, Zaragoza (Spain), 28–31 August 2002.

Magdoff, Harry. *Imperialism: From the Colonial Age to the Present* (New York: Monthly Review, 1978).

Markham, Jerry. *The History of Commodity Futures Trading and Its Regulation* (New York: Prager, 1987).

Marshall, Katherine. *The World Bank* (New York: Routledge, 2008).

Marx, Karl. "The German Ideology," in *The Marx-Engels Reader*, Robert Tucker ed., 2nd edition (New York: WW Norton, 1978), pp. 146–202.

Marx, Karl and Engels, Friedrich. *The Communist Manifesto* (New York: Penguin, 1998).

Masao, Yoshida. *Agricultural Marketing Intervention in East Africa* (Tokyo: Institute of Developing Economies, 1984).

Masters, Michael and White, Adam. "Accidental Hunt Brothers" (July 2008). http://www.loe.org/images/content/080919/Act1.pdf, accessed November 17, 2011.

McKinnon, Ronald. "Futures Markets, Buffer Stocks and Income Stability for Primary Producers." *Journal of Political Economy* 75:6 (1967), 844–61.

Mehrling, Perry. *Fischer Black and the Revolutionary Idea of Finance* (Hoboken: John Wiley & Sons, 2005).

Melamed, Leo. *For Crying Out Loud* (New York: Wiley and Sons, 2009).

Meyers, Robert J. "Incomplete Markets and Commodity-Linked Finance in Developing Countries." *World Bank Research Observer* 7:1 (1992), 79–94.

Miller, Simon. "Weather Builds on Derivatives Sales in 2011." *Financial Risk Today* (May 23 2011).

Mohan, Sushil. "Market-Based Price Risk Management for Coffee Producers." *Development Policy Review* 25:3 (2007), 333–54.

Mohan, Sushil and Love, James. "Coffee Futures: Role in Reducing Coffee Producers' Price Risk." *Journal of International Development* (2004), Vol. 16, 983–1002.

Mojarov, Alexei and Arda, Mehmet. "Commodities," in *Beyond Conventional Wisdom in Development Policy: An Intellectual History of UNCTAD, 1964–2004*, Shigehisa Kasahara and Charles Gore, eds. (New York: United Nations, 2004), pp. 61–72.

Morduch, Jonathan. "Between the State and the Market: Can Informal Insurance Patch the Safety Net?." *The World Bank Research Observer* 14:2 (1999), 187–207.

Morrison, Joanne. "ICE Adds Brazilian Flavor to Coffee Futures Market." *Futures Industry*, (March/April 2011).

Moss, David. *When All Else Fails* (Cambridge: Harvard University Press, 2002).

Murray, Sara. "Most Food Stamp Recipients Have No Earned Income." *The Wall Street Journal*. (September 26, 2011).

Newbery, David and Stiglitz, Joseph. *The Theory of Commodity Price Stabilization* (Oxford: Oxford University Press, 1981).

Newman, Susan. "Financialization and Changes in Social Relations Along Commodity Chains: The Case of Coffee." *Review of Radical Political Economics* 41:4 (2009), 539–59.

Nissanke, Machiko. *A Case for Innovative Commodity Stabilization Measures* (Geneva: Global Commodities Forum, March 2010).

Oliviera, Carlos. "The Silence of the Lambs: Paul Virilio in Conversation." http://www.alchemists.com/visual_alchemy/manifesto/virilio1.html, accessed October 7, 2011.

Osorio, Néstor. "The Global Coffee Crisis: A Threat to Sustainable Development." Submission to the World Summit on Sustainable Development, Johannesburg, 2002

Oxfam. "Dumping Without Borders." *Oxfam Briefing Paper*, August 2003.

Oya, Carlos. "Sticks and Carrots for Farmers in Developing Countries," in *Neoliberalism: A Critical Reader*, Saad Fihlo and Deborah Johnston, eds. (London: Pluto, 2005), pp. 127–134.

Neumann, William and Pollack, Andrew. "U.S. Farmers Cope with Roundup-resistant weeds." *The New York Times* (May 3, 2010).

Nicholson, Marcy. "UPDATE 3-ICE Committee Recommends Brazilian Coffee-trade." *Reuters* (October 14, 2010).

Pallavi, Aparna. "Empty Fields Stare at Farm Widows." *India Together* (August 23, 2007).

Partnoy, Frank. *FIASCO* (New York: Penguin, 1999).

Patel, Raj. *Stuffed and Starved: The Hidden Battle for the World Food System* (Brooklyn, NY: Melville House, 2008).

Peck, Anne. "The Economic Role of Traditional Commodity Futures Markets," in *Futures Markets: Their Economic Role*, Anne Peck, ed. (Washington, D.C.: American Enterprise Institute, 1985), pp. 1–81.

Peck, Anne. "Hedging and Income Stability: Concepts, Implications and an Example." *American Journal of Agricultural Economics* 57:3 (1975), 410–9.

Pindyck, Robert. "The Dynamics of Commodity Spot and Futures Markets: A Primer." *The Energy Journal* 22 (2001), 1–29.

Polanyi, Karl. *The Great Transformation* (Boston: Beacon, 2001).

Pollan, Michael. *The Omnivore's Dilemma* (New York: Penguin, 2006).

Ponte, Stefano. "The 'Latte Revolution'? Regulation, Markets and Consumption in the Global Coffee Chain." *World Development* 30:7 (2002), 1099–122.

Potts, Jason. *Building a Sustainable Coffee Sector Using Market-Based Approaches: The Role of Multi-Stakeholder Cooperation* (Geneva: UNCTAD/IISD, 2003).

Rabach, Eileen and Kim, Eun Mee. "Where is the Chain in Commodity Chains? The Service Sector Nexus," in *Commodity Chains and Global Capitalism*, Gereffi and Korzeniewicz, eds. (Westport, CT: Praeger, 1994), pp. 123–42.

Raynolds, Laura, Murray, Douglas and Taylor, Peter. "The Future of Fair Trade Coffee: Dilemmas Facing Latin America's Small-Scale Producers." *Development in Practice* 16:2 (2006), 179–92.

Rice, Robert. "The Land Use Patterns and the history of coffee in Eastern Chiapas, Mexico." *Agriculture and Human Values* 14 (1997), 127–43.

Rios, Anna R. and Shively, Gerald R. "Farm Size and Nonparametric Efficiency Measurements for Coffee Farms in Vietnam." Prepared for presentation at the American Agricultural Economics Association Annual Meeting, Providence, Rhode Island, July 24–27, 2005.

Roberts, Sheridan. *The Global Information Society: A Statistical View* (Santiago: United Nations, 2008).

Rodrik, Dani. "Goodbye Washington Consensus, Hello Washington Confusion?." *Journal of Economic Literature* 44:4 (2006), 973–87.

Rothstein, Jeffery S. "Economic Development Policymaking Down the Global Commodity Chain: Attracting an Auto Industry to Silao, Mexico." *Social Forces* 84:1 (September 2005), 46–69.

Rutten, Lamon. "Going rural with Smart Finance." *Hindu Business Line* (March 21, 2007).

Rutten, Lamon and Youssef, Rita. *Market-Based Price Risk Management* (Winnipeg: IISD, 2007).

Sarkar, Asani. "Indian Derivatives Markets." From The New York Federal Reserve, http://www.newyorkfed.org/research/economists/sarkar/derivatives_in_india.pdf, accessed November 3, 2011.

Sayer, Geoff. *Coffee Futures: The Impact of Falling World Prices on Livelihoods in Uganda* (London: Oxfam, 2002).

Schaeffer, Robert. *Understanding Globalization* (Lanham, MD: Rowman and Littlefield, 2005).

Schultz, Theodore. "The Theory and Measurement of Price Expectations." *The American Economic Review* 39:3 (1949), 135–49.

Schwartz, Nelson and Creswell, Julie. "Who Created This Monster?" *The New York Times*. March 23, 2008.

Narcis, Serra, Xxx, Spiegel and Joseph, Stiglitz, eds. *The Washington Consensus Reconsidered* (New York: Oxford, 2008).

Shiller, Robert. *The New Financial Order* (Princeton NJ: Princeton University Press, 2003).

Shiller, Robert. "Radical Financial Innovation," *Cowles Foundation Discussion Paper #1461*, Cowles Foundation for Research in Economics, Yale University (April 2004).

Shiva, Vandana. "Development as a New Project of Western Patriarchy," in *Reweaving the World*, Diamond and Orenstein, eds. (San Francisco: Sierra Club, 1990), pp. 189–200.

Shiva, Vandana. "In the Footsteps of Gandhi: An Interview with Vandana Shiva." By Scott London, http://www.scottlondon.com/interviews/shiva.html, accessed October 14, 2011.

Shiva, Vandana. "The Economics of Peace," Speech at the Economics of Peace Conference in Sonoma, CA, October 2009. http://vimeo.com/7429355, accessed October 20, 2011.

Shiva, Vandana. *The Violence of the Green Revolution* (London: Zed Books, 1992).

Sick, Deborah. "Coping with the Crisis: Costa Rican Households and the International Coffee Market." *Ethnology* 36:3 (1997), 255–75.

Smith, Adam. *The Wealth of Nations* (New York: Modern Library, 2000).

Stallman, Bob. "Statement of the American Farm Bureau Federation" To the CFTC, April 22, 2008.

Standing Committee on Food, Consumer Affiars and Public Distribution (2006–07), "Forward Contracts (Regulation) Amendment Bill, 2006," Ministry of Consumer Affairs, Food and Public Distribution, Department of Consumer Affairs, Government of India, 14th Lok Sabha, 17th Report, December 2006.

Stavrianos, L.S. *Global Rift* (New York: William Morrow and Company, 1981).

Steinherr, Alfred. *Derivatives: The Wild Beast of Finance* (West Sussex: John Wiley & Sons, 2000).

Stennis, Earl, Pinar, Musa and Allen, Albert. "The Futures Market and Price Discovery in the Textile Industry." *American Journal of Agricultural Economics* 65:2 (1983), 308–10.

Stiglitz, Joseph. "Globalism's Discontents." *American Prospect* (January 14, 2002).

Stringer, Lindsay, Twyman, Chasca and Gibbs, Leah. "Learning from the South." *The Geographic Journal* 174 (2008), 235–50.

Story, Louise. "A Secretive Banking Elite Rules Trading in Derivatives." *The New York Times* (December 11, 2010).

Talbot, John. *Grounds for Agreement* (Lanham, MD: Rowman and Littlefield, 2004).

Talbot, John. "The Struggle for Control of a Commodity Chain." *Latin American Research Review* 32 (1997), 117–35.

Tawney, R. H. *Land and Labor in China* (New York: ME Sharpe, 1966).

Tickell, Adam. "Unstable Futures," in *Global Capitalism Versus Democracy*, Panitch and Leys, eds. (London, UK: Merlin, 1999).

Tiffen, Pauline and Fernandez, Guido. *Report on the BMI-FEDA Hedging Program, El Salvador* (Washington, D.C.: World Bank/CRMG, October 2005).

Topik, Steven. "Historicizing Commodity Chains," in *Frontiers of Commodity Chain Research*, Jennifer Bair, ed. (Stanford: Stanford University Press, 2009), pp. 37–62.

Turbeville, Wallace. *Derivatives Clearinghouses in an Era of Financial Reform* (Washington, D.C.: Roosevelt Institute, 2010).

Turvey, Calum. "Weather Derivatives for Specific Event Risk in Agriculture." *Review of Agricultural Economics* 23:2 (2001), 333–51.

UNCTAD. *Commodity Policies for Development* (Geneva: UNCTAD, 2005).

UNCTAD. *Enabling Small Commodity Producers and Processors in Developing Countries to Reach Global Markets* (Geneva: United Nations, 2006).

UNCTAD. *Examination of the Effectiveness and Usefulness for Commodity Dependent Countries of New Tools in Commodity Markets: Risk Management and Collateralized Finance* (Geneva: United Nations, 1998).

UNCTAD. *Expert Meeting on the Trade and Development Implications of Financial Services and Commodity Exchanges (Part I), Item 3: Trade and Development Implications of Commodity Exchanges* (Geneva: United Nations, 2007).

UNCTAD. *Farmers and Farmers' Associations in Developing Countries and Their Use of Modern Financial Instruments* (Geneva: United Nations, 2002).

UNCTAD. *Progress in the Development of African Commodity Exchanges* (Addis Ababa: UNCTAD/African Union, 2005).

UNCTAD . *Report of the Expert Meeting on Enabling Small Commodity Producers and Processors in Developing Countries to Reach Global Markets* (Geneva: United Nations, January 2007).

UNCTAD. *Report of the Expert Meeting to Examine the Effectiveness and Usefulness for Commodity-Dependent Countries of New Tools in Commodity Markets: Risk Management and Collateralized Finance* (Geneva: United Nations, 1998).

UNCTAD. *The Development Role of Commodity Exchanges* (Geneva: United Nations, 2007).

UNCTAD . *The Global Trading Village* (Bürgenstock: UNCTAD, 2000).

UNCTAD, FAO, World Bank, et al., "Price Volatility in Food and Agricultural Markets." June 2011.

UNCTAD and SFOA. "The World's Commodity Exchanges," proceedings of the 27th Bürgenstock Conference. Bürgenstock: UNCTAD, 2006.

UNDP. *Commodity Development Strategies in the Integrated Framework* (Geneva: United Nations, 2009).

UNDP. *Uganda Human Development Report, 2007* (Geneva: United Nations Development Program, 2007).

USAID. *Commodity Futures Exchange: An Assessment and Conceptual Framework for Establishing a Commodity Futures Exchange in Egypt* (Washington, D.C.: USAID, 2007).

USDA Economic Research Service. "Farm Risk Management: Risk Management Strategies." http://www.ers.usda.gov/Briefing/RiskManagement/Strategies.htm, accessed on July 7, 2011.

USDA Foreign Agricultural Service. *GAIN Report: Colombia Coffee, Semi-Annual 2008* (Washington, D.C.: USDA, 2008).

Ussher, Leanne. "International Price Stability, Full Employment and Global Balances: The Case for a Commodity Reserve Currency." Draft from Economics Department at Queens College, City University of New York, March 2008.

Varangis, Panos, Larson, Donald and Anderson, Jock. *Agricultural Markets and Risks: Management of the Latter, Not the Former* (Washington, D.C.: The World Bank, 2002).

Varangis, Panos and Larson, Donald. *Dealing with Commodity Price Uncertainty* (Washington, D.C.: The World Bank, 1996).

Campesina, Via "G20 Excludes Poor Countries" (press release). http://www.viacampesina.org/en/index.php?option=com_content&view=article&id=969:G20-exludes-poor-countries-and-pushes-business-as-usual-small-farmers-demand-system-change&catid=15:News-from-the-regions&Itemid=29, accessed October 7, 2011.

Vidal, John and Provost, Claire. "US Universities in Africa Land-Grab." *The Guardian*, June 8, 2011.

Wade, Robert. "The First World Debt Crisis of 2007–2010 in Global Perspective." *Challenge* (July—August 2008).

Wall Street Journal. "US Plans Tougher Rules on Commodities," June 4, 2008.

Woods, Ngaire. *The Globalizers* (Ithaca: Cornell, 2006).

Immanuel, Wallerstein. "The Modern World-System as a Capitalist World-Economy," in *The Globalization Reader*, Lechner and Boli, eds. (Malden, MA: Blackwell, 2008), pp. 55–61.

Wallerstein, Immanuel. *The Politics of the World-Economy* (Cambridge: Cambridge University Press, 1984).

Watson, Kelly. Achinelli, Moira Laura. "Context and Contingency: The Coffee Crisis for Conventional Small-Scale Coffee Farmers in Brazil." *The Geographic Journal* 174:3 (2008), 223–34.

Wheatley, Jonathan. "Brazil Exchanges in Global Party Mood." *Financial Times* (February 28, 2008).

Wild, Antony. *Coffee: A Dark History* (London: Fourth Estate, 2004).

Williamson, John. "Did the Washington Consensus Fail?." Speech before the Peterson Institute for International Economics. Washington, D.C.: November 6, 2002.

Wise, Timothy. "Food Price Volatility" (January 27, 2011). http://triplecrisis.com/food-price-volatility, accessed on September 27, 2011.

World Bank. *Agriculture for Development: World Development Report, 2008* (Washington, D.C.: World Bank, 2008).

World Bank. *Brazil: Access to Financial Services* (Washington, D.C.: World Bank, Brazil Country Management Group, 2004).

World Bank. *Dealing with Commodity Price Volatility in Developing Countries: A Proposal for a Market-Based Approach* (Washington, D.C.: World Bank, 1999).

World Bank. *Managing Agricultural Production Risk* (Washington, D.C.: World Bank/Agricultural and Rural Development Department, 2005).

World Bank. *Rural Finance Innovations: Topics and Case Studies* (Washington, D.C.: World Bank, 2005).

World Bank. *Shocks and Social Protection: Lessons From the Central American Coffee Crisis* (Washington, D.C.: World Bank, 2005).

World Bank. *Social Protection Sector Strategy: From Safety Net to Springboard* (Washington, D.C.: World Bank, 2001).

World Bank. *World Development Report: Agriculture for Development* (Washington, D.C.: World Bank, 2008).

Index